Talk Left,
Walk Right

Talk Left, Walk Right

South Africa's Frustrated
Global Reforms

PATRICK BOND

Cartoons by Zapiro

UNIVERSITY OF KWAZULU-NATAL PRESS

Published in 2004 by University of KwaZulu-Natal Press
Private Bag X01
Scottsville 3209
South Africa
Email: books@ukzn.ac.za
www.uknpress.co.za

© 2004 Patrick Bond

All rights reserved. No part of this publication may be reproduced or transmitted in any form or by any means, electronic or mechanical, including photocopying, recording or any information storage or retrieval system, without prior permission in writing from the publishers.

ISBN 1-86914-054-0

Editor: Charlene Smith
Cover designer: Anthony Cuerden
Cover photograph: Sydney Seshibidi, Sunday Times

Typeset by Alpha Typesetters, New Germany
Printed and bound by Interpak Books, Pietermaritzburg

Contents

Preface and acknowledgements......vii
Lists of figures and tables......xvi
List of abbreviations......xvii

PART ONE: CONTEXT

1 **Introduction**
  Against global apartheid?......3

2 **Global-local power relations**
  Ideology, image and war games......21

PART TWO: ISSUES AND EVENTS

3 **Racism talk-shop, reparations sabotage**
  From reconciliation to amnesia......37

4 **Pretoria's trade off**
  Splitting Africa for the WTO......51

5 **Washington renamed**
  A 'Monterrey Consensus' on finance......75

6 **NEPAD neutered**
  Tragedy or joke?......103

7 **The 'W$$D'**
  Pretoria meets its match......125

8 **Water wars**
  Dams, privatisation and pre-paid meters, from
  Johannesburg to Kyoto and back......143

PART THREE: POLITICAL ANALYSIS, STRATEGY AND ALLIANCES

9 Pretoria talk
Exhausted Leninism and the 'ultraleft' — 179

10 Analysing Washington's agenda
Are there anti-imperial options? — 191

11 Movement strategy
Abolish global apartheid — 211

References — 243

Index — 257

Preface and acknowledgements

So much laudatory fluff is written in the mainstream media and academia about the South African government's international reform agenda, that I am duty bound to offer a review from a critical perspective.

Historians will probably look at 1994–2001 as a warm-up period, where ambitious human rights rhetoric emerged in Pretoria's multilateral, regional and bilateral engagements. However, not only was hypocrisy a problem, ranging from flirtation with the Indonesian dictator Suharto and recognition of the Myanmar military junta as a legitimate government, to the hapless Lesotho invasion and ill-considered arms sales to countries like Algeria, Columbia and Peru with appalling human rights records. Generally, the balance of forces proved hostile to Pretoria. The first period witnessed the Western power bloc's quick dismissal of appeals for relief: from unfair trade rules, debt and financial squeezes, speculative attacks on the currency, foreign investment strikes, and disputed patents on AIDS medicines and, absurdly, the names of geographically-branded exports like 'port' and 'sherry'.

It is to Thabo Mbeki's credit that he did not give up. The period subsequent to the September 11, 2001 terrorist attack against the US might logically, for a less ambitious Third World ruler, have been a time to retreat: to hunker down and sort out domestic and purely subregional politics. But the opposite has transpired. Mbeki moved to the world stage even more aggressively, denouncing 'global apartheid' and offering grand visions of a more equal, just and balanced world. Hence arose the impressions we would all like to have of Mbeki, Trevor Manuel, Alec Erwin and others in the leadership of the New South Africa: enlightened and rational, resolute and ambitious, progressive and democratic, and above all, highly capable.

Now, having seen Pretoria's recent round of global reforms so persistently frustrated, I must confess to mixed feelings. To be sure, the home front remains a disaster in socio-economic terms for most low-income people, especially women, and 5 million HIV-positive South Africans. As just one reflection of their plight, the former head of the Medical Research Council and the present chairperson of the

South African Medical Association (both black, highly-regarded professionals) have publicly described Mbeki's AIDS-denialist posture as 'genocidal'.

Some would say that even the most egregious policies at home should not stop Mbeki having progressive potential on the world stage. Some of Africa's military hot-spots – the DRC, Burundi, Liberia – are cooler in the wake of Pretoria's interventions, even if, as diplomatic and military experts agree, the durability of peace is still to be tested. Manuel and Erwin have been at the top of their form when managing global summits. And many other South Africans have taken up key positions in multilateral agencies or international commissions; testimony to the calibre of people who came through the anti-apartheid struggle, and who are still left with enormous energy to work toward a better world. When compared to their peers in Washington or London, South Africa's governing elite are, without question, preferable. To illustrate, when South African officials drove the international anti-landmine campaign to victory through the United Nations in 1997, such leadership provided at least some optimism for Pretoria's global-scale prospects.[1]

Hence a fresh book-length survey of Mbeki's reform programme is in order, even if, after carefully considering the analysis, strategies, tactics and alliances in various recent initiatives, I am compelled to conclude that Pretoria is engaged in a great scam. The scam is twofold. Not only are locals and international friends alike regularly confused by Mbeki's recourse to radical rhetoric: the left talk. There is an even more debilitating feature of his simultaneous walk right: embracing the global establishment's neoliberal premises and institutions gets South Africa and Africa *nowhere*.

Pretoria's political style may hasten the roll-out of red carpets leading up the stairs to transnational elite gatherings. The *Mail & Guardian* newspaper's year-end 2003 report card of Mbeki may be correct that 'it is in the area of foreign affairs that his legacy will rest'. But it may also constitute an area where history will judge him harshly for the positions he took in those fora, and for his neglect of pressing issues at home.

This book argues that there is little or nothing to show for Mbeki's unprecedented degree of access to the structures of global power. Pretoria's reformers are both 'compradors' – i.e., agents of the global establishment – and failures, when it comes to advancing their stated agenda. Even at Cancun, where the World Trade Organisation ran aground in September 2003, South Africa's rulers simply did not know how – or did not want – to take advantage of the opportunities that began to emerge, once neoliberal policies crashed in east Asia and the rest of the Global South during the late 1990s. The South African economy's dismal performance since 1996, when international competitiveness became the overriding objective via the misnamed 'Growth, Employment and Redistribution' strategy, offers proof that Washington's economic advice was inappropriate. Even Manuel himself now admits as much, as discussed in Chapter Ten.

Instead of progress, all we are left with are radical discursive flourishes. Rand Merchant Bank chief economist Rudolph Gouws recently bragged that Pretoria deals with the profound contradiction between international capitalism and its constituents 'by talking left but acting right'.[2] But Pretoria's skew is so obvious that even *Business Day* editor Peter Bruce was drawn to concede in mid-2003, 'The government is utterly seduced by big business, and cannot see beyond its immediate interests.'[3]

Only Mbeki and his ANC Political Education Unit bother to deny the charge, especially when it comes from the left, as in this 2002 discussion document: 'There are no facts that the anti-neoliberalism can produce to prove its accusations. Its statement characterising the policies pursued by the ANC and our government since 1994 as the expressive of a neoliberal agenda are complete falsification of reality (*sic*).'[4]

The fundamental point of this book is that Mbeki's approach cannot succeed *even on its own terms*. Indeed, Pretoria's frustrated global reformism represents a world-historic failure, a chance missed when in this conjuncture so much more could be done. What might have been possible, had Mbeki and his lieutenants adopted liberatory principles and approaches to the *globalisation of people*, rather than *of capital*?

Instead of selling arms to the Iraq War aggressors – the US and UK – and warmly welcoming George W. Bush a few weeks after his illegal occupation of Baghdad, what if Mbeki had taken the lead of former president Mandela and punished Bush with a snub, and strengthened anti-war resistance and even US/UK boycotts in venues like the Non-Aligned Movement and African Union?

Instead of rejecting reparations to punish international financiers, corporations and the Bretton Woods Institutions for supporting apartheid, what if Mbeki and his colleagues advanced the fight against racism and helped warn big capital off future relations with odious regimes?

Instead of battling against protesters and African trade officials from Seattle through Doha to Cancun, what if Erwin tried uniting the continent and its allies behind a counter hegemonic trade agenda so as to meet popular needs, not those of global capital?

Instead of pooh-poohing debt cancellation as a strategy, what if Manuel joined the Jubilee movement, denounced bogus World Bank and International Monetary Fund plans for crumbs of relief in the midst of amplified neoliberalism, and helped to organise a debtors' cartel?

Instead of a New Partnership for Africa's Development considered, simultaneously, 'philosophically spot on' by the Bush regime and ridiculous by Zimbabweans hoping for pro-democracy pressure, what if Pretoria helped establish a bottom-up African programme for recovery based upon partnerships between Africans themselves?

Instead of exacerbating the World Summit on Sustainable Development's orientation to commodification, not to mention repressing legitimate dissent, what if the ANC leaders tried to harmonise and genuinely implement the agendas of poverty-eradication and environment?

Instead of promoting water commercialisation and large dams, what if South Africa helped establish sound principles of decommodification and respect for nature, both in water catchments at home and in international talk-shops?

But after ten years of practice, South Africa's first democratic government is locked into walking right, the more its politicians and officials talk left. Yet this pattern cannot disguise a simple conclusion: the scale of Mbeki's strategic failure helps explain the paranoia that he and other ANC leaders exhibit when confronted on internationalist terrain by what they term the 'ultraleft', namely the various global justice movements which remain unimpressed by Pretoria's dance.

Although my earlier statement of the problem and potential solutions, in the book *Against Global Apartheid*, ended in technicism – feasible 'policy reform options' – I no longer harbour such pretensions.[5] Many local activists, mainly associated with what is termed the 'Social Movements Indaba' and allied groups, have convinced me instead of their strategic conclusion: eschew the role of the current South African elite and disabuse their international networks of any illusory notions of a common front with Thabo Mbeki against the US-led Empire.

Instead, as the concluding chapter argues, there are many preferable forms of *self-activity*, ranging from the initiative to defund the World Bank, to myriad local struggles for decommodified water, electricity, medicines, education, land, housing and basic income. The seeds of a full-fledged New Freedom Charter and perhaps new left-wing political party are also there, although repression, internal divisions and strategic differences may well kill the seeds before they are grown by the tens of thousands of South Africans who have already moved far beyond Pretoria's agenda at home and abroad. Nevertheless, no matter the difficulties, it is to ever-tighter linkages and programmatic coherence within these local and global-local efforts that, I think, we can all look to with hope.

I am convinced that the activist orientation is more realistic than a new round of less frustrated, or more ambitious, top-down reforms from Pretoria. Mainly, however, Mbeki and his colleagues will continue to serve imperialism. Their subimperial role will be much the same as that of apartheid-era bantustan leaders, who often claimed to be against the system or working to change it from the inside, while in reality they propped it up through logistical support and legitimation.

Over the course of roughly a year and a half, arguments in this book were formally presented to audiences who demanded nuance, better evidence and more convincing political deductions.[6] I was challenged repeatedly by students and colleagues at York and Wits Universities.[7] Perhaps the best learning experience was the infusion of global-scale analysis that all of us in Johannesburg experienced in mid-2002 at the World Summit on Sustainable Development. Sadly, that education necessarily included a police stun-grenade assault on the International Forum on Globalisation conference's candle-light march just outside the Wits University front gate one chilly Saturday evening (Chapter Seven).

Indeed, if Pretoria's persistent, albeit often surreal, attacks on the independent left continue it indicates that the progressive critique of neoliberal policies and practices is not irrelevant. Among revelations from the South African case of repressive neoliberalism is this fact: when Mbeki is stymied or stressed on the international front, such as the World Conference Against Racism in 2001, the WSSD in 2002 or via the Treatment Action Campaign's civil disobedience campaign in 2003, his security forces attack those who see a future where another world, and another South Africa, are possible.

Those activists and organic intellectuals have such extraordinary capacity to think and act globally and locally, that my own analysis pales in comparison to the comprehension they have gained through struggle praxis, of Mbeki's zig-zag talk and walk. The informal workshops I witness in townships always leave me with more than I bring, and it is to these comrades that this book must be dedicated.

Tolerant editors also helped rid the arguments of the most obvious flaws, and I am most grateful for chances to have published excerpts of material in this book during 2003–04, though with substantive changes in this current version.[8] David Moore and particularly Jeremy Seekings are thanked for their publisher reviews. But no readers were as supportive as my mother Moya or aunt Helga who interrupted a holiday to give editorial advice. And none could be as simultaneously rigorous and fun to work with as Charlene Smith, who at the end took the manuscript under her wing, as she has so many better causes, with the nurturing for which she is famous. Glenn Cowley and Sally Hines at the University of KwaZulu-Natal Press remain the favourite publishers of so many South African writers, for many reasons.

As ever, my growing lad Jan was the humanising element, this time in part because he had the task of selecting many of the Zapiro cartoons, which in any case he does regularly from newspapers before I have my own peek. How many others has the tireless, gifted Jonathan Shapiro radicalised in the process of unveiling the persistent ironies and tragedies of the New SA?

Too many other dear friends and comrades go unmentioned this time. Coming next is a work devoted solely to you.

Notes

1. However, even promoting this no-brainer global-scale reform, Pretoria initially faltered. In May 1996, at the Landmine Protocol of the Convention on Conventional Weapons, South Africa officially conceded that the SA National Defence Force would no longer use antipersonnel mines. But Pretoria insisted that 'smart' landmines should still be available for deployment. Finally in February 1997, the position shifted to a full ban. Notwithstanding opposition from the Defence ministry, then run by Joe Modise, SA ambassador to Geneva Jackie Selebi took leadership over the Ottawa Process which generated a full ban in September 1997. One reason for the shift was state-owned Denel's prowess in demining technology and experience; many in the human rights movement cringe upon witnessing the same parastatal and private firms which did so much damage subsequently becoming 'double-dipping' beneficiaries of multi-million dollar contracts across Africa and Eastern Europe (International Campaign to ban Landmines (1999), 'South Africa', New York, Human Rights Watch, http://www.icbl.org).
2. *Independent Online*, 27 October 2002. The phrase may have made an initial appearance in a book I wrote in mid-1999, *Elite Transition*, but it is far more important that Gouws articulates the idea so readily, because for more than a decade he has served as a primary organic intellectual of the financial fraction of South African capital.
3. *Business Day*, 4 June 2003.
4. African National Congress Political Education Unit (2002), 'Contribution to the NEC/NWC Response to the "Cronin Interviews" on the Issue of Neoliberalism', Johannesburg, September; posted on the debate listserve, 25 September 2002. An edited version was published in the *Mail & Guardian*, 11 October 2002: http://archive.mg.co.za/nxt/gateway.dll/PrintEdition/MGP2002/3lv00362/4lv00454/5lv00485.htm.
5. For guidance on positioning I thank *The Ecologist* (June 2003, excerpting Paul Kingsnorth's *One No, Many Yeses*), which quoted comrades racing between anti-neoliberal actions in the Durban townships: '[Heinrich] Bohmke

changes gear determinedly. "But at least people are starting to break through the barrier of illegality," he says. "They've given up expecting the government to do right by them. But then, you know, we have these lefty intellectuals in Jo'burg who are just waiting for Pretoria to have a change of heart and invite them in to sort out the economic programme. Whenever we mobilise for any sort of confrontation here it's always: 'Well, comrade, we support your struggle, but we're worried about your analytical fucking framework and your tactics.' Your tactics, man! People are dying, literally, and they're worried about tactics." '

6. Thanks also to generous hosts. During 2003, these events included the Rosa Luxemburg Stiftung Seminar on Public Goods in Johannesburg (Arndt Hopfmann); the University of Illinois at Urbana-Champaign's Transnational Seminar (Merle Bowen and Faranak Miraftab); the conference on Contested Urban Futures at the University of Minnesota, Minneapolis (Helga Leitner and Eric Sheppard); the York University Department of Political Science Symposium on Empire, Neoliberalism and Resistance (Leo Panitch and Susanne Soederberg); the Ryerson University and Toronto Socialist Project forum on privatisation (Greg Albo and Bryan Evans); the Norwegian Association for Development Research annual conference on Politics and Poverty (Einar Braathen and Arild Schou); the workshop on New Pathways for Mexico's Sustainable Development hosted by the El Colegio de Mexico Department of Economics (Alejandro Nadal and Tania Hernandez) and a Universidad Autonoma Metropolitana-Xochimilco Department of Economics seminar (David Barkin), both in Mexico City; a Detroit workshop on water disconnections with the Welfare Rights Organization, Michigan Green Party, Sweetwater Coalition and EarthFirst (Marie Mason and Maureen Taylor); the Nordiska Afrikainstitutet's Nordic Africa Days in Uppsala, Sweden (Henning Melber); a Carleton University Department of Anthropology seminar in Ottawa (Blair Rutherford); the Philadelphia Social Forum's international weekend (Larry Robin); the Water Wheel of Life conference at the University of California/Santa Barbara (Don George, Philip Grant and Bruce Erickson); a Focus on the Global South and Oxfam symposium on the WTO in Bangkok (Walden Bello); a Heinrich Boell Stiftung and Free University seminar in Berlin on Alternatives to Privatisation (Simon Raiser); the Rand Afrikaans University Department of Sociology Seminar in Johannesburg (Peter Alexander); the Wits Institute for Social and Economic Research and Department of Sociology debate on the book *Empire* (Devan Pillay and Franco Barchiesi); the Marxism 2003 Conference at University of London Union (Alex Callinicos); the International Political Science Association's convention in Durban (David Moore); the Ditsela Workshop on Economic Restructuring in Johannesburg (Steve Faulkner); the Wits University School of Public Health seminar series (Lucy Gilson); the Johannesburg Institute for the Advancement of Journalism's water debate (Joe Hanlon); the University of Pretoria Masters in International Business Studies Programme (Mollie Painter-Morland); Ecologistas en Accion in Madrid (Tom Kucharz); the Conference on the Work of Karl Marx and the Challenges of the 21st Century sponsored by the Institute of Philosophy and Cuban Trade Union Federation in Havana (Jesus Pastor and Michael Lebowitz); Columbia University's Institute of African Studies and the African American Institute Seminar on the Political Economy of NEPAD in New York (Mahmood Mamdani and Kiki

Edozie); the 50 Years is Enough seminar on Third World debt for US congressional staff on Capitol Hill (Njoki Njehu); the South African Parliament Portfolio Committee on Water Affairs and Forestry in Cape Town (Liane Greef); the African Social Policy Group of the UN Research Institute for Social Development at Rhodes University, Grahamstown (Jimi Adesina); the World Council of Churches Dialogue with the World Bank and IMF in Geneva (Rogate Mshana); the University of Stellenbosch Sustainability Institute Seminar on Sustainable Development (Mark Swilling); Cambridge University's HRH Prince of Wales Inaugural Southern Africa Senior Executives Seminar in Stellenbosch (Peter Willis); and in Porto Alegre, the World Social Forum's 'Democratising Democracy' roundtable (Virginia Vargas and Lilian Celiberti), the TransNational Institute's New Politics Seminar (Fiona Dove and Daniel Chavez) and other WSF events (TNI on energy, World Council of Churches on water, and *Z*'s Life After Capitalism on cities). During the latter half of 2002, I was hosted at Chulalongkorn University's Social Research Institute in Bangkok (Nicola Bullard); the Warwick University Local Government Centre seminar on Social Exclusion and Inequality in Coventry (Jonathan Davies); the Freedom of Expression Institute NEPAD seminar in Johannesburg (Jane Duncan); the Zimbabwe Law Society's Nyanga summer school (Sternford Moyo); the University of Cape Town Business School Seminar on Globalisation (Thomas Koelble); the Afrodad, Mwengo, Zimcodd and American Friends Service Committee conference on Alternatives to NEPAD in Harare (Nancy Kachingwe, Davie Malungisa and Ezekiel Pajebo); the Critical Methods Society conference on 'Something for Nothing' at the University of South Africa Institute for Social and Health Science (Martin Terre Blanche); the Heinrich Boell *Jo'burg-Memo* debate in Johannesburg (Stefan Cramer and Wolfgang Sachs); a Goethe Institute debate with Ernst von Weizaecker; the Wits Journalism Programme briefing on the WSSD (Darryl Accone); the Wits Planning Department's WSSD seminar (Mzwanele Mayekiso); and the African Social Forum's Johannesburg forum on NEPAD (MP Giyosi, George Dor and Trevor Ngwane).

7. In late 2003, as this book came to an end, one of the most interesting places in the world was a suburban wasteland in northern Toronto, home to York's unique, critical mass of political economists. Leo Panitch and Sam Gindin arranged my sabbatical stay, and Colin Leys, John and Pat Saul, Richard Saunders and Christina Zarowsky generously broke me in to the Canadian scene. I benefited from discussions at York with Greg Albo, Rob Albritton, Isa Bakker, Shannon Bell, Julie-Anne Boudreau, Uli Brandt, George Comninel, Matt Davies, Stephen Gill, Judy and Steve Hellman, Roger Keil, Minqi Li, Ute Lehrer, David McNally, Nicky Short and others in Leo's Empire seminar, and especially York's multitude of brilliant post-grad students. The city's many friendly internationalists include John Clarke, Janet Conway, Bryan Evans, Paul Jay, Naomi Klein, Avi Lewis, Jess McKenzie, Justin Podur, Emma Ruby-Sachs and Ernie Tate. Back home, for keeping me on track in local and regional ways, I have to thank the recent Wits P&DM crew of Thulani Guliwe and Ebrahim Harvey (who doubled as able research associates), Thandi Henson, Simba Manyanya, Tawanda Mutasah, Trevor Ngwane and Horacio Zandamela, as well as my tolerant Parktown colleagues. Other participants in the Advanced Topics in Political Economy seminar at Wits P&DM during 2001–03 acted as a critical sounding board, and I am also

grateful to the Open Society Initiative of Southern Africa for bringing activists and grassroots leaders from the region to several of our executive courses during 2002–03, as well as for the roles played by Jimi Adesina and George Dor in these brainstorms. Additional research support on related projects was provided by Equinet in Harare, the Ford Foundation in Johannesburg and New York, the Free University Department of Political Science in Berlin, the International Development Research Centre in Ottawa, Kairos Europa in Frankfurt, the Rosa Luxemburg Stiftung, UN AIDS and the UN Research Institute on Social Development in Geneva, the University of Natal School of Development Studies, the World Council of Churches in Geneva and the World Resources Institute in Washington.

8. The following journals were most comradely, providing helpful suggestions from reviewers (and editors): *Austrian Journal of Development Studies* (Bettina Koehler); *Capitalism, Nature, Socialism* (Jim O'Connor and Barbara Laurence); *Development Update* (Firoz Khan and Nicol Colling); *Focus on Trade* (Nicola Bullard); *Foreign Policy in Focus* (John Gershman); *Futures* (Mammo Muchie); *Historical Materialism* (Liam Campling and Sebastian Budgen); *International Journal of Health Services* (Vicente Navarro); *Journal of Peacebuilding and Development Studies* (Erin McCandless); *Links* (John Percy); *Monthly Review* (John Foster and Claude Misukiewicz); *Organisation for Social Science Research in Eastern and Southern Africa Newsletter* (Samuel Tesfamichael); *Society in Transition* (Dawid Venter); *South African Journal on Human Rights* (Stuart Wilson); and *South Atlantic Quarterly* (Garth Farred and Rita Barnard). The following recent or forthcoming edited collections also carried versions of material I draw upon in this book: *African Development Perspective Yearbook* (Karl Wohlmuth); *Anti-Capitalism* (Rachel Neumann); *Banking on Hegemony* (David Moore); *Contesting Public Sector Reforms* (Pauline Dibben); *Democratising South African Foreign Policy* (Janis van der Westhuizen); *For a Fistful of Dollars* (Nina Momsen); *Neoliberalism* (Alfredo Saal-Filho); *The Global Crisis* (Boris Kagarlitsky and Alan Freeman); *Globalization* (Gernot Koehler and E.J. Chavez); *Governance in the New South Africa* (Omano Edigheji and Guy Mhone); *Nordiska Afrikainstitutet Occasional Papers* (Henning Melber); *Power and Negotiations in the Aid Industry* (Lisa Bornstein and Bill Munro); *Rosa Luxemburg Stiftung Policy Papers* (Arndt Hopfmann); and *Transforming South Africa* (Armin Osmanovich). The following are popular publications where short versions were first tried out during 2002–04: *Al Qalam*; *Arena*; *Bundmagazin*; *City Press*; *GreenLeft Weekly*; *L'Humanite*; *The Independent*; *Multinational Monitor*; *New Internationalist*; *Pambezuka*; *Le Passant Ordinaire*; *Political and Economic Weekly* (India); *Red Pepper*; *South African Labour Bulletin*; *Sowetan*; *Third World Quarterly*; *This Day*; *Z*; and *ZNet Commentary* (special thanks to Michael Albert for allowing a monthly column at http://www.zmag.org which brings great feedback from amazing subscribers).

Figures and tables

Figure 1: Income inequality worsens during globalisation: International Gini coefficients, 1950–1999 — 5
Figure 2: Uneven global development: Country category gaps, 1970–2000 — 6
Figure 3: Inequality, 1820–1999: Ratio of wealth between richest and poorest 20% of individuals — 6
Figure 4: Africa's falling terms of trade, 1970–1999 — 7
Figure 5: Africa's debt crisis during globalisation, 1980–2000 — 7
Figure 6: Africa's net debt inflows and outflows, 1980–2000 — 8
Figure 7: Divergent water pricing strategies, Johannesburg (2001) v. ideal tariff for large household — 164
Figure 8: US corporate profits: Percentage breakdown by key components — 196
Figure 9: The long-term record of sovereign bankruptcy: Percentage of countries in default, 1820–1999 — 203

Table 1: Five international ideological currents — 23
Table 2: Five ideological currents in South Africa — 26
Table 3: Water and sanitation apartheid, with social movement solutions — 149

Abbreviations

ACP	African-Caribbean-Pacific
AEC	Anti-Eviction Campaign
AGOA	African Growth and Opportunity Act
ANC	African National Congress
ART	antiretroviral
AU	African Union
BWI	Bretton Woods Institution
CoJ	City of Johannesburg
Cosatu	Congress of South African Trade Unions
DPLG	Department of Provincial and Local Government
DRC	Democratic Republic of Congo
DUPE	Decline, Unemployment and Polarisation Economics
Dwaf	Department of Water Affairs and Forestry
EIR	Extractive Industries Review
FFD	Financing for Development (UN)
GEAR	Growth, Employment and Redistribution
GM	genetically modified
HIPC	Heavily Indebted Poor Countries
HSRC	Human Sciences Research Council
IDA	International Development Association
IFG	International Forum on Globalisation
IMF	International Monetary Fund
IPWA	International Private Water Association
JW	Johannesburg Water
LDC	less developed country
NEPAD	New Partnership for Africa's Development
NGO	non-governmental organisation
ODA	Official Development Assistance
OWCC	Orange Farm Water Crisis Committee
PPP	public-private partnership
PRSP	Poverty Reduction Strategy Papers
R&D	research and development
RDP	Reconstruction and Development Programme
SACP	South African Communist Party
Sapa	South African Press Association
SMI	Social Movements Indaba

SOLD	Survivors of the Lesotho Dam
TAC	Treatment Action Campaign
TRC	Truth and Reconciliation Commission
TRIPS	Trade-Related Intellectual Property Rights
VIPs	Ventilated Improved Pitlatrines
WCAR	World Conference Against Racism
WEF	World Economic Forum
WHO	World Health Organisation
WSSD	World Summit on Sustainable Development
WTO	World Trade Organisation
ZANU (PF)	Zimbabwe African National Union (Patriotic Front)

PART ONE

CONTEXT

1
Introduction
Against global apartheid?

'South Africa is what she is today because, driven by the spirit of human and international solidarity, you, the peoples of the world took a stand and said that apartheid in South Africa will not pass!'

With these words, Thabo Mbeki welcomed dignitaries to the World Summit on Sustainable Development (WSSD) in August 2002. He continued:

> We have converged at the Cradle of Humanity to confront the social behaviour that has pity neither for beautiful nature nor for living human beings. This social behaviour has produced and entrenches a global system of apartheid. The suffering of the billions who are the victims of this system calls for the same response that drew the peoples of the world into the struggle for the defeat of apartheid in this country.[1]

Mbeki expressed similar sentiments after his October 2003 return from a Sao Paolo, Brazil, gathering of allied political parties, of a mainly European, formerly social democratic and subsequently 'Third Way' hue. Within that misnamed 'Socialist International', he aimed to 'engage all progressive forces in our country, in Africa and rest of the world':

> The critically important task to end the poverty and underdevelopment in which millions of African are trapped, inside and outside our country, cannot be accomplished by the market. If we were to follow the prescriptions of neo-liberal market ideology, we would abandon the masses of our people to permanent poverty and underdevelopment . . . Poor as we might be, and precisely because we are poor, we have a duty to contribute to the elaboration of the global governance concept . . . opposing the neo-liberal market ideology, the neo-conservative agenda, and the unilateralist approach.[2]

To any progressive those words are inspiring, but perhaps scepticism is necessary.[3] Since democracy in 1994, South Africa has had many opportunities to put those words into action. In the African National Congress' first seven years of rule, Mbeki and other South African officials presided over the Non-Aligned Movement, the UN Conference on Trade and Development, the Commonwealth, the Organisation of African Unity, the African Union, the Southern African Development Community, the board of governors of the International Monetary Fund (IMF) and World Bank and other important international bodies. But little came of these efforts. Indeed, global apartheid worsened considerably, in part, because Pretoria gave legitimacy to the *status quo*.

This book tackles the main challenges facing orthodox global governance since September 2001, beginning with a review of international political economy, geopolitics and competing ideologies. It does not include a full critique of global capitalism; nor initial failed reforms,[4] but nevertheless a short review helps set the stage.

Capitalism, crisis and global 'minority rule'

The phenomenon of 'global apartheid' is defined by Washington-based Africa advocates Salih Booker and Bill Minter as 'an international system of minority rule whose attributes include differential access to basic human rights, wealth and power'.[5] It is the outcome of political power associated with late 20th century economic crisis, and the ideology of 'neoliberalism'. The neoliberal approach to state policy, namely to rely upon much more upon markets, exacerbated the underlying contradictions of capitalism.

Evidence is found in the growing inequity between countries (as measured by the 'Gini coefficient': 0 is perfect equality, 1 perfect inequality, in Figure 1), types of countries (as measured by Gross Domestic Product per person in Figure 2), and people (Figure 3). These trends follow from global apartheid's two main internal systems for the exploitation of Third World countries: worsening 'terms of trade' whereby exports cheapen as import costs rise (Figure 4); and the foreign debt trap, which forces a desperate Africa to repay 'odious' loans made to elites (Figures 5 and 6).

Because of economic and geopolitical control largely emanating from Washington, capitalism survives – even if many Africans do not – by 'shifting and stalling' two core contradictions of capitalism: 'overaccumulation crisis' and 'uneven development'.[6] This jargon means that *too much has been produced, and its distribution is too unequal, for the capitalist system to readily reproduce in a way that assures continual growth and stability.*

The momentum of neoliberalism and the Washington/Wall Street axis slowed somewhat during the late 1990s, but capital's vulnerabilities remain extremely serious. There appears little scope for genuine

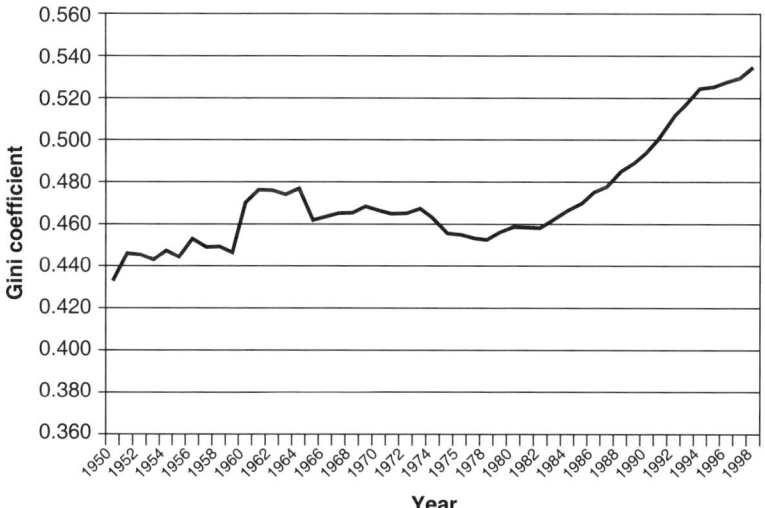

Figure 1: Income inequality worsens during globalisation: International Gini coefficients, 1950–1999.

Source: Branco Milanovic, World Bank, website

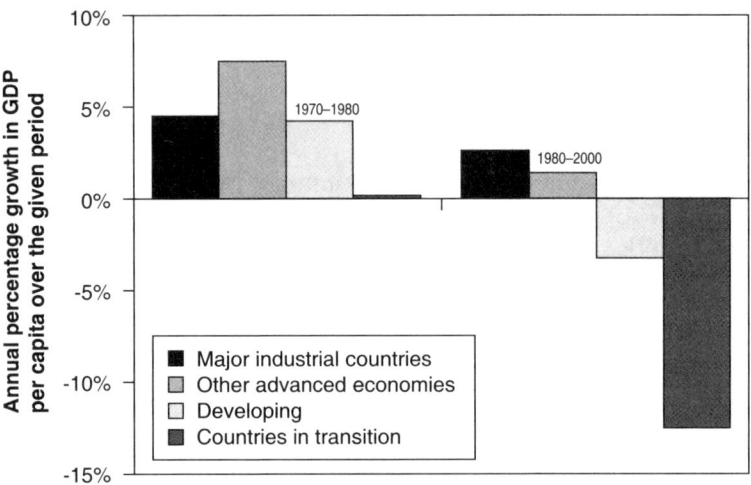

Figure 2: Uneven global development: Country category gaps, 1970–2000.

Source: Alan Freeman, Greenwich University, website

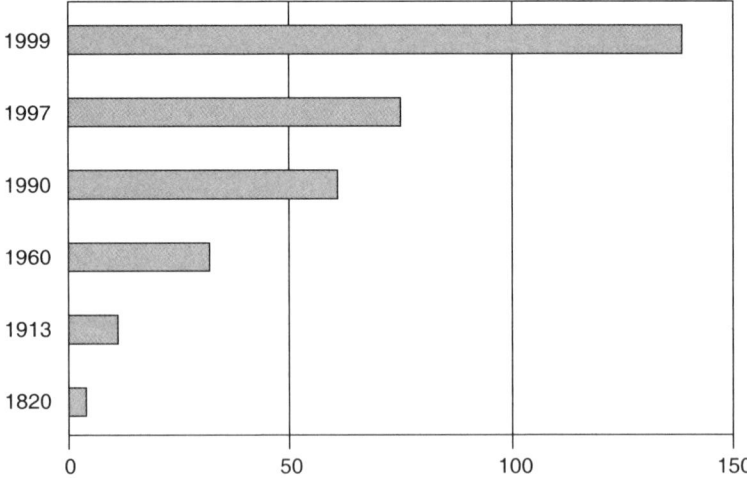

Figure 3: Inequality, 1820–1999: Ratio of wealth between richest and poorest 20% of individuals.

Source: United Nations Development Programme

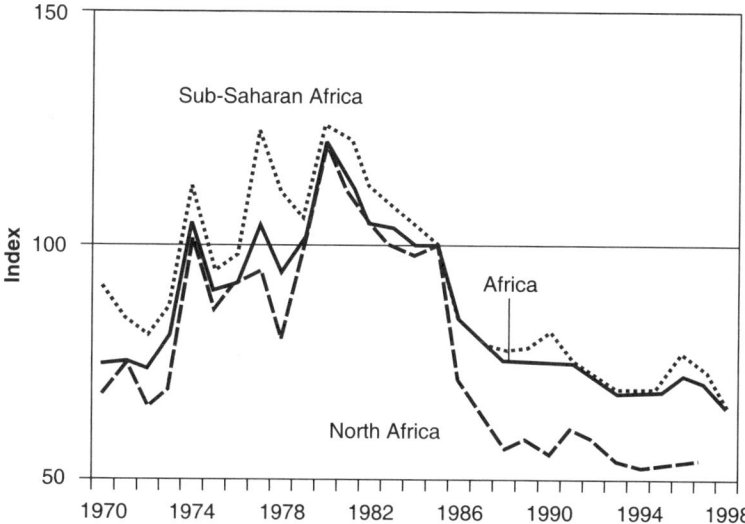

Figure 4: Africa's falling terms of trade, 1970–1999.
Source: UN Conference on Trade and Development

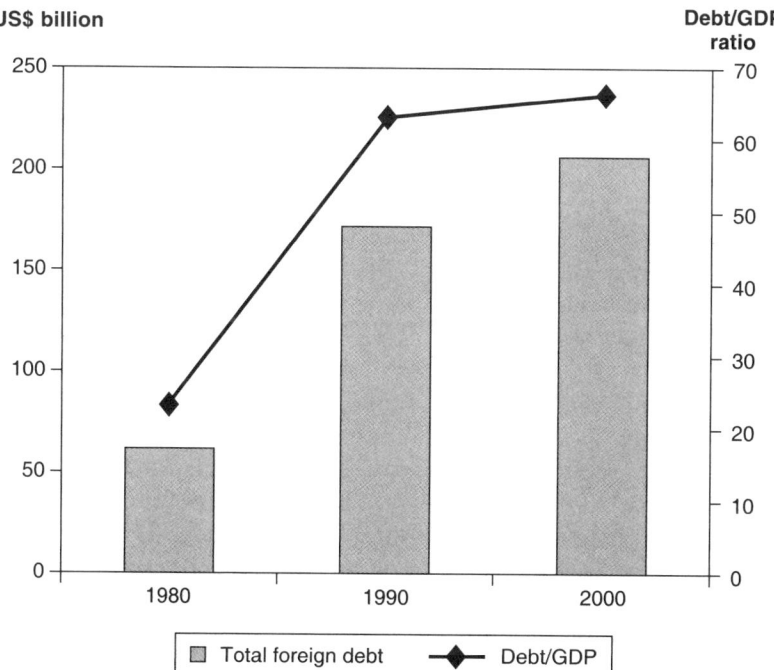

Figure 5: Africa's debt crisis during globalisation, 1980–2000.
Source: World Bank

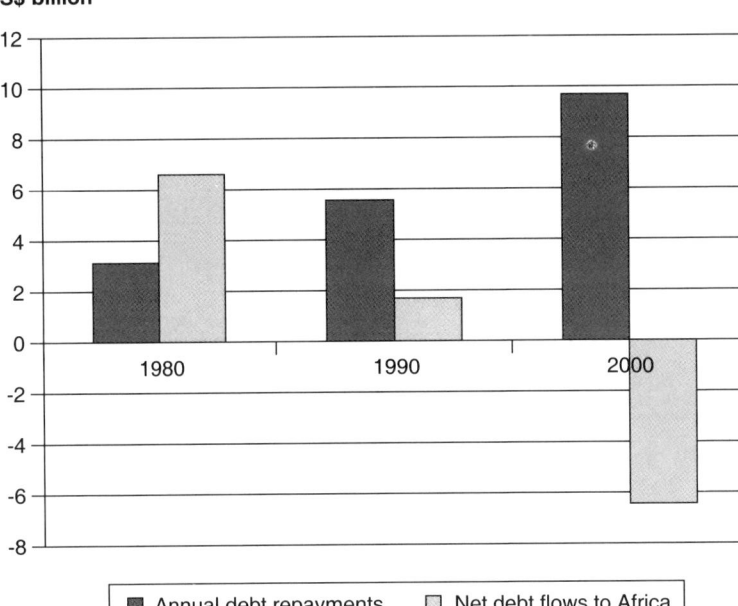

Figure 6: Africa's net debt inflows and outflows, 1980–2000.
Source: World Bank

reform. One necessary task is to discipline financial power with more serious intent, which probably entails combining the 'deglobalisation' of capital with the 'decommodification' of many aspects of life that are now being colonised by business. It is to this global/local strategy that we will return in conclusion.

To this argument must be added the urgent need to counter the rise of right-wing military power from Washington, especially since the post-September 11, 'clash of fundamentalisms', US Empire versus Radical Islam,[7] as the great Pakistani writer, Tariq Ali, puts it. The social justice movements responded with an impressive show of street heat on 15 February 2003, when more people around the world came out to demonstrate for a single cause, peace, in opposition to the threatened war against Iraq by the USA and Britain, than at any time in history. Although termed the world's 'second superpower,' the movement lacked sufficient clout to deter George W. Bush from his manic trajectory. Nevertheless, there remain opportunities to withstand Washington's economic and geopolitical aggression by principled, democratic organisations.

What does this mean for South Africa? The central thesis of this book is that the period immediately before and after September 11, 2001 was a time of conclusive failure for Pretoria's international reforms of global apartheid. It also became the moment at which South Africa's new left opposition emerged as an important social force.[8]

Certainly, the African National Congress (ANC) and its two main Alliance partners – the South African Communist Party (SACP) and Congress of South African Trade Unions (Cosatu) – maintain a self-reinforcing political bloc, even though, as back-seat drivers, communists and workers have only fruitlessly signalled a left turn. Beyond that alliance are church leaders, non-governmental organisation (NGO) officials and a section of the community movement. Middle class and wealthier communities have realised that ANC rule is broadly favourable to their interests and provide tacit support.

Mbeki and his colleagues have pursued the same approach to broad-based alliance-building internationally. Self-congratulatory press statements tell us that Pretoria benefited, as host or in high-profile roles, at many important meetings: the World Conference Against Racism in Durban (August–September 2001); the launch of the New Partnership for Africa's Development in Abuja, Nigeria (October 2001); the Doha, Qatar ministerial summit of the World Trade Organisation (November 2001); regular World Bank/IMF meetings (e.g., November 2001 in Ottawa); a World Economic Forum meeting in New York City (February 2002); the UN's Financing for Development

conference in Monterrey, Mexico (March 2002); the G8 summit in Kananaskis, Canada (June 2002); the Southern African World Economic Forum meeting in Durban (June 2002); the African Union launch in Durban (July 2002); the World Summit on Sustainable Development in Johannesburg (August–September 2002); a UN heads of state summit (September 2002); the Evian G8 Summit (June 2003); the Cancun WTO ministerial (September 2003); the World Bank/IMF annual meeting in Dubai (September 2003); and the Socialist International in Sao Paolo (October 2003).

In only a few recent cases – the World Economic Forum at Davos (January 2003), the Addis Ababa Economic Commission on Africa (June 2003), the Cancun WTO summit, and the Commonwealth summit in Abuja (December 2003) – did Pretoria express frustration at inadequate progress. It is perhaps, thus, not surprising that conventional wisdom in South Africa celebrates Mbeki's ambitions. The *Mail & Guardian*'s editorialists provided a 2003 'report card' on Pretoria, giving Mbeki a 'C' grade, but praising his global agenda:

> As Mbeki nears the end of his first term in office, it is in the area of foreign affairs that his legacy will rest . . . South Africa always has a reserved seat at the head table at powerful multilateral organisations and associations and Africa is now a high agenda item at the summits of the G8 major economies. If Mbeki were to be rated on his performance on the international stage, he would pass with flying colours.[9]

Yet Pretoria's global and continental reforms have been systematically frustrated, partly by design and partly through forces beyond Mbeki's control. Official South African analyses, strategies, tactics and alliances reflect excessive caution, while Mbeki has confused matters with his tendency to talk in a radical manner, while he acts to preserve the overall premises of capitalist globalisation.[10]

Dissatisfaction with Mbeki's local and global initiatives began driving South African activists to seek allies and networks abroad.[11] Left community groups, environmentalists and non-governmental organisations, a few independent trade unionists, and disparate critics provide ongoing critiques. The January 2001 founding of the World Social Forum in Porto Alegre, Brazil, brought some of these activists together. It was followed by activism at the World Conference Against Racism in 2001 and led to the Johannesburg launch of the Social Movements Indaba (SMI) in mid-2002. The SMI used the WSSD and other high-profile events to charge global neoliberalism with inaction against poverty and unemployment, and with ecological destruction and state repression (as documented in Chapter Seven). Periodically,

South African activists have united with international critics of neoliberalism to castigate local, African and global establishments.

An excellent example of a popular movement harnessing globalised information networks is the Treatment Action Campaign's (TAC's) attempt to acquire antiretroviral medicines to prevent and treat HIV in a country with some 5 million infections. In April 2001, government and the TAC won a significant court battle against pharmaceutical companies, which allowed the local production or import of generic substitues. International pressure against Big Pharma played an important role in the victory. But, for another two and a half years, Mbeki and his health and trade ministers, Manto Tshabalala-Msimang and Alec Erwin, failed to substantively change policy or to override patents for generic production or inexpensive imports, even after the Constitutional Court made clear that the denial of medicines to pregnant, HIV-positive women was unconstitutional.

The TAC declared victory in November 2003, after a government medicines roll-out strategy was finally announced: 'The combination of the Constitutional Court decision on mother-to-child transmission prevention, the Stand Up for Our Lives march [of 15 000 people on parliament] in February, the civil disobedience campaign and international protests around the world have convinced Cabinet to develop and implement an ARV rollout plan.'[12] Another factor, of

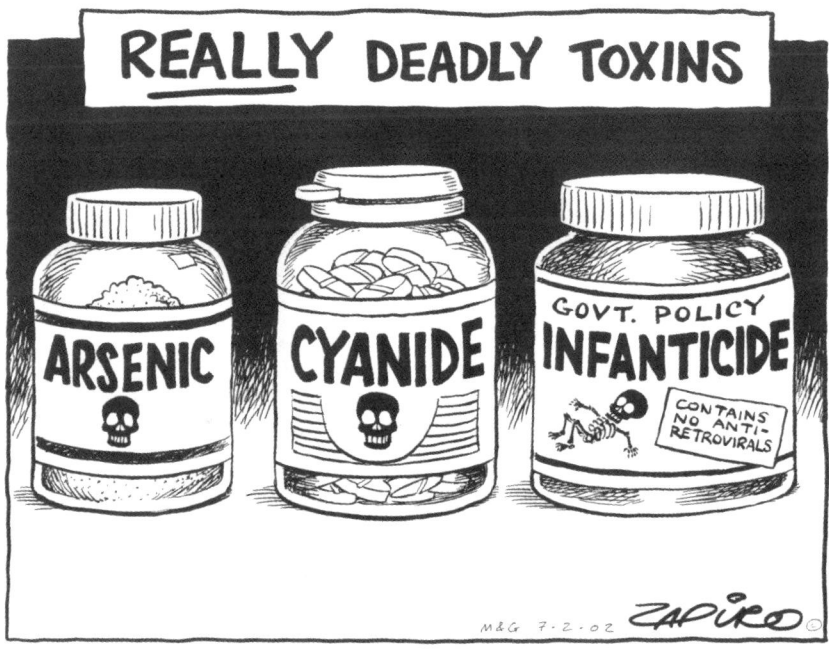

course, was the 2004 presidential election. But by early 2004, the government was already foot-dragging on medicines procurement, according to TAC secretary Mark Heywood: 'It is a totally unwarranted delay, with the result that it could be months before any antiretrovirals get to hospitals. Once again, the AIDS programme is not a priority for government.'[13]

Pretoria's reluctance to save millions of lives would remain a persistent basis for grievance. A few weeks before Cabinet's decision, Mbeki – in full denialist mode – remarked to the *New York Times*, 'Personally, I don't know anybody who has died of AIDS.'[14] Prior to that, Pretoria's regulatory agency for medicines tried to recall a drug commonly used to prevent mother-to-child HIV infection, Nevirapine, because of paper-work mistakes following Ugandan trials many years earlier. This was despite many international agencies, including the US National Institutes for Health, assuring the SA government that those problems had nothing to do with the drug's safety or efficacy. However, the repeated barriers to treatment do probably reflect minister Tshabala-Msimang's viewpoint, reported from the 2002 Barcelona AIDS conference, that such medicines are 'poison'.[15]

From apartheid to class divisions

Mbeki has generated rising left-wing opposition, like the TAC's rights-based medicines strategy and SMI opposition to the WSSD and local neoliberalism, in the course of replacing racial apartheid with 'class apartheid'. The structured processes of division and segregation are comparable in outcome, as reflected in rising alienation and discontent. Shockingly, 'the number of black people who believe life was better under the apartheid regime is growing,' according to a 2002 survey conducted by the Institute for a Democratic Alternative in South

Africa. 'More than 60% of all South Africans polled said the country was better run during white minority rule . . . Only one in ten people believed their elected representatives were interested in their needs and fewer than one in three felt today's government was more trustworthy than the apartheid regime. Black people were only slightly more positive than white and mixed-race groups about the government, with 38% deeming it more trustworthy than before.'[16]

A government agency, Statistics South Africa, released a report in October 2002 confirming that in real terms, average black 'African' household income declined 19% from 1995–2000, while white household income was up 15%. Households with less than R670 per month income – mainly those of black African, coloured or Asian descent – increased from 20% of the population in 1995 to 28% in 2000. The poorest half of all South Africans claimed a mere 9.7% of national income, down from 11.4% in 1995, while the richest fifth grabbed 65%.[17] Matters didn't improve; Cosatu stated in a year-end 2003 message to workers, 'Far from us turning the corner, in 2003 the nightmare of unemployment and poverty got steadily worse . . . [with] at least 22 million people living in desperate poverty and 5.3 million South African children suffering from hunger.'[18]

The official measure of unemployment rose from 16% in 1995 to 31.5% in 2002.[19] Add to that figure frustrated job-seekers and the percentage of unemployed people rises to 43%. Superficially, Cosatu is correct in concluding, 'The main reason for this jobs carnage is that after ten years of liberation, our economy remains largely unrestructured with the structural problems we inherited from apartheid mismanagement still in place. The economy remains firmly in white hands, dominated by the few companies operating in the mining and financial sectors.'[20]

Moreover, at least 10 million people had their water disconnected for non-payment, and a similar number experienced the same for not paying electricity bills. Rising water and electricity prices together accounted for 30% of the income of those earning less than R500 per month.[21] Even more had telephone services terminated. Millions have been evicted from their homes or land since 1994.[22] A January 2004 press statement from the Landless People's Movement observed that in nearly a decade since liberation, Pretoria failed to deliver on its promise to 'redistribute 30% of the country's agricultural land from 60 000 white farmers to more than 19-million poor and landless rural black people and more than 7-million poor and landless urban black people within five years . . . Studies show that just over 2.3% of the country's land has changed hands through land reform.'[23]

One of the most obvious ways in which apartheid was constructed was in residential terms: who could live where. Such segregation did not end in 1994, but took on a class-based character. This can be directly attributed to public policy, ironically designed by the then chairperson of the South African Communist Party, Joe Slovo. As the first democratic housing minister, he adopted World Bank advice that included smaller housing subsidies than were necessary and more reliance upon banks for credit. The policy was to give R16 000 per unit, leaving scant funds for foundations, permanent building materials and sound construction. It also saw greater reliance upon banks and commercial developers, instead of state and community-driven development strategies.[24] Nine years later, Gauteng Province housing minister Paul Mashatile admitted that the resulting landscape had become an embarrassment: 'If we are to integrate communities both economically and racially, then there is a real need to depart from the present concept of housing delivery that is determined by stands, completed houses and budget spent.' His spokesperson, Dumisani Zulu, added, 'The view has always been that when we build low-cost houses, they should be built away from existing areas because it impacts on the price of property.'[25]

Lew Geffen, who heads one of Johannesburg's large real estate corporations, insists that 'low-cost houses should be developed in outlying areas where the property is cheaper and more quality houses (can) be built'.[26] Given the power relations in the housing industry, it is reasonable to anticipate continuity, not change, in Johannesburg's geography, featuring more such 'quality' houses, i.e., half as large, and constructed with flimsier materials than during apartheid; located even further from jobs and community amenities; characterised by disconnections of water and electricity; with lower-grade state services including rare rubbish collection, inhumane sanitation, dirt roads and inadequate storm-water drainage.[27]

Worsening class division and social segregation appear to be the inexorable outcome of South Africa's elite transition. All of this makes a mockery of Mbeki's challenge, in the wake of the WSSD, to his cabinet:

> As a host country the successful outcome of the Johannesburg World Summit places a special responsibility on us to be – in our own habits and practices – among the global leaders in sustainable development. Just as South Africa provided the leadership required of it at the Summit and . . . hosted with widely acclaimed success the biggest-ever multilateral event, so too must South Africa serve as a shining example in putting into action the Johannesburg Plan of Implementation [the main WSSD declaration].[28]

Long after the WSSD, Mbeki's attack on global apartheid aimed high rhetorically, but conclusively failed to reverse inequities at home. Pretoria's neoliberalism generates deepening poverty and also despoils the ecosystem.

Eco-decay and environmental racism

Consider some of the sources of ecological strife. South Africa has scarce water resources, yet Pretoria permits extreme inequality in their distribution, with respect to natural surface and groundwater (since apartheid land dispossession), and in water consumption norms, with wealthy urban families enjoying swimming pools and English gardens, and rural women queuing at communal taps in the parched ex-bantustan areas for hours.

South Africa also contributes more to global warming than nearly any economy in the world if CO_2 emissions are corrected for both income and population. Greenhouse gas emissions are 20 times higher than even the United States by that measure, and the emissions have been worsening over the last decade. Notwithstanding good solar, wind and tides potential, renewable energy is desperately underfunded. Instead, vast resources are devoted to nuclear energy R&D (including huge investments in pebble-bed nuclear reactors) and construction of Africa's largest hydropower facilities.

South Africa boasts extraordinary natural biodiversity, but controversy and conflict continue over natural land reserves, including ongoing displacement of people, the impact of industrialisation on biodiversity, the protection of endangered species, intellectual property rights, especially indigenous knowledge and organic flora and fauna. South Africa has become a subimperial site for the corporate penetration of Africa through genetic modification for commercial agricultural purposes.

Marine regulatory systems are overstressed and hotly contested, given the desire of black economic empowerment entrepreneurs to access fishing quotas in waters strained by overfishing from European and East Asian fishing trawlers.

South Africa's use of exotic timber plantations (mainly gum and pine) is extremely damaging to grasslands and indigenous forests. Soil degradation with the use of these plants creates the potential for flood damage, and the spread of alien-invasive plants into water catchment areas across the country, nothwithstanding a small countervailing effort to eradicate alien vegetation.

Commercial agriculture is heavily reliant upon fertilizers and pesticides, and pays little attention to potential organic farming markets.

South Africa's failure to prevent toxic dumping and incineration has led to a nascent but portentous group of mass tort (class action) lawsuits that may graduate from asbestos victims to residents who suffer persistent pollution in several extremely toxic pockets (South Durban, Sasolburg, Steel Valley).[29]

Explaining Pretoria's frustrations

To make sense of all this global and local damage, we need to consider the array of forces lined up for and against capitalist globalisation, alongside admiration for Pretoria's increasingly active globe-trotting reformism. But our respect for Mbeki's energy and ambition to tackle global apartheid must be tempered by a clear assessment of victories and defeat.

In Chapter Two we review international and local power relations including the rise of US militarism. We then examine Pretoria's frustrated attempts to dent global apartheid at the main world summits on racism (Chapter Three), trade (Chapter Four), finance (Chapter Five), G8-African relations (Chapter Six), sustainable development (Chapter Seven) and water (Chapter Eight).

The impact of these international processes upon local politics, at a time of unprecedented political paranoia in Pretoria, is of great interest. The ruling party responded to challenges from the independent left with an exceptional burst of 'talking left' while 'walking right' (Chapter Nine). Meanwhile, in the context of more explicit imperial ambitions emanating from Washington, even some former insider-reformers began to understand the need for more radical measures (Chapter Ten). Finally, I assess the lessons learnt and attempt to predict a way forward for the global justice movements (Chapter Eleven).

Notes
1. Mbeki, T. (2002), 'Address by President Mbeki at the Welcome Ceremony of the WSSD', Johannesburg, 25 August.
2. Mbeki, T. (2003), 'Letter from the President', *ANC Today*, http://www.anc.org.za, 31 October.
3. One pro-business political commentator, Harald Pakendorf, asked: 'Why did the market not take fright at this bold statement of a reversal in fundamental economic approach?' His answer: the market knows Mbeki 'will not abandon the fundamental economic approach the ANC has been following from about 1993 onwards: fiscal discipline, reducing the budget deficit, making the country attractive to investors, giving the private sector room to grow'. As for the slight Keynesian turn indicated in a 3% deficit/GDP ratio (higher than any recent year), Pakendorf explains that Mbeki

respects the political importance of 'welfare departments and infrastructure. That started two budgets ago, but the money has not yet trickled through the economy. Just before an election, you step up that programme. If you then verbally denounce that which makes your alliance partners – the SACP and Cosatu – unhappy, there is an added advantage: you take one issue off the table.' In sum, says Pakendorf, 'Mbeki is doing the old classical political thing: talking left but doing right' (*Business Report*, 12 November 2003).

4. Background covering the structural conditions and political processes prior to September 2001, as well as South Africa's wretched experience in international currency markets since, is found in Bond, P. (2003) [2001], *Against Global Apartheid: South Africa Meets the World Bank, IMF and International Finance*, Cape Town, University of Cape Town Press and London, Zed Books.

5. Booker, S. and W. Minter (2001), 'AIDS is a Consequence of Global Apartheid', *The Nation*, 2 July.

6. For details, see Harvey, D. (2003), *The New Imperialism*, Oxford, Oxford University Press and Harvey, D. (1999) [1982], *The Limits to Capital*, London, Verso, especially the analysis of 'spatial and temporal fixes' to the overaccumulation problem.

7. Ali, T. (2002), *The Clash of Fundamentalisms*, London, Verso.

8. Considerations about domestic politics are treated in depth in Bond, P. (2004) [2000], *Elite Transition: From Apartheid to Neoliberalism in South Africa*, London, Pluto Press and Pietermaritzburg, University of Natal Press. I recommend several websites: http://www.nu.ac.za/ccs, http://www.aidc.org.za, http://southafrica.indymedia.org; and numerous books written mainly by independent leftists over the last dozen or so years. These give a flavour of the depth and breadth of the radical political-economic critique (there are still others from critical gender and race perspectives): Legassick, M. (forthcoming), *Towards Socialist Democracy*, Pietermaritzburg, University of KwaZulu-Natal Press; Saul, J. (forthcoming), *The Next Liberation Struggle*, London, Merlin Press, New York, Monthly Review Press and Pietermaritzburg, University of KwaZulu-Natal Press; Barchiesi, F. and T. Bramble (eds) (2003), *Rethinking the Labour Movement in the 'New South Africa,'* Aldershot, Ashgate; Kimani, S. (ed.) (2003), *The Right to Dissent: Freedom of Expression, Assembly and Demonstration in the New South Africa*, Johannesburg, Freedom of Expression Institute; Alexander, N. (2002), *An Ordinary Country*, Pietermaritzburg, University of Natal Press; Jacobs, S. and R. Calland (eds) (2002), *Thabo Mbeki's World*, London, Zed Books and Pietermaritzburg, University of Natal Press; Hart, G. (2002), *Disabling Globalisation*, Pietermaritzburg, University of Natal Press and Berkeley, University of California Press; Desai, A. (2002), *We are the Poors*, New York, Monthly Review Press; McDonald, D. (ed.) (2002), *Environmental Justice in South Africa*, Cape Town, University of Cape Town Press; McDonald, D. and J. Pape (eds) (2002), *Cost Recovery and the Crisis of Service Delivery in South Africa*, London, Zed Books and Pretoria, HSRC Publications; Duncan, J. (2002), *Broadcasting and the National Question*, Johannesburg, Freedom of Expression Institute; Bell, T. and D. Ntsebeza (2001), *Unfinished Business*, Cape Town, RedWorks; Adams, S. (2001), *Comrade Minister*, New York, Nova Science Publishers; Marais, H. (2000),

South Africa Limits to Change, London, Zed Books and Cape Town, University of Cape Town Press; Bond, P. (2000), *Cities of Gold, Townships of Coal*, Trenton, Africa World Press; Bond, P. and M. Khosa (eds) (1999), *An RDP Policy Audit*, Pretoria, HSRC Publications; Desai, A. (1999), *South Africa Still Revolting*, Durban, Natal Newspapers; McKinley, D. (1997), *The ANC and the Liberation Struggle*, London, Pluto Press; Levin, R. and D. Weiner (eds) (1997), '*No More Tears*', Trenton, Africa World Press; Bernstein, H. (ed.) (1996), *The Agrarian Question in South Africa*, London, Frank Cass; Fine, B. and Z. Rustomjee (1996), *The Political Economy of South Africa*, London, Christopher Hurst and Johannesburg, Wits University Press; Mayekiso, M. (1996), *Township Politics*, New York, Monthly Review; O'Meara, D. (1996), *Forty Lost Years*, London, James Currey; Murray, M. (1994), *Revolution Deferred*, London, Verso; Mokonyane, D. (1994), *The Big Sell Out*, London, Nakong ya Rena; Saul, J. (1993), *Recolonization and Resistance in Southern Africa*, Trenton, Africa World Press; Alexander, N. (1993), *Some are More Equal than Others*, Cape Town, Buchu; Callinicos, A. (1992), *South Africa Between Apartheid and Capitalism*, London, Bookmarks; Fine, R. and D. Davies (1991), *Beyond Apartheid*, London, Pluto Press; and Bond, P. (1991), *Commanding Heights and Community Control*, Johannesburg, Ravan Press.
9. *Mail & Guardian*, 24 December 2003.
10. In mid-2003, Mbeki's agenda was explained by former International Monetary Fund managing director Michel Camdessus, subsequently France's personal G8 representative to Africa, in the following way: 'The African heads of state came to us with the conception that globalisation was not a curse for them, as some had said, but rather the opposite, from which something positive could be derived . . . You can't believe how much of a difference this [home-grown pro-globalisation attitude] makes' (http://www.g7.utoronto.ca/ summit/2003evian/ briefing_apr030601.html).
11. Bond, P. (2004), 'Labour, Social Movements and South African Foreign Economic Policy,' in P. Nel and J. van der Westhuizen (eds), *Democratising South African Foreign Policy*, New York, Lexington Books and Cape Town, University of Cape Town Press.
12. What was behind the 19 November Cabinet statement? Pretoria cited factors which included: 'a fall in the prices of drugs over the past two years . . . new medicines and international and local experience in managing the utilisation of ARVs . . . [sufficient] health workers and scientists with skills and understanding . . . and the availability of fiscal resources to expand social expenditure in general, as a consequence of the prudent macro-economic policies pursued by government.' However, these factors are minor compared to intense activist pressure and the rising pre-election alienation, for an AC Nielsen survey in November 2003 confirmed that Mbeki's AIDS policy was hurting the ANC's chances of turning out the vote. For more, see http://www.tac.org.za. My own pessimism about the deeper structural forces at work is recorded in *Against Global Apartheid*, Chapters Eight and Nine; *Elite Transition*, second edition; Bond, P. (2003), 'Can AIDS Medicines Victory Catalyse Deeper Changes?', *ZNet Commentary*, http://www.zmag.org, 1 December; and Bond, P. (2002), 'The Social Costs of Corporate HIV/AIDS Policies', *Sowetan/Sunday World*, 14 July.
13. *Financial Times*, 20 January 2004.

14. *New York Times*, 29 September 2003.
15. According to the 8 July 2002 *Newsday* (a respected New York paper): 'Health Minister Manto Tshabalala-Msimang told *Newsday* of her unhappiness with the ruling [by South Africa's Constitutional Court, forcing government to treat HIV-positive pregnant women], and her characterisation of the drug nevirapine as "poison" may signal an intention to continue to thwart use of the drug. In comments later she said, with obvious rage, "We will implement because we are forced to implement. The High Court has decided the Constitution says I must give my people a drug that isn't approved by the FDA. I must poison my people," she said.' Later, Tshabalala-Msimang denied saying this, but *Newsday* did not retract.
16. Carroll, R. (2002), 'More Blacks believe Apartheid Country ran Better', *Mail & Guardian*, 13 December.
17. Statistics South Africa (2002), *Earning and Spending in South Africa*, Pretoria; *Business Day*, 22 November 2002. Apartheid-era terminology is occasionally utilised throughout this book, not by way of endorsement, but because this is the way statistics are most readily disaggregated.
18. Cosatu (2003), 'End of Year Statement', Johannesburg, 22 December, p. 2.
19. Statistics South Africa (2001), *South Africa in Transition*, Pretoria, for 1995, and Statistics South Africa (2003), *Labour Force Survey, September 2002*, Pretoria, p. iii for 2002.
20. Cosatu, 'End of Year Statement', p. 3. There is a deeper argument, as well, relating to South Africa's own organic overaccumulation problems (Bond, *Elite Transition*, Chapter One).
21. Statistics South Africa (2002), 'Database on Expenditure and Income, 2000'.
22. http://www.queensu.ca/msp. Although Pretoria has disputed the figures, they may be understatements. The issue is reviewed in Chapter Eight.
23. Landless Peoples Movement (2004), 'Press Statement,', Johannesburg, 8 January.
24. Full details are provided in Bond, *Elite Transition*, Chapter Four and *Cities of Gold, Townships of Coal*, Part Four.
25. *Saturday Star*, 7 June 2003.
26. *Saturday Star*, 7 June 2003.
27. See ongoing documentation of these problems at the Municipal Services Project website at http://www.queensu.ca/msp.
28. Mbeki, T. (2002), 'Response to Questions in the National Assembly of Parliament', Cape Town, 19 September.
29. These and related issues – along with critiques of megaprojects like the Coega port and industrial development zone and the Lesotho Highlands Water Project – are discussed in Bond, P. (2002), *Unsustainable South Africa: Development and Social Protest*, London, Merlin and Pietermaritzburg, University of Natal Press. See also McDonald, *Environmental Justice in South Africa*; and Clarke, J. (2002), *Coming Back to Earth: South Africa's Changing Environment*, Johannesburg, Jacana. For more background to the historic impact of state and capital, see Dovers, S., R. Edgecombe and B. Guest (eds) (2002), *South Africa's Environmental History: Cases and Comparisons*, Cape Town, David Philip and Athens, Ohio University Press; and for an important case study, see Jacobs, N. (2002), *Environment, Power and Injustice: A South African History*, Cambridge, Cambridge University Press.

2
Global-local power relations
Ideology, image and war games

What is the array of global forces Pretoria confronted after Sepember 2001? At least five ideological categories have emerged and solidified:
- Global justice movements
- Third World nationalism
- Post-Washington Consensus
- Washington Consensus
- Resurgent Rightwing.

This chapter seeks to map these groups and explore their beliefs, contradictions, institutions and leading personalities. The five currents are recognisable by the political traditions from which they have evolved, their political-economic agenda, leading institutions, internal disputes and noted public proponents.

Semantics need not detain us. Debates over ideology are so well advanced in South Africa that virtually no government official would claim to be 'neoliberal' given the word's demonisation since the late 1990s. Across the world, many individuals have moved, not merely rhetorically, but also substantively, from one camp to another. For example, economist Joseph Stiglitz has rapidly shifted left since the late 1990s, while Brazilian president Luis 'Lula' Ignacio da Silva has repositioned to the right of his Workers' Party base. Some, like Mbeki, stand in more than one camp at once, and their outlook depends partly upon the political 'scale' which they are contesting: global, continental, national or local.

How does Pretoria relate to the five core ideologies? Mbeki and his top political aides have articulated strong, but ultimately hypocritical, opposition to the Rightwing Resurgence, especially the 2003 war against Iraq. With regard to the Washington Consensus, Pretoria did not hesitate to implement the full range of neoliberal policies at home and sought to relegitimise the WashCon across the continent via the New Partnership for Africa's Development. At the same time, Mbeki,

Manuel, Erwin and others offer rhetorical support for the Post-Washington Consensus – yet, can claim no obvious progress when leading elite processes, such as international summits. There is a residual commitment within the ANC-Alliance to the Third World nationalist tradition of enlightenment and liberation – although as Fanon would have anticipated,[1] a degenerate, exhausted nationalism is often on display in Pretoria, and as we see in subsequent chapters, an intense fear of the global justice movements. Hence, while Mbeki made repeated overtures to Washington, the possibilities for co-operation across the divides on the left were generally ignored or even actively sabotaged by Pretoria.

Tables 1 and 2 are self-explanatory, although several obvious caveats apply, not least of which is the highly subjective, snapshot nature of such an exercise. The ideological currents are rough approximations, sometimes proudly worn as labels, sometimes not.

Learning from war

To illustrate the wavering alliances, Pretoria formally opposed the 2003 US/UK war against Saddam Hussein's Iraq – or, more precisely, a war without UN Security Council approval. A few ANC leaders engaged in occasional pickets at US consulates in Cape Town, Durban and Johannesburg. But had Washington's bullying of several Security Council swing votes succeeded in achieving a Council endorsement of the war, Pretoria would no doubt have fallen into line.

The rhetoric was predictably intense. On 19 February 2003, at a demonstration of 4 000 people outside the US embassy in Pretoria, ANC secretary-general Kgalema Motlanthe pronounced: 'Because we are endowed with several rich minerals, if we don't stop this unilateral action against Iraq today, tomorrow they will come for us.'[2] Health minister Tshabalala-Msimang reportedly said: 'South Africa cannot afford drugs to fight HIV/AIDS . . . because it needs submarines to deter attacks from nations such as the US.'[3]

To its credit, the ANC-Alliance put together a Stop the War Campaign with the South African Council of Churches. The campaign co-ordinator, ANC policy director Michael Sachs, argued the merits of 'uniting around the broadest possible alliance in opposition to war and imperialism . . . George W. Bush has drawn a line in the sand, and we must decide on which side we stand.'[4] However, the independent left's Anti-War Coalition did far more mobilising for demonstrations, especially on the date of global anti-war protests: 15 February 2003. Sachs told a co-ordinating meeting that ANC leaders

Table 1: Five international ideological currents.

Political current	Global justice movements	Third World nationalism	Post-Washington Consensus	Washington Consensus	Resurgent right wing
Political tradition	socialism and anarchism	*national* capitalism	(lite) social democracy	neoliberal capitalism	neoconservatism
Main agenda	'deglobalisation' of capital (not *people*); 'globalisation-from-below'; anti-war; anti-racism; indigenous rights; womens liberation; ecology; 'decommodified' state services; radical participatory democracy	increased (but fairer) global integration via reform of interstate system, based on debt relief and expanded market access; democratised global governance; regionalism; rhetorical anti-imperialism; and Third World unity	fix 'imperfect markets'; add 'sustainable development' to existing capitalist framework via UN and similar global state-building; promote global Keynesianism (maybe); oppose US unilateralism and militarism	rename neoliberalism (PRSPs, HIPC and PPPs) but with some provisions for 'transparency' and self-regulation; more effective bail-out mechanisms; (hypocritical) financial support for US-led Empire	unilateral petro-military imperialism; crony deals, corporate subsidies, protectionism and tariffs; reverse globalisation of *people* via racism and xenophobia; religious extremism; patriarchy and social control
Leading institutions	social movements; environmental justice activists; indigenous people; autonomist groups; radical activist networks; leftist labour movements; left think-tanks (e.g., Focus on the Global South, FoodFirst, GX, IBASE, IFG, IPS, Nader centres, TNI); left media (Indymedia, Pacifica, zmag.org); semi-liberated zones (Porto Alegre, Kerala); sectoral or local coalitions allied to World Social Forum	Non-Aligned Movement, G77 and South Centre; self-selecting regimes (often authoritarian): Argentina, China, Egypt, India, Iraq, Libya, Malaysia, Nigeria, Pakistan, Palestine, Russia, South Africa, Turkey, Zimbabwe with a few – Brazil, Cuba and Venezuela – that lean left (but others pro-Empire, e.g., East Timor, Ecuador and Eritrea); and supportive NGOs (e.g., Third World Network, Seatini)	some UN agencies (e.g., Unctad, Unicef, Unifem, Unrisd); some int'l NGOs (e.g., Care, Civicus, IUCN, Oxfam, TI); large enviro. groups (e.g., Sierra and WWF); big labour (e.g., ICFTU and AFL-CIO); liberal foundations (Carnegie, Ford, MacArthur, Mott, Open Society, Rockefeller); Columbia U. economics department; the Socialist International; and some Scandinavian governments	US state (Fed, Treasury, USAid); corporate media and big business; World Bank, IMF, WTO; elite clubs (Bilderburger, Trilateral Commission, World Economic Forum); some UN agencies (UNDP, Global Compact); universities and think-tanks (U. of Chicago economics, Cato, Council on Foreign Relations, Adam Smith Inst., Inst. of International Economics, Brookings; and most G8 governments	Republican Party populist and libertarian wings; Project for New American Century; right-wing think-tanks (AEI, CSIS, Heritage, Manhattan); the Christian Right; petro-military complex; Pentagon; rightwing media (Fox, *National Interest, Weekly Standard, Washington Times*); and proto-fascist European parties – but also Israel's Likud and perhaps Islamic extremism

Table 1: (cont)

Political current	Global justice movements	Third World nationalism	Post-Washington Consensus	Washington Consensus	Resurgent right wing
Internal disputes	role of state; party politics; fix-it v. nix-it for int'l agencies; gender & racial power; divergent interests (e.g., Northern labour and environment vs Southern sovereignty); tactics (symbolic property destruction)	degree of militancy against North; divergent regional interests; religion; Islam; ego & internecine rivalries large vs small countries;	some look left (for alliances) while others look right to the Wash. Consensus (in search of resources, legitimacy and deals); and optimal reforms	differing reactions to US Empire due to divergent national-capitalist interests and domestic political dynamics	disputes over US imperial reach, religious influence, protection culture, patriarchy and state sovereignty
Exemplary proponents	E. Adamovsky M. Albert T. Ali S. Amin C. Augiton M. Barlow D. Barsamian H. Belafonte W. Bello A. Bendana F. Betto H. Bonafini J. Bove J. Brecher R. Brenner D. Brutus N. Bullard A. Buzgalin L. Cagan A. Callinicos L. Cassarini J. Cavanagh C. Chalmers N. Chomsky A. Choudry A. Cockburn T. Clarke K. Danaher A. Escobar E. Galeano S. George D. Glover A. Grubacic M. Hardt D. Harvey D. Henwood J. Holloway B. Kagarlitsky P. Kingsnorth N. Klein M. Lowy Marcos A. Mittal	Y. Arafat F. Castro H. Chavez L. da Silva M. Gaddafi Hu J. M. Khor N. Kirshner R. Lagos Mahathir M. N. Mandela T. Mbeki R. Mugabe O. Obasanjo D. Ortega V. Putin Y. Tandon	Y. Akyuz K. Annan L. Axworthy N. Birdsall Bono G. Brundtland S. Byers B. Cassen J. Chretien P. Eigen J. Fischer A. Giddens W. Hutton P. Krugman W. Maathai P. Martin T. Mbeki T. Mkandawire G. Monbiot M. Moody-Stuart K. Naidoo T. Palley J. Persson John Paul II M. Robinson D. Rodrik J. Sachs W. Sachs A. Sen G. Soros J. Stiglitz J. Sweeney G. Verhofstadt E. von Weizaecher K. Watkins	T. Blair G. Brown M. Camdessus J. Chirac B. Clinton A. Erwin V. Fox S. Fischer M. Friedman T. Friedman A. Greenspan S. Harbinson A. Krueger P. Lamy M. Malloch Brown T. Manuel T. Mbeki R. Prodi K. Rogoff R. Rubin G. Schroeder Supachai P. J. Snow L. Summers J. Wolfensohn E. Zedillo R. Zoellick	E. Abrams J. Aznar S. Berlusconi O. Bin Laden C. Black Z. Brzezinski P. Buchanan G. Bush D. Cheney D. Frum N. Gingrich J. Haider J. Howard R. Kagan H. Kissinger W. Kristol J.M. le Pen R. Limbaugh R. Murdoch J. Negroponte G. Norquist M. Peretz R. Perle O. Reich C. Rice K. Rove D. Rumsfeld R. Scaif A. Scalia A. Sharon P. Wolfowitz J. Woolsey

Table 1: *(cont)*

Political current	Global justice movements	Third World nationalism	Post-Washington Consensus	Washington Consensus	Resurgent right wing
	M. Moore E. Morales R. Nader V. Navarro A. Negri T. Ngwane N. Njehu G. Palast M. Patkar M. Pheko J. Pilger A. Roy J. Sen V. Shiva J. Singh B. Sousa Santos A. Starr J. Stedile P. Waterman T. Teivainen, V. Vargas G. Vidal H. Wainwright L. Wallach M. Weisbrot R. Weissman H. Zinn				

Table 2: Five ideological currents in South Africa.

Political current	Global justice movements	Third World nationalism	Post-Washington Consensus	Washington Consensus	Right wing
South African institutions	'anti-neoliberal' social movements (e.g., SMI, APF, Durban Concerned Citizens Forum, Education Rights Project, Environ. Justice Networking Forum, Jubilee SA, Khulumani, Limpopo Movement for Delivery, Palestine Solidarity C'te, SECC, TAC, WC Anti-Eviction Campaign, Youth for Work, sometimes Lamosa, LPM and Sangoco); media (debate, Indymedia, Khanya); think-tanks/ training institutes (AIDC, CEJ-SA, Khanya, groundWork, Ilrig, U. Natal Centre for Civil Society); some unions; campaigns for ARV drugs, free water and electricity, land, housing, reparations, security from sexual violence; Anti-War Coalition	African National Congress, SA Communist Party and some other political parties (PAC, Azapo, Inkatha); ANC Youth League and ANC Women's League; SA Ministry of Foreign Affairs; Africa Institute and African Renaissance Institute; some currents within Cosatu head office and member unions (e.g., NEHAWU, NUMSA and NUM); some media (City Press, Enterprise, New Agenda and Sowetan and most SABC); Black Economic Empowerment Commission; some civil society mvts and NGOs (e.g., SA Council of Churches, SA National Civic Org., SA Non-Governmental Organisations Coalition); Stop the War Campaign	Nedlac; liberal media (e.g., Mail & Guardian, Sunday Independent); some think-tanks (CPS, IGD, Naledi, Niep); some parastatals (HSRC, Human Rights Comm); development NGOs (e.g., Black Sash, IDT, Mvula); mainstream environment groups (EWT, IFAW, IUCN, WWF); SANew Economics network; some funders (FES, Ford, Mott, Open Society, etc.)	business associations (Business Unity SA, Chamber of Commerce and Industry SA, Banking Council); some media (e.g., Business Day, Leadership, Business Report, Financial Mail, SA Jnl of Econ); SA Treasury; dti; Min. of Public Enterprises; DEAT; Reserve Bank; DBSA; DA and NNP; bank and university economics depts; think-tanks (Free Market Foundation, Business-Map, CDE, SAIIA); int'l funders (DFID, GTZ, USAid); NEPAD secretariat	Boeremag

Table 2: (cont)

Political current	Global justice movements	Third World nationalism	Post-Washington Consensus	Washington Consensus	Right wing
South African internal disputes	relations with ANC, SACP, Cosatu; whether to form a left political party; fix-it v. nix-it strategies for int'l agencies; sectarianism; Zimbabwe land issue and imperialist-aligned opposition	relations with 'ultraleft'; fear of (or desire for) split in ANC-SACT-Cosatu Alliance; race (especially role of whites); Int'l alignments; militance vis-à-vis the North; egos and internecine rivalries	some look leftward (for broader alliances) while others look right to the Wash. Consensus (in search of resources, legitimacy and deals)	extent of corporate co-operation with ruling party; and whether Democratic Alliance is too shrill as opposition	strategy for ethnic homeland and language policy

were uncomfortable with the anti-imperialist language of the Anti-War Coalition.[5] After Sachs claimed credit for the 15 February protest in the media, the Coalition refused – churlishly, some members felt – to allow ANC speakers on the stage of the Johannesburg rally.[6] Many felt Pretoria had drawn its own line, and stood on the side of war profits, ignoring Anti-War Coalition calls to withdraw permission for three Iraq-bound warships to dock and refuel in Durban, and to halt arms sales to the US and UK governments. The state-owned weapons manufacturer Denel sold R25 million in ammunition shell-casing, R1.3 billion in artillery propellants, and 326 hand-held laser range finders to the British army, and 125 laser-guidance sights to the US Marines.[7] In the days prior to the USA and UK bombing of Iraq in March 2003, Mbeki deployed deputy foreign minister Aziz Pahad and a technical team to assist in the search for and demobilisation of alleged Iraqi weapons of mass destruction. None were located, and in early 2004 even the US government's main official withdrew from the search in exasperation.

The most outspoken ANC leader was Nelson Mandela:

> All Bush wants is Iraqi oil, because Iraq produces 64% of oil and he wants to get hold of it . . . Their friend Israel has weapons of mass destruction but because it's [the US] ally, they won't ask the UN to get rid of it . . . Bush, who cannot think properly, is now wanting to plunge the world into a holocaust. If there is a

> country which has committed unspeakable atrocities, it is the United States of America . . . They don't care for human beings.⁸

After the fall of Baghdad, Mandela condemned Bush again when he met French foreign minister Dominique de Villepin: 'Since the creation of the United Nations (in 1945) there has not been a World War. Therefore, for anybody, especially the leader of a superstate, to act outside the United Nations is something that must be condemned by everybody who wants peace. For any country to leave the United Nations and attack an independent country must be condemned in the strongest terms.'⁹ However, notwithstanding the laudable opposition of several UN Security Council members to the invasion, the merits of the UN as a site for adjudicating US power was thrown into question after Saddam's regime collapsed and reconstruction was debated. A commentator in the *Jordan Times*, Hasan Abu Nimah, explained:

> The latest Security Council resolution on Iraq, 1483, has been a flagrant betrayal of the UN Charter, a scandalous result of power politics and opportunistic superpower compromises, and a dangerous submission to the *fait accompli* of war and aggression, at the expense of principle and international legality. Earlier, in the weeks leading to the war, the council stood firm in the face of immense American and British pressure, boldly refusing to prematurely undercut the arms inspection programme in favour of a resolution providing legal international cover for the military action against Iraq which was already planned by the US and Britain . . . On May 22, the council dramatically abandoned its steadfast position by suddenly legitimising aggression, endorsing devastation of an innocent country and its weary people, and by licensing their indefinite, unwarranted occupation.¹⁰

Added to the UN's role in the death of as many as a million Iraqis during the 1990s imposition of anti-Saddam sanctions, these problems are reason enough to question Mandela's respect for the world body.

Bush declared an end to the combat on 1 May, a declaration immediately followed by a rise in guerrilla activity. Within days, Mbeki and colleagues returned to their uncritical relationship with Washington. Talk of new trade deals drowned out the option of boycotting US products which had been proposed by progressives in civil society. Pretoria provided the right noises via the New Partnership for Africa's Development (NEPAD), which was termed 'philosophically spot-on' by the White House's main Africa expert, Walter Kansteiner.¹¹

Bill Fletcher, director of the Washington-based TransAfrica Forum observed: 'The US interest in Africa is in direct relationship to oil in the ground. Angola, yes. Equatorial Guinea, yes. But Democratic Republic of the Congo, no. The international community just doesn't care. Over two million people dead. So what?'[12] NATO's Supreme Allied Commander for Europe, General James Jones, confirmed those US interests in May 2003: 'The carrier battle groups of the future and the expeditionary strike groups of the future may not spend six months in the Mediterranean Sea but I'll bet they'll spend half the time down the West Coast of Africa.'[13] Within weeks, that coast was graced by 3 000 US troops deployed offshore from Liberia (and briefly onshore to stabilise the country after Charles Taylor departed). Potential US bases were suggested for Ghana, Senegal and Mali, as well as the North African countries of Algeria, Morocco and Tunisia.[14] Another base was occupied by 1 500 US troops in the small Horn country of Djibouti. Botswana and Mozambique were also part of the Pentagon's strategy, and South Africa would remain a crucial partner.

A telling conflict emerged on the eve of Bush's first-ever Africa trip in July 2003, when the Pentagon announced it would withdraw $7.6 million worth of military aid to Pretoria, because the South African government – along with 34 military allies of Washington (and 90 countries in total) – had not signed a deal that would give US citizens immunity from prosecution at The Hague's new International Criminal Court. Botswana, Uganda, Senegal and Nigeria, also on Bush's itinerary, signed these blackmail-based immunity deals and retained US aid.[15]

Nonetheless, Bush noted during a June 2003 speech to the Corporate Council on Africa: 'I look forward to going to South Africa, where I'll meet with elected leaders who are firmly committed to economic reforms in a nation that has become a major force for regional peace and stability.'[16]

The best spin on Bush's visit was provided by SACP secretary-general, Blade Nzimande: 'Let us use this visit to impact as best as possible on the consciences of the American electorate. It would, we believe, be a mistake to press for a cancellation of the visit. But it would be equally mistaken to present the invasion of Iraq as a "thing of the past", as "something we've put behind us", as we now return to bi-national US/SA business as usual.'[17] The Anti-War Coalition countered: 'The ANC and SACP claim to be marching against the war ... while hosting the chief warmonger, George Bush. The ANC's public relations strategy around the war directly contradicts their actions, which are pro-war and which have contributed to the deaths of thousands of Iraqi civilians.'[18]

Bush was welcomed to Africa uncritically by Mbeki, in contrast to Mandela, who pointedly refused to meet the US president. Johannesburg's *Business Day* editorialised that the 'abiding impression' left from Bush's Pretoria stopover 'is of a growing, if not intimate trust between himself and president Thabo Mbeki. The amount of public touching, hugging and backpatting they went through was well beyond the call of even friendly diplomatic duty.' What was apparent, wrote this arbiter of South African neoliberalism, was that 'Bush trusts Mbeki probably more than do many South Africans'. *Business Day* continued, 'Damage with Africans that may have built up internationally due to Mbeki's positions on AIDS and Zimbabwe will have been greatly eased.'[19]

Similarly, among Bush's European critics, what initially appeared as potential inter-imperial rivalry gave way to co-operation. Tariq Ali observed:

> Schroeder owed his narrow re-election to a pledge not to support a war on Baghdad, even were it authorised by the UN. Chirac, armed with a veto in the security council, was even more voluble with declarations that any unauthorised assault on Iraq would never be accepted by France. Together, Paris and Berlin coaxed Moscow into expressing its disagreement with American plans. Even Beijing emitted a few cautious sounds of demurral. The Franco-German initiatives aroused tremendous excitement and

consternation among diplomatic commentators. Here, surely, was an unprecedented rift in the Atlantic alliance. What was to become of European unity, of Nato, of the 'international community' itself if such a disastrous split persisted? Could the very concept of the west survive?

Such apprehensions were quickly allayed . . . Unsurprisingly, the UN security council capitulated completely, recognised the occupation of Iraq and approved its re-colonisation by the US and its bloodshot British adjutant . . . The UN has now provided retrospective sanction to a pre-emptive strike. Its ill-fated predecessor, the League of Nations, at least had the decency to collapse after its charter was serially raped.[20]

A veil of radical rhetoric

As is apparent from its slippery stance on the 2003 Iraq war, the South African government entered the 21st century slogging through the ideological swamp that is world politics. Pretoria politicians often deployed Third World nationalist rhetoric amongst friends, but Post-Washington Consensus advocacy was the preferred globalist discourse, with the application of Washington Consensus philosophy at home and anywhere South African business interests were at stake in Africa. Remarked neoliberal Democratic Alliance leader Tony Leon,

> Our foreign policy pronouncements have become increasingly politically schizophrenic. The president reassures Parliament that South Africa's relations with the US are still good, and the next day ANC secretary general Kgalema Motlanthe claims that South Africa is the target of an American invasion. The ANC retains an idealised, wounded, radical posture, while the president maintains an air of statesmanship and moderation. So runs the division of labour. This charade cannot go on much longer without running up against its own embarrassing contradictions.[21]

But it can and will continue, especially if Leon is correct that Mbeki's 'focus on global inequality is partly an attempt to mobilise the mass support that he otherwise lacks, and (to) marginalise opposition parties even further'.

Talking left and walking right was perhaps most useful when Mbeki and his colleagues had the job of hosting, chairing or otherwise leading major international events of a diplomatic nature, where – as discussed in subsequent chapters – ideological clarity was inappropriate. In addition, NEPAD was launched to great acclaim in late 2001 and given standing at important meetings of the world's political and business elite. In sectors such as water and venues such as the World Water Forum in Kyoto, South Africans were also extremely prominent.

It was also in Mbeki's interests to muddy the terrain so that it was not immediately evident whose interests Pretoria favoured. Radical rhetoric veiled the reproduction of global apartheid.

Notes
1. Fanon, F. (1961), *The Wretched of the Earth*, New York, Grove Press, Chapter Three: Pitfalls of National Consciousness. Pretoria's claim to support a human rights agenda characteristic of Third World nationalist enlightenment traditions falls apart when we consider policies on Zimbabwe, Burma and arms sales, for example.
2. *Business Day*, 20 February 2003.
3. Tshabala-Msimang told the British *Guardian* that South Africa needed to deter aggressors: 'Look at what Bush is doing. He could invade.' After publication, she called the citation a 'gross misrepresentation' of her comments, yet a clarifying report from the health ministry confirmed that buying AIDS medicines should not undermine 'other important issues such as ensuring the SA National Defence Force was able to carry out its duties including the protection of South Africa's sovereignty and interests' (Sapa, 19 December 2002).
4. Sachs, M. (2003), 'A Line in the Sand, *Khanya Journal*, 3, March.
5. Interview, Salim Vally, June 2003.
6. Co-operation between the groups was more civil in Cape Town, and there were apparently no divisions at a Port Elizabeth rally.
7. Andy Clarno pointed out, 'Trevor Manuel wants to privatise 30% of Denel's Aerospace division in 2003. This commitment to neoliberal capitalism prevents the government from taking a principled stance against imperialism and war. By participating in the contemptible practice of profiting from the war, the South African government has not only refused to challenge imperialism – it has become complicit and is establishing its position clearly within the global capitalist empire' (Clarno, A. (2003), 'Denel and the South African Government: Profiting from the War on Iraq', *Khanya Journal*, 3, March.)
8. *Independent Online*, 30 January 2003.
9. Reuters, 28 June 2003.
10. *Jordan Times*, 28 May 2003.
11. Gopinath, D. (2003), 'Doubt of Africa', *Institutional Investor Magazine*, May.
12. *Socialist Worker* 405, 25 June 2003. For an excellent summary of geopolitical processes and Zimbabwe's predatory role in the DRC, see Campbell, H. (2003), *Reclaiming Zimbabwe: The Exhaustion of the Patriarchal Model of Liberation*, Cape Town, David Philip.
13. allAfrica.com, 2 May 2003.

14. *Ghana News*, 11 June 2003.
15. Sapa, 2 July 2003. Other African countries where US war criminals are safe from ICC prosecutions thanks to military-aid blackmail are the DRC, Gabon, The Gambia, Ghana, Kenya, Mauritius, Sierra Leone and Zambia.
16. Bush, G. (2003), 'Remarks by the President to the Corporate Council on Africa's US-Africa Business Summit', Washington, 26 June.
17. *Umsebenzi*, 2 July 2003.
18. Anti-War Coalition Press Statement, 1 July 2003.
19. *Business Day*, 11 July 2003.
20. Ali, T. (2003), 'Business as Usual', *The Guardian*, 24 May 2003.
21. Leon, T. (2003), 'South Africa's Policy Conundrum', *South African Journal of International Affairs*, p. 127.

PART TWO

ISSUES AND EVENTS

3
Racism talk-shop, reparations sabotage
From reconciliation to amnesia

The August–September 2001 World Conference Against Racism (WCAR) in Durban was the site at which South Africa's 'Social Forum' alternative to the standard NGO parallel summit began to gel. However, the official WCAR talk-shop itself was considered an historic defeat for those insisting on advancing social justice.

The key demands made by the activists who gathered – namely, reparations for slavery, colonialism, apartheid and neocolonialism, and a more profound censure of Israel – failed to move the UN meeting, or even gain the host's support. Neither Thabo Mbeki nor Kofi Annan deigned to meet the main delegation of 20 000 demonstrators who marched to within a few metres of the Durban International Convention Centre entrance. The WCAR showed the distance between the managers of global apartheid, in all its class/race/gender manifestations, and the South African activists and internationalists arrayed against imperialism.

Marching for justice

Pretoria politicians and officials alike must have been badly shaken by events prior to the WCAR. In his book *Dispatches from Durban*, Los Angeles community leader Eric Mann describes Cosatu's strike against privatisation, including a large march, timed for the moment that thousands of delegates flew in to South Africa:

> In the second day of the strike, some 40 000 people filled the streets of Durban with wave upon wave of union contingents. This was not a trade union rally for a better contract; it was a political strike by Black working class and poor people for the future of their country. The call to strike? 'We did not fight for liberation so that we could sell everything we won to the highest bidder!' . . .

Similar to anti-globalisation and antiracist groups in the US that used the Democratic or Republican national conventions as international media arenas to popularise their demands, Cosatu is taking advantage of Mbeki's tactical vulnerability during the WCAR. At a time when Mbeki wants to showcase South Africa as a center for world tourism and to use tourism as a source of urgently needed foreign exchange funds, a two-day general strike is the last thing he wanted. This contributed to the greater leverage and impact of the march, but also to the bitterness of the exchanges between its leaders and the South African government.[1]

However, that bitterness was quickly redirected by trade union leaders, who joined the SACP and ANC for an anti-racism march the day after the furious Durban Social Forum protest of 20 000. The mild-mannered Alliance event drew little more than 7 000 supporters.

Just before the official WCAR began, Mbeki spoke to the formal gathering of NGOs at their alternative summit plenary. Mann reports that at a press conference set up by South Africa's new Indymedia Centre, civil society leaders 'criticised Mbeki's opening speech to WCAR, publicised the demands of the Palestinians, and supported the Durban Social Forum coalition's critique of South African neoliberalism, in particular, the privatisation of public services such as water, and its

RACISM TALK-SHOP, REPARATIONS SABOTAGE 39

support for the demands of the landless movement'.[2] That press conference put South African society on notice that Mbeki was considered an enemy of Durban's poor.

On subsequent days, the streets came alive with campaigns for reparations and Palestinian liberation, supported with great vigour by groups as diverse as Jubilee South affiliates, South Africa's large Muslim community and thousands of international anti-racism activists. The NGO parallel summit also generated a progressive resolution. All of this increased pressure on the official delegates who issued vaguely progressive sentiments inside the WCAR, which saw the US and Israeli governments storm out because of references to racism within both those countries.

Reparations rupture

The official conference also splintered over a demand from NGOs and some African governments that payment be made to compensate for centuries of colonial plunder, whose effects continue contributing to vastly imbalanced economies, societies and international power relations. The EU's chief negotiator, Belgian foreign minister Louis Michel, justified his own country's appalling history at a press conference: 'Colonialism could not be considered a crime against humanity, for at the time it was a sign of economical good health.'[3] UN human rights commissioner Mary Robinson broke off discussions

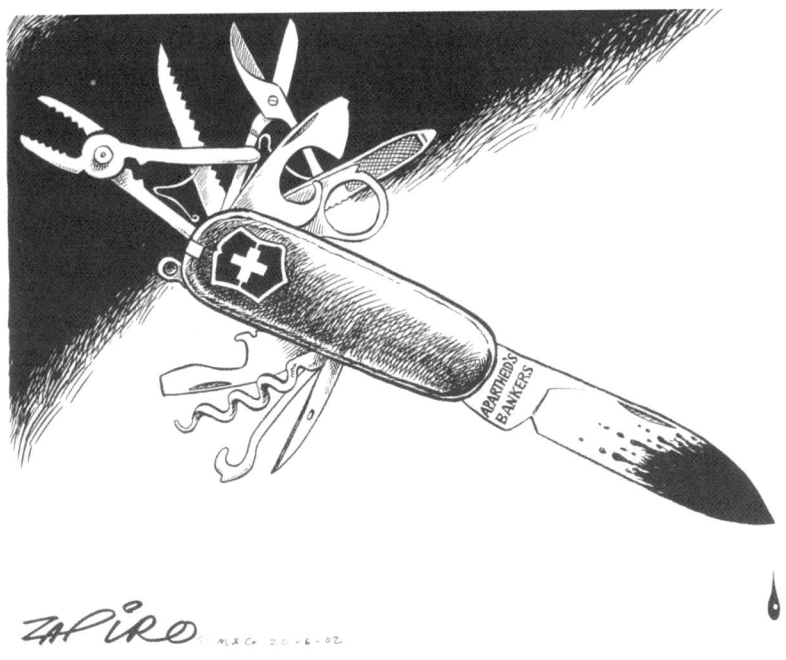

with activists because the NGO petition calling for reparations and Palestinian rights was, for her, too radical.

Ironically, even though Nigerian president Olusegun Obasanjo endorsed reparations along with other African official delegates, Mbeki and his foreign minister, Nkosazana Dlamini-Zuma, refused support, saying merely that more donor aid was needed. 'Nigeria has chosen to ditch SA and align itself with other African hardliners over the slavery issue,' lamented a *Business Day* editorial under the headline 'Trapped in the Middle'. It continued, 'The difficulties that SA has encountered in Durban trying to move the rest of the continent to a more moderate position in negotiations between Africa and Europe over an apology and reparations for slavery, highlight the gulf, and sometimes deceit, that underlies relations between this country and the rest of the continent . . . When will our real friends in Africa stand up and be counted?'[4]

Reparations demands were absent from the final WCAR document, and moreover, also soon led to a rupture between the ANC government and civil society activists. Frustrated by the failure of the WCAR to advance their agenda, leaders of Jubilee South Africa, the Khulumani apartheid-victims group and other faith-based activists turned to the US and Swiss courts. Civil cases for billions of dollars in damages were filed on behalf of apartheid victims against large multinational corporations which made profits from South African investments and loans (by 2003, Anglo American, Gold Fields and Sasol were added to the corporate defendants' list).[5] The Bush regime and corporate lobbies pleaded with US courts, initially unsuccessfully, to nullify an interpretation of the Alien Tort Claims Act that made apartheid-reparations suits possible.[6]

Mbeki first reacted to the court applications with 'neither support nor condemnation'. However, in April 2003, in the wake of Archbishop Desmond Tutu's final Truth and Reconciliation Commission (TRC) report which recommended a reparations payment by businesses which benefited from apartheid, Mbeki changed tack. Now, he said, it was 'completely unacceptable that matters that are central to the future of our country should be adjudicated in foreign courts which bear no responsibility for the well-being of our country, and the observance of the perspective contained in our constitution of the promotion of national reconciliation'. He expressed 'the desire to involve all South Africans, including corporate citizens, in a co-operative and voluntary partnership'. But Mbeki failed to reflect upon numerous such attempts by the Reparations Task Force and Cape Town's Anglican Archbishop Njongonkulu Ndungane for some years prior to the lawsuits.[7]

Always a strong advocate for business interests, Alec Erwin joined Mbeki during an April 2003 parliamentary discussion. Pretoria was

'opposed to, and contemptuous of the litigation', Erwin said. Any findings against companies 'would not be honoured' within South Africa, he added, and a wealth tax – as recommended by the TRC – would be 'counterproductive'.[8]

A few weeks later, the director-general in Mbeki's office, former liberation theologian Frank Chikane, attacked the morals of those filing the reparations lawsuits: 'I have seen [apartheid] victims being organised by interest groups who make them perpetual victims. They will never cease to be victims because they [interest groups] need victims to advance their cause. I think it is a dehumanising act.' Chikane argued that lawsuits against banks and corporations would lead 'businesses here to lose money and therefore to lose jobs'. As for the TRC wealth tax, 'My view has always been that healing will happen only if the victimiser stands up and says, "let us make it right". It will not happen if the government says so.'[9]

In July 2003, Mbeki and justice minister Penuell Maduna went to even greater lengths to defend apartheid-era profits, arguing in a nine-page brief to a US court hearing a reparations case, that by 'permitting the litigation', the New York judge would discourage 'much-needed foreign investment and delay the achievement of the government's goals. Indeed, the litigation could have a destabilising effect on the South African economy as investment is not only a driver of growth, but also of unemployment.'[10] As a friend of the court on behalf of the claimants (alongside Tutu), Nobel laureate Joseph Stiglitz replied that the comments by Mbeki and Maduna had 'no basis', because, 'those who helped support that system, and who contributed to human rights abuses, should be held accountable . . . If anything, it would contribute to South Africa's growth and development.'[11]

But by late August, even Nelson Mandela decided that the activist pressure on the foundations of global capitalism, namely, corporations' right to make profits no matter how egregious the regime, was out of control. Hosted by Africa's richest man, Nicky Oppenheimer, at the Rhodes Building in Cape Town, Mandela gave his name to a new foundation, 'Mandela Rhodes', and used the occasion to attack the apartheid reparations lawsuits as 'outside interference'. Mandela commented, not incorrectly: 'I am sure that Cecil John Rhodes would have given his approval to this effort to make the South African economy of the early 21st century appropriate and fit for its time.'[12]

At the same time, London's *New Left Review* published an interview with Soweto community leader Trevor Ngwane, who did not mince words: 'Without detracting from those twenty-seven years in jail – what that cost him, what he stood for – Mandela has been the real sellout, the biggest betrayer of his people.'[13]

Maduna's letter to the US court requested that the lawsuits be dismissed 'in deference to the sovereign rights of foreign countries to legislate, adjudicate and otherwise resolve domestic issues without outside interference'. But in August 2003, at the opening plenary of a major Reparations Conference, Jubilee SA's Berend Schuitema reported that Maduna made an extraordinary confession: 'The reason why he had made the objection was that he was asked for an opinion on the lawsuit by Colin Powell. He gave Powell his written response, whereupon Powell said that he should lodge this submission to the Judge of the New York Court. Howls from the floor. Jubilee SA chairperson M.P. Giyose pointed out the bankruptcy of the sovereignty argument.'[14]

Given Pretoria's supine posture in relation to Washington and transnational capital, it should not be surprising that as early as September 2001, activists realised that a more public form of protest was crucial. Enough Durban communities had suffered such brutal attacks – evictions, water and electricity disconnections, and violent police repression – by Mbeki's national government and their own municipality that they not only spurned the official WCAR but also dismissed the NGO summit, no matter how progressive its resolutions, as a mere distraction. Their instinct, to take to the streets, catalysed a new style of South African protest, linking the fights against global and local capitalism.

NGO conferencing or community protest?

The chaos associated with the parallel summit at Durban was captured in one lament by a local NGO functionary: 'There were no commissions yesterday. Today the delegates are wandering around aimlessly; the panels are in a mess; commissions have failed and will fail. The deadline for the submissions of the inputs is tomorrow. What will the nature of the final document be, considering that the thematic commissions will not have had any opportunity to provide substantive input?'[15]

In contrast to the NGO summit, radical anti-racism activists and community-based organisers were motivated by two great elders of the progressive movement: sociologist Fatima Meer and poet Dennis Brutus. They proceeded to hold a 'pavement summit' and stage creative protests. Ashwin Desai, in his book *We are the Poors*, offered acclamatory, but also critical, analysis of the leading Durban community coalition, the Concerned Citizens Forum (the core of the Durban Social Forum):

> From the beginning, it was clear that the WCAR mobilisations would, to a certain extent, be opportunistic. While most Concerned Community Forum members were, in their bones, anti-racists too, it would be fair to say that the dominant motive in pulling together public demonstrations during the race conference was to exploit the platform this provided to make telling points about class. Activists realised they would have to do a lot of work to explain to foreigners that, despite the superficial, if dramatic, advances that had been made on the race front in South Africa, these did not compensate for the deepening misery of the majority of the poor (and Black) people of this country. Even if they failed to make a dent in the epistemological wall that hides evidence of South Africa's failed revolution, actions during the WCAR would be an ideal test of strength against a government that was bound to recommence evictions and cutoffs as the last delegates boarded their Boeings home.[16]

This was similar to what would emerge at the WSSD 12 months later. Mann summed up the WCAR's importance: 'The antiracist forces at Durban did not win many concrete demands. Still, as a dress rehearsal for future world struggles, WCAR was an important and, at times, amazing event, the high points of which were the complete disgrace and isolation of the US government and its self-exposure as a racist bully, the spirited show of support for the Palestinian liberation

struggle, and the strong NGO document against racism – even if rejected in its essence by the world's governments.'[17]

Racism and reparations out, terrorism and state control in

The international campaign for reparations is probably vital to the objective of realigning society so that ingrained racial (and gender) oppression is mitigated, and so that communities of black and brown survivors of colonialism and slavery are not continually disadvantaged by the locked-in forms of racism that persist so strongly today. Beyond the restitution needed for past wrongs, reparations provide a strategy for present and future social justice, as a disincentive to corporate financing of repressive regimes. Henry Ford and Thomas Watson warmly supported Adolf Hitler, and because their firms, Ford and IBM, made no reparations to the victims of Nazism, they then both nurtured apartheid South Africa for decades. As church activist Neville Gabriel explained, 'Reparations is not just about money . . . it's about acknowledging that what was done in the past was wrong, should not have happened and should not happen again.'[18] The Burmese junta today depends upon major foreign corporations for resources, and so the US Alien Tort Claims Act is being invoked to break the close relationship between capital and fascism.

Disincentivising such repression through reparations is critical. Recognising the far-reaching implications, Clinton-era US deputy treasury secretary Stuart Eizenstat, a supporter of reparations claims against pro-Nazi corporations, provided 'talking points' in November 2002, to help capital fight the Alien Tort Claims Act. Eizenstat worried that if South African reparations activists 'can galvanise public opinion and generate political support . . . they may achieve some success despite legal infirmities'.[19] The New York courts may ultimately decide against the various claimants, partly because of infighting between the two sets of legal teams. But the unveiling of Pretoria's own pro-corporate orientation during mid-2003 left public opinion aghast, and increased political support for reparations campaigners.

In the process, Mbeki revealed surprising loyalties that conflicted with the ANC's political history. A South African correspondent for the British magazine *Private Eye* picks up the story:

> Bizarrely, in the week of George Orwell's centenary, our ever-progressive ANC government began broadcasting slick TV and radio adverts from the secret services, boasting how our spooks are working overtime to keep us safe and happy.
>
> In an echo of the bad old days of BOSS, when Big Brother really was watching us, it was also discreetly announced that three top apartheid-era spooks had been signed up to serve the new regime. Neil Barnard and Mike Louw are former heads of the old National Intelligence Service, while Richard Knollys 'spooked' for the nasty tin-pot Bantustan, Bophutatswana. All three will 'advise' current minister of intelligence Lindiwe Sisulu.
>
> Cynics wonder, however, if this has more to do with keeping us in the dark than keeping us safe. Barnard had been collaborating on a book, while Louw had begun to talk to select journalists about the murky past, dropping hints about hitherto unexposed collaborators with the old regime. Both could confirm or deny widespread rumours about which of our present 'liberation' leaders, even possibly current ministers, had been suborned. Both have abruptly gone mum. Spooky, eh?
>
> Simultaneously the government has gone to great lengths to fib about 'missing' documents from the Truth and Reconciliation Commission, set up to hear evidence of atrocities under apartheid. It claims it was conducting an investigation, knowing perfectly well that the 34 boxes of documents were in the possession, illegally, of Lindiwe Sisulu's National Intelligence Agency (NIA). Among 'sensitive' papers are those relating to the mysterious 1988 assassination of the ANC representative in Paris, Dulcie September.

We're often told we now have the most liberal constitution in the world, and under the access to information act all ministries had till the end of August to reveal what information they hold. Until, that is, justice minister Penuell Maduna recently gave Lindiwe Sisulu a reprieve by quietly gazetting a regulation which exempted the NIA for five years. That may become permanent. Critics compare this to practices prevalent under our final old school white president, P.W. Botha.

But then history is being rewritten by the day. The burial of apartheid's greatest stooge and collaborator (also in the week of Orwell's centenary) proved the perfect opportunity for revisionist fabrication. Chief Kaizer Matanzima was the venal, brutal ruler of the Transkei, apartheid's first Bantustan. Yet Matanzima was accorded an official funeral, attended by president Thabo Mbeki. In his memorial oration, Mbeki urged us to 'take up' the malevolent dictator's unfinished work – as tasteful as if, say, Churchill had honoured Oswald Mosley with state pomp at Westminster Abbey, acclaiming the old blackshirt to be an anti-Nazi patriot.

Apartheid Kaizer's rehabilitation was on Sunday. That week Mbeki had refused to meet a delegation of veterans from Umkhonto we Sizwe, the former military wing of the ANC. The ex-combatants wished to present a memorandum, pointing out that though they'd fought for the liberation of the country, they were now completely ignored by their own government. Some had even been in exile with Mbeki. Majestically, the prez declined to receive their memo – perhaps because he was too busy practising his new passion. On Saturday, you see, President Mbeki was due to play in the inaugural round of his Presidential Golf Classic at the exclusive Woodhill Country Club outside Pretoria.[20]

The tragic story of apartheid collaboration within the ANC will continue to emerge, long after the fall-out of the great scandal of 2003: failed spying allegations against the national prosecutor Bulelani Ngcuka by deputy president Jacob Zuma's financial advisors and former Umkhonto we Sizwe comrades (brothers Mo and Schabir Shaikh, and Mac Maharaj). However, especially worrisome is the continuity, not change, from apartheid-style social control under conditions of state demonisation.

Matters may degenerate further thanks to inclement 'anti-terrorism' legislation. A week after the racism conference ended, the September 11 terrorist attacks took the WCAR's failure off the international radar screen. Maybe the most important result of the disastrous terrorist attack for South Africa and many other countries was the ubiquitous drafting of laws to curtail civil liberties. Pretoria's draft bill was unconstitutional, as Mandela's long-time legal associate George Bizos informed parliament.[21] Added Cosatu, the bill 'conflicts with virtually every demand in the *Freedom Charter*'s section on democratic rights. The Freedom Charter demanded that no one should be imprisoned, deported or restricted without a fair trial, or condemned by the order of any government official. It declared that the law shall guarantee to all, their right to speak, organise, meet together, publish, preach, worship and educate their children, and that the privacy of the house from police raids shall be protected by law.'[22] Johannesburg's Freedom of Expression Institute requested that the bill be withdrawn because it violates 'reasonability and justifiability' provisions of the Constitution, and 'seeks to limit key fundamental rights and freedoms'. Moreover, 'there are other less restrictive means to achieve the objectives sought'.[23]

The degree of repressive intent that might explain that draft law was witnessed in the months that followed, especially at the World Summit on Sustainable Development, as discussed in Chapter Seven. But too, Pretoria's attention to global-scale reform switched again. Within weeks of the WCAR, debates over international commerce found Pretoria again advancing Washington's agenda while posturing against the unfairness of global economic apartheid. Trade minister Alec Erwin played a crucial role in the World Trade Organisation's Doha ministerial summit, and again at Cancun two years later. As in Durban, the stage was set for more opportunities to talk left, and act right.

Notes
1. Mann, E. (2002), *Dispatches from Durban*, Los Angeles, Frontline Books, pp. 47, 51; also on Black Radical Congress listserve.
2. Mann, *Dispatches from Durban*, p. 127. See http://southafrica.indymedia.org.
3. Cashdan, B. (2002), *Globalisation and Africa: Whose Side are We On?*, video, Johannesburg, Seipone Productions.
4. *Business Day*, 7 September 2001. Three days earlier the same editorial column carried these words: 'There is a new and powerful breed of African leader in Africa, democrats such as Mbeki and Obasanjo, who are determined to end war and want and who also know their economics.'
5. South African Institute of Race Relations director John Kane-Berman, a hard-core neoliberal ideologue, called the lawsuits 'superficial' because they included charges of apartheid as 'genocide' and a 'crime against humanity'. After all, the black population grew during apartheid, Kane-Berman

observed. *Business Day*, 3 June 2003 and Charles Abrahams' letter-to-the-editor rebuttal of 26 June 2003.
6. *Business Day*, 17 June 2003.
7. For coverage see, for example, *Financial Times*, 19 May 2003. According to Jubilee SA secretary George Dor, writing to *Business Day* in the wake of the late August 2003 Reparations Conference, 'Attempts to engage the foreign corporations were initiated as long ago as 1999 and this had been met with an obstinate refusal to talk. Business reiterated its non-cooperative stance by failing to take the opportunity to address this conference.'
8. *Financial Times*, 19 May 2003.
9. *Sunday Independent*, 15 June 2003.
10. *Sunday Independent*, 25 July 2003. Replying to this logic a month later, prize-winning Indian author Arundhati Roy told BBC radio, 'In what ought to have been an international scandal, this same government officially asked the judge in a US court case to rule against forcing companies to pay reparations for the role they played during apartheid. Its reasoning was that reparations – in other words justice – will discourage foreign investment. So South Africa's poorest must pay apartheid's debts so that those who amassed profit by exploiting black people can profit more?' (BBC, 24 August 2003).
11. *Sunday Independent*, 9 August 2003.
12. *Sowetan*, 26 August 2003.
13. Ngwane, T. (2003), 'Sparks in the Township', *New Left Review*, July–August 2003. Ngwane noted: 'The ANC was granted formal, administrative power, while the wealth of the country was retained in the hands of the white capitalist elite, Oppenheimer and company. Mandela's role was decisive in stabilising the new dispensation; by all accounts, a daring gamble on the part of the bourgeoisie.'
14. e-debate listserve, 30 August 2003. The organisations represented included Jubilee SA, Khulumani, Cosatu, the Anti-Privatisation Forum, Sanco, the Landless People's Movement, the South African Council of Churches and the Environmental Justice Networking Forum. Notwithstanding important divisions over loyalty to the ANC-Alliance, there was no dispute that Mbeki had erred in his attempt to sabotage the reparations campaign.
15. Cited in Mann, *Dispatches from Durban*, p. 126.
16. Desai, A. (2002), *We are the Poor*, New York, Monthly Review Press, p. 123.
17. Mann, *Dispatches from Durban*, p. 106.
18. *New African*, July 2003.
19. *New African*, July 2003.
20. *Private Eye* 1085, 25 July 2003.
21. Sapa, 1 July 2003.
22. Cosatu (2003), 'Statement on the Anti-Terrorism Bill', Johannesburg, 25 June.
23. Freedom of Expression Institute (2003), 'FXI urges Parliament to Withdraw Anti-Terrorism Bill', Johannesburg, 25 June.

4
Pretoria's trade off
Splitting Africa for the WTO

Tension was palpable ahead of the World Trade Organisation meeting in Cancun, Mexico, in September 2003. Malaysia's *Straights Times* reported on an apparent change of heart by Thabo Mbeki, expressed during a seminar in the capital, Kuala Lumpur:

> From South Africa's past experience, it helped to have strong anti-apartheid groups in developed countries to lobby its case. In the same way, he suggested linking up with groups in developed countries which were concerned about the negative effects of globalisation – which seemed to cause greater imbalances and disparity among the rich and poor nations. 'They may act in ways you and I may not like and break windows in the street but the message they communicate relates.'[1]

The week after Mbeki's remark, the WTO's failure to reach agreement at Cancun was celebrated by activists, but not by trade minister Alec Erwin. Indeed, since the December 1999 debacle at the WTO's infamous Seattle ministerial summit, Pretoria had been extremely cautious about relations with the WTO's critics, whether in the streets or in other African states.[2]

At Seattle, according to the critics, democracy, environment, labour conditions, indigenous people's rights and other social struggles were not taken seriously by trade negotiators. Third World delegates were alienated from the high-level 'Green Room' discussions conducted between a select group of influential delegates from the US, EU, Japan, Canada, South Korea, Singapore, India and South Africa.[3] Disrespectful treatment of African delegations, including removal of translators and microphones by the US hosts, led to a formal 'denial of consensus' by the offended ministers.[4] The Africa Group used stern language about the lack of transparency, which Erwin managed to moderate slightly, although he could not persuade the continent's delegates that his Green Room negotiations were in their interest.

Erwin's final plenary statement at Seattle condemned the 70 000 protesters who blocked his entrance to the summit for a day, as well as the US government for 'bad management'. The demonstrations, he baldly and sarcastically misinterpreted, were 'designed to give us some insight into the pressures' on US negotiators from their own constituencies.[5] He repeated this slur in his report-back to Parliament after the 2003 Cancun fiasco: '[In Seattle,] the USA ensured – by intent or by disingenuous conduct – that the talks were held in chaotic conditions and added to this an insistence on the labour standard issue.'[6] In other words, the protesters were dupes of Bill Clinton. Trevor Manuel told a seminar eleven months later, 'If the governments and civil society of the developed world are serious about the fight against global poverty, they should be more comfortable taking a dose of the "free trade" medicine that they so liberally prescribe to the developing world.'[7] But, no serious civil society activists were supportive of blatant G8 protectionism, and none prescribed neoliberalism in the Third World.

In contrast, Pretoria's environment minister, Mohammed Valli Moosa, claimed in a 2002 interview, 'Seattle clearly struck a chord with many of us in developing countries, even in government. Frankly, those people in the streets of Seattle were speaking for us.' Moosa's intention was apparently to artificially distinguish the good Seattle protesters from the later, bad Johannesburg protesters, who, he alleged, 'were trying to replicate the dramatic events of Seattle in a completely wrong context'.[8]

Making friends

Erwin's alienation from both African negotiators and civil society activists grew before and after the November 2001 WTO ministerial summit in Doha, Qatar. As one of South Africa's leading international analysts, Dot Keet, explained, Pretoria 'failed, within and after Seattle, to use its political/moral weight and democratic kudos to actively prioritise real institutional reforms as an essential pre-condition to any other discussions in, or on, the WTO'. Erwin also disappointed observers by accepting a controversial 'Friend of the Chair' position, which made him responsible for negotiating WTO rules. Civil society critics called him one of five 'Green Men', since the function of the WTO chair's 'friends' was to replicate the secretive Green Rooms, within what Keet described as Doha's 'even more flagrantly inequitable and undemocratic processes'.[9] An African civil society summit declaration repeated this point in June 2003: 'The manipulative and undemocratic practices initiated at Doha, such as the appointments of

Friends of the Chair in informal working groups, which make undemocratic decisions on key issues, is being institutionalised at the WTO in the run up to Cancun.'[10]

As the November 2001, Doha conference agenda emerged, social movement critics united with the more ambitious African delegations. Erwin viewed their arguments with disdain: delegates from some other African nations and developing world countries 'merely articulate extremely basic positions and very seldom get beyond that'.[11] He chose to work closely with Egypt, even though reportedly the most effective African ministerial delegations to the WTO meetings were from Nigeria, Tanzania, Uganda, Kenya and Zimbabwe. During the five months prior to Doha, several interim meetings were held in which Erwin ejected the NGO advisers to African governments, and carefully advanced the pro-WTO position in favour of a so-called 'new round' or 'broad-based agenda'. He did so again at a Southern African Development Community ministerial summit in Pretoria, at a summit of Lesser Developed Country ministers in Zanzibar, at an Eastern/Southern African ministerial in Cairo,[12] and at the Abuja meeting of African trade ministers before Doha.[13]

By the time the Doha meeting took place, Erwin had acquired what the WTO's then director-general, Mike Moore, termed 'very useful African leadership',[14] even though there were vigorous complaints by African state and civil society groups about the draft text to be considered at the ministerial summit.[15] For Erwin, however, 'our overall approach was to defend the overall balance in the draft text'.[16]

Making friends with WTO leaders necessarily entailed creating conflict with others, such as the delegations from Cuba, the Dominican Republic, Haiti, India, Jamaica, Kenya, Pakistan, Peru, Uganda, Venezuela and Zimbabwe. The latter's ambassador complained that 'the small consultations held by [Friends of the Chair] were not inclusive. People had problems getting into those consultations.'[17] Montesquieu once remarked, 'Commerce makes the manners mild,' but this obviously did not apply in Doha, or to Erwin's treatment of fellow African ministers and civil society trade experts.

Twisting arms

Thanks to the WTO-pliant Green Men, the *modus operandi* changed somewhat from Seattle, but the insider elite retained power against the world's majority. Dissenting delegates were threatened that trade preferences would be withdrawn. At one point, a live microphone picked up Moore's discussion with the Qatari host trade minister about how to stop the Indian delegation from taking the floor.

Save the Children's main trade analyst, John Hilary, concluded, 'Bullying and blackmail have become an integral part of how the WTO works, as we saw all too clearly at the Doha ministerial. Time and again, developing countries have been forced to abandon negotiating positions as a result of economic, political and even personal threats to their delegates.'[18] Aileen Kwa of Focus on the Global South reported, 'What broke Africa in the final two days, was when the US and the EU contacted heads of state such as President Obasanjo of Nigeria and other African leaders. This led to delegations in Doha receiving calls from their capitals. While Nigeria had earlier been quite firm in its opposition, it suddenly went silent in the final 13th November meetings.'[19]

The possibility of a coerced deal became tangible when Erwin met the African, African-Caribbean-Pacific (ACP) and less developed countries (LDC) group on the final day of the Doha negotiations. Keet's review of Pretoria's WTO behaviour records that Erwin

> advised them that they had no choice but to accept the text, which was 'the best possible outcome for them in the circumstances.' According to participants and eyewitnesses, there were a number of angry responses to the South African minister, some even asking rhetorically who he represented and whose interests he was serving . . .
>
> The joint meeting dissolved in disarray. This was the final maneuver that dissipated the resistance of a major grouping of developing countries that many had hoped would repeat (at) Doha their role in Seattle. This was not to be. All the pressures and persuasions, manipulations and maneuvers only managed to secure what one Member of the European Parliament characterised as 'a resentful acquiescence.'[20]

Subimperial South Africa

Erwin's own Doha agenda was first exposed to local audiences in the *Mail & Guardian*, which reported that although 'Africa got a sop in the form of a promise to the developing world to help build capacity', the overall outcome was negative. The *Mail & Guardian* reported:

> South Africa led a Southern African Development Community breakaway from the consensus of key African countries this week at the World Trade Organisation ministerial meeting in Doha, Qatar. There are fears that the split between South Africa and many of its SADC partners on the one hand, and other African

countries on the other, has compromised the continent's unified bargaining position.

The original strategy of most African countries, along with much of the developing world, was to block a new WTO negotiations 'round' until issues – still unresolved after the 1986–1994 Uruguay round and perceived as essential to boost developing nations' interests in the world trade system – are addressed. But on the eve of the WTO's fourth ministerial meeting, held in Doha from November 9 to 13, the South African government embarked on a broad drive to get African countries to consider a new round of WTO trade negotiations.

The South African government managed to take the SADC along with it, but failed to reach consensus with other African countries, says the South African Institute of International Affairs . . . This situation, says institute researcher Carin Voges, 'might signify to the Africa group of countries that South Africa, a prominent leader of the continent, does not have their best interests at heart, thereby compromising the future of the African renaissance.'[21]

This concession from the main South African voice of liberal globalist capitalism was repeated in mid-2003. The institute's pro-WTO analyst Peter Draper issued a report, 'To Liberalise or not to Liberalise?', which noted that 'it is debatable whether the majority of African states have an interest in a broad round of WTO negotiations.' He suggested that African governments would view Erwin 'with some degree of suspicion'.[22] Erwin, meanwhile, described the 'Doha Developmental Agenda' – for all practical purposes the 'new round' so strongly opposed by African and civil society critics of the WTO – as a 'fantastic achievement'.[23] This meant, according to a fanciful *Business Day* reporter, that 'South Africa is now part of the Big Five of global trade', alongside the US, EU, Japan and Canada.[24]

The manoeuvres and inflated claims surrounding trade negotiations were reminiscent of the way Erwin and other South African officials had earlier handled multi-billion rand arms purchases. These also made other African countries justifiably nervous of Pretoria's ambitions, especially in light of the incompetent manner in which the South African National Defence Force invaded Lesotho in September 1998, ostensibly to restore order while allowing part of Maseru's central business district to burn to the ground. Pretoria's troops flew to Katse Dam, killing dozens of sleeping Basotho soldiers. What new use would be made of fighter airplanes, submarines and high-speed corvettes in view of the lack of genuine threats to South African territory? When George Bush visited Pretoria in July 2003, afer all, the potential role of South Africa as a gendarme for the US Empire became clearer, highlighted by the comment that Mbeki was his 'point man on Zimbabwe'.

The R43 billion-plus arms deal remained rife with controversy. Bribery extended high into Erwin's department, requiring the sacking of a senior aide. Erwin and defence minister Masiuoa Lekota claimed that arms manufacturers would establish R104 billion worth of 'offset' investments. One East London condom factory meant to be funded by a German submarine manufacturer never materialised, and investments in the Coega industrial complex, purportedly the main site of offset deals, were rife with environmental, social and economic contradictions.[25]

Under the circumstances, Keet concluded, 'South Africa's role is not so much a bridge *between* the developed and developing countries, but rather a bridge for the transmission of influences *from* the developed to the developing countries.'[26] Draper too, warned of likely worsening 'African suspicion' of Erwin in the run up to the Cancun summit: 'It will be difficult for South Africa to co-operatively develop and maintain common African positions in the WTO negotiations.'[27]

Doha drove forward where Seattle stalled, according to Raj Patel of FoodFirst, largely because at that stage (although not subsequently

in Cancun), US trade representative Robert Zoellick acted as 'a dealer, a broker of accord, a merchant of consensus. This new-found humility evidently pushed the buttons of the developing country elite. So they signed [the Doha deal]. This should come as no surprise. These are the elites that milk and pimp the majority of people in their countries. It's hard to see why putting them in five-star accommodation and making them feel important might make them less venal.'[28]

In the end, the critics were defeated and Erwin prevailed. The geographical distance from activist centres, the high levels of WTO security, and the generally repressive conditions within Qatar meant Doha was an impossible platform for staging public protests.

For the moderate wing of civil society, protest was not on the agenda in any case. Some labour and non-governmental representatives joined Pretoria's delegation at occasional summits, including Seattle, with the myopic hope of being part of a corporatist deal. According to two National Economic Development and Labour Council officials,

> In both the Geneva and Seattle ministerial meetings of the WTO, representatives of business, trade unions and community were active participants of the South African government delegation, enabling South Africa to speak with one voice in international fora and to strategically engage with global processes. In this context, social dialogue offers opportunities for developing countries like South Africa not only to respond to globalisation but also to shape its form and outcomes.[29]

In reality, the corporatist option was foreclosed because Erwin quickly retreated from Cosatu's Social Clause strategy, which aimed to penalise countries with exports emanating from child labour, union repression, safety or health violations and environmental destruction.[30] Cosatu and community representatives received nothing from the frustrated reform strategy. 'There is extremely limited scope for effective alternative inputs,' concluded Keet. But as 'one voice' was silenced, others soon emerged.[31]

Erwin's critics included regional colleagues, who occasionally spoke out in anger. As the *Sunday Times* reported, SADC delegates argued at a Dar es Salaam regional summit prior to Cancun that 'Pretoria was "too defensive and protective" in trade negotiations ... [and] is being accused of offering too much support for domestic production "such as duty rebates on exports" which is killing off other economies in the region.'[32]

US and EU gratitude

But it was soon clear that Erwin's reform agenda was not succeeding. Faced with a protectionist onslaught from the US shortly after Doha – huge steel, apparel and footwear tariffs and agricultural subsidies which negated claims of progress at the WTO summit – Erwin announced an alliance with Brazil, Australia, and the 18-nation Cairns group of food exporting countries. In a rare talk-left moment, Erwin declared, 'we will fight this out.'[33] A year later, he confessed defeat: 'The position is not particularly favourable . . . I think we are heading for a very difficult time in Cancun.'[34]

In 2002, other deadlines were missed by trade negotiators concerning the 'special and differential treatment' required by the Third World, and the health sector's need for exemptions from Trade-Related Intellectual Property Rights (TRIPS) pharmaceutical patent provisions. But, by mid-2003 there was still no procedure and the Cairns Group strategy was conclusively frustrated.

Difficulties with the US were obvious throughout the post-Doha period. US Treasury undersecretary John Taylor explained away the Bush regime's hypocrisy: 'You take steps forward and move back. That's always the case.'[35] Before the G8 Summit at Evian, France in June 2003, Bush and Blair announced their opposition to host president Jacques Chirac's plan to halt dumping of subsidised Western food in Africa.[36] Bush proposed increasing his government's aid-

related subsidies on agricultural exports and argued that 'European governments should join – not hinder – the great cause of ending hunger in Africa', by adjusting agricultural subsidies and permitting trade in genetically-modified foodstuffs.[37]

Six leading African global justice movements that met near Evian issued a statement: 'The 2003 G8 was a disaster for African farmers. It failed to adopt even limited proposals for a moratorium on reducing European and American tariff duties and subsidies for US and European agriculture. These policies are perverse. While millions of African farmers, and most women's livelihoods, are ruined by these policies, European livestock are ensured major state subsidies.'[38]

The 'terms of trade' between Africa and the rest of the world deteriorated steadily (Chapter One, Figure 4), thanks in part to the artificially low prices of subsidised crops. The UN Conference on Trade and Development revealed that if instead of falling since 1980, the relative prices of imports and exports had been constant, Africa would have twice the share of global trade it did 20 years later; per capita GDP would have been 50% higher; and annual GDP increases would have been 1.4% higher.[39] But the subsidies stayed in place.

At this very point of US mendacity, Erwin emphasised bilateralism with the US, specifically a US-Southern African Customs Union free trade area that Zoellick began promoting energetically in early 2003 at a Mauritius trade conference. It was a proposal that would give

Pretoria and its neighbours practically no additional benefit beyond the Africa Growth and Opportunity Act (AGOA).⁴⁰ The benefits to South Africa from AGOA far outstripped those of other African countries, whose trade to the US increased only a quarter as fast as South Africa's (10% from 2001–02).⁴¹ In 2001, 84% of all exports from sub-Saharan African countries – which total just 1% of all US imports – were sourced from only four countries: South Africa, Nigeria, Kenya and Angola.⁴² In mid-2003, the AGOA applied to 39 countries; the remaining 13 African states were vetoed by the White House for various reasons. AGOA came under fire because its conditionalities include adopting neoliberal policies, privatising state assets, removing subsidies and price controls, ending incentives for local companies, and endorsing US foreign policy. On the latter point, Burkina Faso was deemed inelegible because, Washington ruled, the country 'undermined . . . US foreign policy interests'. Numerous civil society groups across Africa and the US opposed the deal, decrying it as a vehicle for US imperialism.⁴³

Although South Africa increased exports to the US under AGOA, the plan offers few durable benefits to the African masses. Most AGOA job creation has been short-term, low-paid and unstable, especially when Asian firms relocate for trade benefits. Practically no backward-forward linkages exist between the new exports and the economy. Moreover, the alleged democracy premium that AGOA would bring was unwittingly exposed as a sham by King Mswati of Swaziland, who intensified repression while attracting R30 million in new Taiwanese and Chinese sweatshop investments which took advantage of AGOA garment trade concessions.⁴⁴ Tiny changes were made in the Swazi Industrial Relations Act to comply with AGOA, but a major study of the trade deal's impact there by a South African university and Dutch NGO, found its garment sector is characterised by 'low wages, unhealthy and unsafe workplaces, substantial and often compulsory overtime, lack of adequate monitoring by buyers of products, trade union repression by employers and government, extra hardships experienced by pregnant workers, and lack of worker protection by government'. The Swaziland Federation of Trade Unions attacked the garment sector investments as unsustainable because the five-year tax holiday typically becomes permanent, as factories change paper-ownership names and demand another five years of new-investor benefits.⁴⁵

Another example of the Bush regime's imposition of unsustainable development on Africa was the genetically-modified (GM) food controversy. The EU, Australia, Japan, China, Indonesia and Saudi

Arabia (i.e., more than half the world) banned GM trade and production, so Bush was clearly desperate for new markets, as he revealed to the US-Africa Business Summit shortly before his July 2003 trip:

> To help Africa become more self-sufficient in the production of food, I have proposed the initiative to end hunger in Africa. This initiative will help African countries use new high-yield bio-tech crops and unleash the power of markets to dramatically increase agricultural productivity.
> But there's a problem. There's a problem. At present, some governments are blocking the import of crops grown with biotechnology, which discourages African countries from producing and exporting these crops. The ban of these countries is unfounded; it is unscientific; it is undermining the agricultural future of Africa. I urge them to stop this ban.[46]

The Southern African Catholic Bishops Conference responded, 'We do not believe that agro-companies or gene technologies will help our farmers to produce the food that is needed in the 21st century. We think it will destroy the diversity, the local knowledge and the sustainable agricultural systems that our farmers have developed for millennia and that it will undermine our capacity to feed ourselves.' Lori Wallach, director of Public Citizen's Global Trade Watch, commented: 'The Bush administration is not straightforward. It is not poverty in Africa that is the most important issue for the administration but business considerations on behalf of the US technology and agricultural sector.' As InterPress Service reported, 'Zambia, citing health concerns, rejected GM corn in both grain and milled forms. One year later, president Levy Mwanawasa announced that Zambia will nearly double the 600 000 tonnes of grain it harvested last season, providing fuel to the argument that GM technology is not necessary for reducing hunger in Africa.'[47]

In his speech to the US-Africa Business Summit, Bush threatened: 'Money will go to developing nations whose governments are committed to three broad strategies: First, they must rule justly. Second, they must invest in the health and education of their people. And third, they must have policies that encourage economic freedom.'[48] It could be confidently predicted that the latter would trump the first two. Meanwhile, South Africa, under Erwin's direction, continued its irresponsible invitations to Monsanto and other genetically modified food producers to sell or grow the tainted crops on African soil.

Cancun dissent

Washington had generated too many contradictions in world trade to easily get its way at the September 2003 Cancun ministerial summit. Consider this mid-conference report from Dot Keet:

> What is amazing, and inspiring, is that the many colourful banners and placards, flags and chants, songs and drumming, each with their distinctive cultural characteristics, all carry similar messages against the World Trade Organisation, against the unjust and destructive economic system it is being used for, against the damages to the world environment, to livelihoods and lives – as expressed dramatically in the symbolic suicide of the Korean farmer, Lee Kyung Hae . . . With our distinctive black and green t-shirts and banner proclaiming that 'Africa is Not for Sale, Africa no esta a la venta', the African people's organisations in Cancun are sending a clear message to the WTO and African governments that we are here to demand that the needs and rights of our people are not sold off by our governments.
>
> We are deeply suspicious that in the Convention Centre from which we are barred by twelve foot steel and concrete barriers ten kilometers away – symbolic of the vast gulf in understanding and experience between officials on 'the inside' and people on 'the outside' – the insider wheeling-and-dealing between governments might produce yet another sell-out of their countries and their people . . . While we are demanding that there be 'No New Issues' to expand the powers of the WTO; (and) are determined to 'Stop the GATS-Attack' on our public services; (and) warning our governments not to accept further Industrial Tariff Liberalisations that will destroy more jobs; we were told in a meeting here with South African Deputy Minister of Trade, Lindiwe Hendrickse, that the South African negotiators are preparing to make 'trade-offs', although she 'cannot as yet tell what these will be.'
>
> African activists are urging African governments to stand firm on their agreed positions, and on the issues that African peoples' organisations prioritise. Some African governments, led by Kenya, Uganda, Tanzania, Nigeria, Zambia and Zimbwabwe, are playing a leading role in developing country alliances against the power of 'the majors', drawing developing countries such as India, Indonesia, Malaysia, Philippines and others around them . . .
>
> From afar it appears that South Africa has at last taken a stand after recent inaction reflecting the loss of their chosen strategic

direction. The intransigence of the majors in Geneva over the last two years has blown apart the compromise so-called 'development agenda' that South Africa helped broker in Doha.[49]

However, Keet continued, Erwin's choice of Brazil, India and other 'G21' countries as allies, instead of other Africans, appeared a threat to popular interests:

> No African countries [aside from South Africa] have joined this group because it essentially reflects the interests of big agricultural exporters and does not support the needs of small producers. There is no mention of the Special and Differential Terms that are key to the defence of the policy flexibilities of smaller and weaker countries in the WTO, and that should be at the centre of the Cancun agenda, as promised in the Doha declaration. Most problematically, the G21 has adopted the overall position that, if there is 'movement' (a rather ill-defined notion) on agriculture by the majors, they will consider negotiating their other demands. This flies in the face of the position of the African and other developing countries in Asia and Latin America (numbering more than 70 in total) that the controversial new issues must not be linked to any possible agriculture 'concessions'. In fact, these new issues, above all towards the global liberalisation of international investment and capital flows, must NOT become negotiating subjects at the WTO.

Looking at Cancun from the top down, the US and EU roles were explicit: no concessions on matters of great importance to Africa – this included the decimation of West African cotton exports due to subsidies and grain dumping. There was a rigid insistence on moving the corporate agenda forward. Among their ambitions were four 'Singapore issues' that had been placed on hold since the 1996 WTO summit at Cancun – Zoellick and Lamy insisted they be revitalised. These issues included equal treatment of foreign investors; the prevention of laws that favour local ownership; more open competition and antitrust policies so that foreign companies could penetrate local markets more easily; more transparency in government purchasing to open up procurement to international trade; and trade facilitation through customs simplification.

The position of most Third World countries was that until the huge hypocrisies associated with G8 subsidies and tariffs were sorted out, and items from earlier rounds were addressed, it was disadvantageous to introduce complex new issues. Many countries' socio-economic objectives, e.g., more balance in local ownership (as Malaysia achieved through its 'bumipatra' system of preferences for indigenous Malaysians or as Pretoria claims to seek via black economic empowerment) or environmentally sensitive development, would be sabotaged if negotiations began on the Singapore issues, leading to further erosion of state sovereignty and the blunting of local economic development tools. Writing just before the final breakdown at Cancun, Riaz Tayob of the Southern and Eastern African Trade and Investment Negotiations Initiative accused the South African minister of selling out on the Singapore issues:

> Erwin consulted with civil society in South Africa where he gave the assurance that he would not open up new issues for discussion until the requirements of the Doha Development Agenda (had) been met. Contrary to what he informed us, during the Green Room [meeting] last night, he took the position that he would move on the new issues if the imperialists conceded on agriculture. Alec Erwin misrepresented his position to civil society and is playing a game of speak left and act right.[50]

This game was not well understood at home, notwithstanding the public acknowledgement of Erwin's contradictory stance by the South African Institute of International Affairs.[51] However, the US and EU behaviour at Cancun was so obnoxious that the G21 middle-income countries, led by Brazil, held up negotiations at the outset. Then, the African-Caribbean-Pacific countries, joined by some low-income Asian allies, refused to accept a draft text which left out the crucial cotton sector. As at Seattle, there was no way to reach consensus. The African Union commissioner for trade, industry and economic affairs, Vijay Makhan, was scathing about the experience:

> Everybody knew the African position. But what disturbed us was that it was not taken onboard . . . I have my own feeling that all the facilitation was a question of formality rather than to inject anything into the final text. When you look at the final text . . . from the chairman, that text left the position expressed by Africa on many issues, to the side . . . Africa will have to take a political decision, whether it is worthwhile to stay in an organisation that is not proving its worth.[52]

Erwin tried, repeatedly, to paper over the cracks that loomed wide at Cancun. He expressed 'disappointment', while the majority of the Third World cheered their negotiators' resolve against Zoellick and

Lamy. Talking left, Trevor Manuel told a World Customs Organisation conference in Fourways, Johannesburg, in late September 2003, that Cancun's 'result' was 'an important moral and political victory, which sought to constrain the dominance of the powerful countries'.[53]

In contrast, Erwin offered a convoluted explanation which blamed the victims. 'After the good work of unifying African positions during the Doha meeting, the complexities of agriculture began to worm into this fragile structure,' he told parliament after returning from Cancun. Because so many African countries relied on 'preferences' in the form of special quotas for their cash crop exports to Europe, the G21's proposed liberalisation was not in their interests. As Erwin explained, 'The agricultural protectionists lost no time in mobilising this vulnerability. Africa was chaired by Mauritius – a more preference dependent economy is hard to find – and the result was rather chaotic. In the sad hurly-burly of the meeting, Mauritius ended up actually joining a hardy band of agricultural protectionists led by Switzerland, Norway and Japan.' Who was at fault? Erwin concluded, 'Strange partners hold hands in a fog of nervousness. The G21 absorbed so much of their resources in the battle with the big two – USA and Europe – that they could not divert sufficient resources to speaking to the Africa, ACP and LDC group.'[54]

Again and again, Erwin failed, as efforts to repair the damage at the WTO secretariat came to naught. Nevertheless, Erwin's persuasiveness meant that from a 'D+' in 2002, he was promoted to a 'B' grade in the *Mail & Guardian*'s 2003 report card, largely because of his global reform agenda:

> Alec Ewin wears the exhausted look of a minister whose energy has been sapped by tireless campaigning for rules of world trade to be fairer for developing countries. However, the result is that he is recognised internationally as a determined, hard-nosed trade negotiator who is leading the developing world in its efforts to ensure a rules-based international trade system. Immediately after the collapse of the Cancun round of the world trade talks he set about revitalising them by getting developing countries together to try to save efforts to open the global economy. If he succeeds, the medium- to long-term benefits to South Africa, an exporting economy, are significant.[55]

If South Africa's interests markedly diverge from those of the rest of the continent, that conclusion may be true. Erwin repeatedly undermined the long-term possibility of more balance between South

Africa and Africa – appropriate industrialisation, ecological sustainability and less uneven regional development – by buying into the neoliberal free-trade strategy. This was also evident in the most crucial campaign of all: to save millions of lives in the most HIV-infected region of the world by ensuring an example of political leadership, through access to life-saving medicines and appropriate care.

Trading life and death

Northern-dominated trade rules have generated not only underdevelopment, but also death through the corporate application of intellectual property rights that prevent access to affordable medicines in the Global South. According to a mid-2003 *Business Day* report, Erwin conceded that 'a key issue for the developing world was agreement to allow developing countries to import or manufacture generic drugs to deal with major public health crises without running into patent problems. Erwin urged those pharmaceutical companies which were applying pressure to block a deal to come on board. The US government is holding up a deal, under pressure from its pharmaceutical lobby.'[56]

Although Bush promised $15 billion in new AIDS funding from 2003–06, it would mainly benefit US pharmaceutical corporations. Bush soon backpeddled on his pledge by cutting the 2003–04 allocation in half, underfunding the Global Fund set up to combat AIDS, malaria and TB by the United Nations, and linking AIDS spending to Washington's discredited aid bureaucracy, whose ultraconservative, and oft-criticised, reproductive policies extended to denying support to NGOs and Third World agencies engaged in sex education and reproductive rights.[57] The *Wall Street Journal* reported, 'President Bush plans to ask Congress for relatively small funding increases to fight AIDS and poverty in the developing world, stepping back from his highly publicised pledge to spend huge sums to help fight them.'[58]

The logic appeared to be that if too many Africans received AIDS medicines that they could not afford to buy without substantial subsidies, it could undermine the global pharmaceutical industry. A differential pricing system would have two negative impacts on drug company profits: first, black market deals might emerge and allow wealthy northerners to gain access to cheap antiretroviral medication (ARVs); and the basic principle of intellectual patents would be so undermined that poor people in the industrialised world would also be justified in demanding free or low-cost treatment access.

In May 2003, NGO critics accused the Bush regime of having 'an almost blind belief in the Intellectual Property system, without regard for the reality for patients in desperate need of newer, more effective health technologies and access to existing essential medicines. In view of the HIV/AIDS crisis, and the massive problems expressed by many World Health Assembly delegates in guaranteeing equitable and sustainable access to affordable antiretroviral medicines, [there is an] impression that the US has lost touch with reality.' The US insisted that intellectual property protection was the best way to promote pharmaceutical research and development. But NGO critics rebutted, 'Of the 1,393 new drugs approved between 1975 and 1999, only 16 (or just over 1%) were specifically developed for tropical diseases and tuberculosis, diseases that account for 11.4% of the global disease burden.'[59] Figures were not given for HIV drug research and development.

The importance of intellectual property rights is witnessed by the Bill and Melinda Gates Foundation AIDS drugs strategy. US investigative journalist Greg Palast wrote a critique of a fawning *New York Times* Gates profile:

> The bully billionaire's 'philanthropic' organisation is currently working paw-in-claw with the big pharmaceutical companies . . . Gates' game is given away by the fact that his Foundation has invested $200 million in the very drug companies stopping the shipment of low-cost AIDS drugs to Africa. Gates says his plan is to reach one million people with medicine by the end of the decade. Another way to read it: he's locking in a trade system that will effectively block the delivery of medicine to over 20 million. The computer magnate's scheme has a powerful ally. 'The president could have been reading from a script prepared by Mr. Gates,' enthuses the *Times*' cub reporter, referring to Mr. Bush's AIDS plan offered up this week to skeptical Africans.
>
> The US press does not understand why Africans don't jump for Bush's generous handout. None note that the money held out to the continent's desperate nations has strings attached or, more accurately, chains and manacles. The billions offered are mostly loans at full interest which may be used only to buy patent drugs from US companies at a price several times that available from other nations.
>
> What Africans want, an end to the devastating tyranny of TRIPS and other trade rules, is dismissed by the Liberator of Baghdad. We are all serfs on Microsoft's and Big Pharma's 'intellectual

property.' If Gates' fake philanthropy eviscerates the movement to free Africans from the tyranny of TRIPS, then Bill and Melinda's donations could have the effect of killing more Africans than then even their PR agents claim they have saved.[60]

Erwin, too frightened to challenge transnational capital, had lost touch with the realities faced by his constituents. He consistently refused to use his regulatory power in terms of the 1997 Medicines Act to lower drug prices. The Treatment Action Campaign accused him of failure to prevent the 'premature, predictable and avoidable deaths' of several hundred thousand people who died of AIDS during the early 21st century. On Human Rights Day in 2003, at the commemoration of 69 people shot dead at Sharpeville in 1960, Erwin and health minister Tshabalala-Msimang were charged by the TAC with culpable homicide. According to the docket filed at police stations, 'During the period 21 March 2000 to 21 March 2003 in all health care districts of the Republic of South Africa, both accused unlawfully and negligently caused the death of men, women and children. They also breached their constitutional duty to respect, protect, promote and fulfil the right to life and dignity of these people.'[61]

Erwin ignored 'repeated requests' to issue compulsory licences for antiretroviral treatment and 'to ask pharmaceutical companies to give voluntary licences for the manufacture of generics'. Erwin 'consciously ignored the efforts of scientists, doctors, nurses, trade unionists, people living with HIV/AIDS, international agencies, civil society organisations, communities and faith leaders'. Instead, he and Tshabalala-Msimang 'repeatedly delayed the implementation of the Medicines and Related Substances and Control Amendment Act and its Regulations'. Erwin was 'aware of the measures implemented in other countries, like Brazil, to increase access to essential medicines, including anti-retrovirals, but has denied offers by such countries to transfer technology and provide other assistance'. Instead, he and Tshabalala-Msimang 'directed their will towards ensuring government policy is the non provision of anti-retrovirals. Accused knew and foresaw that this would cause the deaths of many people but remained undeterred by this probability.' Erwin's 'conduct in failing to make these medicines available to people who need them does not meet the standards of a reasonable person', the TAC concluded. Characteristic of the growing paranoia in Pretoria, the police did not take the case seriously, and used violence against peaceful TAC protesters in Durban.

An ongoing, unnecessary daily death toll of 600 people to AIDS in South Africa represents an horrific tragedy. Governments cannot escape accountability in failing to move rapidly to end a holocaust. The tragedy of Erwin's pro-liberalisation trade strategy, then, was not only failure on its own limited terms, but also the damage that adherence to neoliberalism caused more broadly. The same is true of Manuel's approach to international finance, as we see next.

Notes
1. *The Straights Times*, 3 September 2003.
2. Further coverage of Erwin's role at Doha can be found in Bond, P. and Manyanya, M. (2003), *Zimbabwe's Plunge: Exhausted Nationalism, Neoliberalism and the Search for Social Justice*, London, Merlin Press, Pietermaritzburg, University of Natal Press and Harare, Weaver Press, pp. 142–145.
3. Tandon, Y. (1999), 'A Blip or a Turnaround?', *Journal of Social Change and Development*, 49, December. For more, see any of the excellent publications of the Harare-based training/research NGO, Seatini, including Tandon's personal recollections of indignity at Doha. Tandon – once a Ugandan marxist guerrilla and briefly a culture minister – has bridged the global justice movements and the best Third World nationalist civil servants, in the manner of Martin Khor and Third World Network.
4. The story is told in detail in Keet, D. (2002), *South Africa's Official Role and Position in Promoting the World Trade Organisation*, Cape Town, Alternative Information and Development Centre.
5. Erwin, A. (1999), 'Statement to the World Trade Organisation Plenary', Seattle, 1 December.
6. Erwin, A. (2003), 'Statement on the 5th Ministerial Meeting of the World Trade Organisation held in Cancun Mexico in September 2003', Speech to the SA Parliament National Assembly, Cape Town, 26 September. On the basis of an agreement in the National Economic Development and Labour Council, Erwin himself was mandated to maintain a strong position in favour of labour clauses at Seattle, so his remark to parliament in 2003 is especially revealing.
7. Manuel, T. (2000), 'Address to the Seminar on South Africa's Relations and Creation of National Wealth and Social Welfare', Rand Afrikaans University Centre for European Study in Africa, Johannesburg, 20 October.
8. *New Agenda*, 8, 2002.
9. Keet, *South Africa's Official Role and Position in Promoting the World Trade Organisation*, p. 23.
10. *The Nation*, 19 June 2003.
11. *New Agenda*, 3, 2001.
12. At the Cairo meeting, Erwin successfully requested of the chair that African NGO delegates be excluded (Keet, *South Africa's Official Role and Position in Promoting the World Trade Organisation*, p. 26).
13. The Abuja meeting included an incident described by Keet, *South Africa's Official Role and Position in Promoting the World Trade Organisation*

(p. 28): 'In their determination to prevent African trade officials and ministers from hearing the views of NGOs, members of the SA delegation were openly hostile toward the NGOs present. This included a direct personal attack on internationally recognised NGO expert on the WTO, Martin Khor, director of the Third World Network based in Malaysia, who had been invited by the OAU to provide specialist advice to African trade officials.'

14. *Business Day*, 12 February 2002.
15. Hormeku, T. (2001), 'Text a Slap in the Face for African Countries', *Business Day*, 8 November.
16. Cited in Keet, *South Africa's Official Role and Position in Promoting the World Trade Organisation*, p. 35.
17. Cited in Kwa, A. (2002), *Power Politics in the WTO*, Bangkok, Focus on the Global South, p. 23.
18. Cited in Lynas, M. (2003), 'Playing Dirty at the WTO', *Third World Network Features*, Penang, Malaysia, June.
19. Kwa, *Power Politics in the WTO*, p. 24.
20. Keet, *South Africa's Official Role and Position in Promoting the World Trade Organisation*, p. 35.
21. *Mail & Guardian*, 16 November 2001.
22. *Business Day*, 2 June 2003.
23. *Business Report*, 16 November 2001.
24. *Business Day*, 7 March 2002.
25. Bond, *Unsustainable South Africa*, Chapter Two.
26. Keet, *South Africa's Official Role and Position in Promoting the World Trade Organisation*, p. 44.
27. Draper, P. (2003), 'To Liberalise or Not to Liberalise? A Review of the South African Government's Trade Policy', SA Institute of International Affairs Working Paper, Johannesburg, p. 18.
28. http://voiceoftheturtle.org/articles/raj_doha.shtml.
29. Edigheji, O. and K. Gostner (2000), 'Social Dialogue: The South African Experience', *Labour Education,* 3, 120, pp. 89–90.
30. As argued in Bond, *Against Global Apartheid*, Chapters Ten and Eleven, Cosatu's plan to end eco-social oppressions through a WTO reformed by the Social Clause was utopian, divisive and counterproductive. It was closer to AFL-CIO and ICFTU reformism than to the analysis, strategies and tactics of Third World labour and social movements.
31. Keet, *South Africa's Official Role and Position in Promoting the World Trade Organisation*, p. 44.
32. *Sunday Times*, 24 August 2003.
33. http://enn.com/news/wire-stories/2002/05/05222002/reu_47285.asp.
34. *Business Day*, 20 May 2003.
35. *New York Times*, 1 June 2003.
36. That plan failed to gain even EU support. According to George Monbiot (*The Guardian*, 3 June 2003), 'Chirac's proposals addressed only part of the problem, but they could have begun the process of dismantling the system which does so much harm to our pockets, our environment and the lives of some of the world's most vulnerable people. We might have expected Tony

Blair, who created a major diplomatic incident last year when he savaged Chirac for refusing to budge, to have welcomed the heavily subsidised sheep into the free-market fold. But our prime minister has single-handedly destroyed the French initiative. The reason will by now be familiar. George Bush, who receives substantial political support from US agro-industrialists, grain exporters and pesticide manufacturers, was not prepared to make the concessions required to match Chirac's offer. Had the EU, and in particular the member which claims to act as a bridge across the Atlantic, supported France, the moral pressure on Bush may well have become irresistible. But (once) Blair made it clear that he would not back Chirac's plan, the initiative was dead. Thanks to our conscience-stricken prime minister, and his statesmanlike habit of doing whatever Bush tells him to, Africa is now well and truly stuffed.'

37. *The Guardian*, 23 May 2003.
38. African Women's Communication and Development Network, African Women's Empowerment Network, Congress of South African Trade Unions, Council for the Development of Social Science Research in Africa, Crisis in Zimbabwe Coalition and Mwelekeo wa NGO (2003), 'Joint Statement: G8 Summits 2002 to 2003: From a Trickle to a Drop', Geneva, 3 June.
39. Cited in Dembele, D. (2003), 'PRSPS: Poverty Reduction or Poverty Reinforcement?', *Pambezuka News* 136, 11 December.
40. Cosatu economist Neva Makgetla (who supported AGOA, albeit by ignoring its regional distributional impacts) wrote, 'The proposed free-trade agreement harbours a host of risks, but promises few tangible benefits beyond what AGOA already provides.' She expressed concern because 'Zoellick included demands that reach beyond the traditional focus of trade negotiations. They include: Opening up government procurement to US firms. It is not clear how this would affect preferences for black empowerment or the Proudly SA campaign. Stronger patent protection for US goods. This might block local production of generic medicines. Increased trade in services. That could add to pressure to privatise basic infrastructure and social services in the name of allowing foreign investors to participate. US proposals on settling disputes are worrying. Other countries have signed free-trade agreements that let US companies sue governments directly, but it is usual for only states to lodge trade disputes. Company-to-state disputes can contradict development policies. The proposals rule out one free-trade measure that would benefit SA: a reform of antidumping rules to ensure they can't be used as a protectionist measure' (*Business Day*, 11 July 2003).
41. *Business Day*, 6 June 2003.
42. Feldman, G. (2002), 'US-African Trade Profile', US Department of Commerce, Washington, March.
43. Lallah, R. (2003), 'AGOA – Consolidating US Imperialism in Africa', *Khanya Journal*, 3, March.
44. *Business Day*, 6 June 2003.
45. According to the study, 'The manufacturers interviewed complained that labour costs in Swaziland need to be reduced. They indicated that their presence in the country was directly linked to trade facilitation agreements and the promulgation of the AGOA. They (said) their best opportunities in

Swaziland lay in the four years in which the MultiFibre Agreement and the AGOA overlapped. They argued that once these ended it would be difficult for them to compete with Asian based producers. Some indicated that they would shift their operations to China.' Trade Union Research Project and Center for Research on Multinational Corporations (2001), 'Taking the Devil's Rope: Findings from Swaziland', Durban and Amsterdam; and (2003), *Made in Southern Africa*, Amsterdam and Durban.
46. Bush, 'Remarks by the President to the Corporate Council on Africa's US-Africa Business Summit'.
47. InterPress Service, 19 June 2003.
48. Bush, 'Remarks by the President to the Corporate Council on Africa's US-Africa Business Summit'. This bullying was not uncommon; see Tibbett, S. (2003), 'The Spoils of the War on Poverty: The West's Rhetoric about Foreign Aid Conceals a Greedy Self-Interest', *The Guardian*, 2 July.
49. Keet, D. (2003), 'Contrasts and Counter-Positions in Cancun', Report on behalf of the African Peoples Caucus, Cancun, 16 September.
50. Balancing Peter Draper's honesty about Erwin's unpopularity in Africa, SAIIA *eAfrica* editor Ross Herbert (a US citizen) penned the following fibs in an article, 'Asessing George W. Bush', in the newsletter's August 2003 edition (p. 4): 'Many African and European politicians display attitudes towards the US that seek to publicly challenge and condemn Bush's unilateral moves. On trade, Iraq and genetically modified foods, Africa has largely aligned itself with Europe, all of which look like strategic mistakes. Particularly on trade, the US and the more radical Cairns Group are both natural allies to the African bloc and represent the only plausible alliances with sufficient clout to bring down devastating agricultural subsidies, which Europe stridently defends . . . US trade concessions to Africa are heavily influenced by the US goal of ensuring stability by boosting economic growth . . . in many cases America can be persuaded to follow its nobler instincts' (*sic*).
51. Tayob, R. (2003), 'South Africa at Cancun', Unpublished paper, Seatini, Harare, 14 September. In a further example of Erwin's degenerating relations with civil society, a telling incident occurred in the run up to Cancun, when Mohau Pheko, a talented African justice movement activist and intellectual, had the following run in with Erwin:
    (1) Friday 15 August: Mohau Pheko invited to be on the official [South African] government delegation going to the WTO 5th Ministerial meeting by the Department of Trade and Industry.
    (2) Tuesday 19 August: Mohau Pheko invited to speak at a government consulation on the WTO [Pheko was extremely critical].
    (3) Wednesday 20 August: Minister Alec Erwin downsizes the delegation to enable only one member of civil society to attend the 5th Ministerial, Mohau Pheko kicked off the delegation.
    (4) Thursday 21 August 2003: Mohau Pheko in leaked document from the Mexican government listing her as one of the activists from South Africa on Mexico's Watchlist for the WTO Cancun meeting.
    (Gender and Trade Network in Africa (2003), 'Mohau Pheko in Mexican Gov't Leaked "Enemies List" of Activists toward Cancun', Johannesburg, email alert, 22 August).

52. Irin news service, 18 September 2003.
53. Cited in *This Day*, 1 December 2003.
54. Erwin, 'Statement on the 5th Ministerial Meeting of the World Trade Organisation'.
55. *Mail & Guardian*, 19 December 2003.
56. *Business Day*, 20 May 2003.
57. *Business Day*, 3 July 2003.
58. *Wall Street Journal*, 10 December 2003.
59. Medecins Sans Frontieres, Health GAP, Health Action International, ACT UP Paris, Peoples Health Movement, Oxfam (2003), 'Joint NGO response to US proposal on Intellectual Property Rights, Innovation and Public Health at the 56th World Health Assembly', Geneva, 21 May.
60. Greg Palast Weblog, http://www.gregpalast.com, 14 July 2003.
61. Treatment Action Campaign (2003), 'The People's Docket: Indictment Against South African Government Ministers', Cape Town, 21 March.

5
Washington renamed
A 'Monterrey Consensus' on finance

In the Mexican city of Monterrey, the United Nations' Financing for Development (FFD) Conference in March 2002 was the first major international opportunity to correct global capital markets since the spectacular late 1990s emerging markets crises. South Africa's volatile currency was the freshest evidence, but similar problems with international financial markets spread from Mexico (1995) through Latin America (1995), to Eastern Europe and South Africa (1996), to Thailand, Indonesia and Malaysia (1997), then South Korea, Russia and South Africa again (1998), to Brazil (1999), and on to Turkey and Argentina (2000), and back to Argentina and South Africa (2001).[1]

South African finance minister Trevor Manuel and former International Monetary Fund managing director Michel Camdessus[2] were UN secretary general Kofi Annan's special envoys at the conference. In addition to 'speaking to heads of state and high-level politicians to convince them to make a commitment to a concrete outcome' (his UN mandate),[3] Manuel was a key ideological functionary.[4] He served as chairperson of the key IMF/World Bank policymaking body, the Development Committee.[5] Mbeki also addressed the conference plenary, declaring, 'We must accept the Monterrey Consensus.'

Throughout the conference, the September 2000 UN Millennium Development Goals were referred to in reverential terms. United Nations General Assembly resolution 55/2 set seven targets:
- To reduce the proportion of people living in extreme poverty by half between 1990 and 2015;
- enrol all children of school age in primary schools by 2015;
- make progress toward gender equality and empowering women by eliminating gender disparities in enrolment in primary and secondary education by 2005;
- reduce infant and child mortality ratios by two-thirds between 1990 and 2015;

- reduce maternal mortality ratios by three-quarters between 1990 and 2015;
- provide access for all who need reproductive health services by 2015; and
- implement national strategies for sustainable development by 2005, to reverse the loss of environmental resources by 2015.

Official development assistance (ODA) shortfalls and external debt were considered the main constraints, whereas global financial volatility, while recognised as a problem, was not explicitly linked to development goals. Achieving the targets would cost $54 billion per year, according to IMF and World Bank estimates.[6]

Civil society critics argued that the FFD conference was tainted from the outset, given that Mexico's ex-president Ernesto Zedillo effectively managed the process. The Yale-trained neoliberal economist's five-year term in Mexico City was notable for repression, failed economic crisis-management, and the end of his notoriously corrupt party's 85-year rule. Controversially, Zedillo appointed as his main advisor (and document author) John Williamson of the Washington-based Institute for International Finance, a think-tank primarily funded by the world's largest commercial banks. Williamson is considered one of the establishment's most vigorous neoliberal ideologues, and takes credit for coining the term 'Washington Consensus' in 1990. His November 1995 visit to South Africa included strong advocacy of Washington's agenda.[7]

Pretoria's image and power

As for South Africa's role at Monterrey, expectations were raised by Manuel's periodic bragging. The prior Bank/IMF conference at which Manuel had substantial influence was in Prague in September 2000. It was a disastrous meeting, which had to be truncated to one day because of the intense global justice movement protest outside. Nevertheless, speaking to an audience at Johannesburg's Rand Afrikaans University shortly afterwards, Manuel (who used the royal 'we') was buoyant:

> Last month we chaired the annual meetings of the IMF and World Bank in Prague, where we put on the table the most serious issue facing the world today: the growing and desperate impoverishment of almost half the world's people who live on less than $2 a day . . . These are issues that we are now in a position to take up because we can walk in the world with our heads held high.

Next week, we go to the G20 meeting in Canada – a group that includes 'systemically significant' countries. Countries, like ourselves, influential, although not powerful, countries with a voice; with potential. The G20 provides us with an opportunity to make new allies among the middle powers to engage with the G7; to push for structural change in a world where the inequalities are often reinforced by what, in the post Cold War era, has been a completely lopsided balance of power. We do this for ourselves, but we also need to engage on behalf of our neighbours. If our neighbours fall by the wayside, we are dragged down too.[8]

The global financial establishment decided to hunker down in late 2001. No structural change in international finance was implemented by the G20, G8 or any other group. Neighbours continued to fall by the wayside. Even before the September 11 terrorist attacks on the World Trade Centre and Pentagon, the 2001 IMF and World Bank annual meeting, originally scheduled for a fortnight later, was dramatically reduced in scope because of the prospect of 100 000 global justice movement protesters and, after the attacks, was relocated to Ottawa.

A few months before Monterrey, Cosatu education officer Mahlengi Bengu observed in an interview with the US-based *Democracy Now* radio show, how Pretoria had moved 'front and center stage within the global community, but more particularly within the financial institutions'. She added that the aims of a liberated South African society were 'largely inconsistent with the policies within the WTO, within the IMF, and within the World Bank'. Bengu noted, 'South Africa, as a component of the UN system and a number of financial institutions, has not been able to challenge [them] in the manner in which we would like to see that happening.'[9]

Was Manuel genuinely interested in challenging the power or the ideology behind Monterrey? The FFD's central premises were straightforward: deeper integration of developing countries into the global financial system to promote economic growth and development; and combination of World Bank, IMF, WTO and donor government powers, so as more consistently to armtwist Third World countries, aided by allies like Pretoria. These are also the implicit premises of NEPAD.

In Monterrey, Manuel endorsed privatisation during his high-profile address to business elites: 'Public-private partnerships are important win-win tools for governments and the private sector, as they provide an innovative way of delivering public services in a cost-effective manner.'[10] At the same time, PPPs were also being promoted

vigorously within NEPAD. But back in South Africa, such PPPs were nearly universally failing, from the standpoint of workers and consumers, and sometimes also businesses, in water, sanitation, electricity, telecommunications, the postal system, forestry, air and road transport, ports and road construction.[11] In August 2001 and October 2002, Cosatu held two-day mass stayaways against private parternships involving essential public services. They targetted Manuel and minister of public enterprises Jeff Radebe, who was subsequently voted off the SACP central committee by angry communists. Manuel didn't mention these problems, even as caveats, nor did he concede Pretoria's repeated failure to reach revenue targets from state asset sales.

Crumbs of debt relief

While the Monterrey final report that Manuel helped steer through the conference contained some pleasing rhetoric, it promotes only orthodox strategies. The report observed 'dramatic shortfalls in resources required to achieve the internationally agreed development goals'.[12] But it endorsed the Heavily Indebted Poor Countries (HIPC) initiative as 'an opportunity to strengthen the economic prospects and poverty reduction efforts of beneficiary countries'. NEPAD carries a similarly worded endorsement of HIPC.[13] Manuel suggested that 'the HIPC Trust Fund be fully funded, and that provision is made for topping-up when exogenous shocks impact on countries' debt sustainability', as if the programme was otherwise satisfactory.[14]

Within a year of Monterrey, the World Bank admitted some of HIPC's mistakes. The Bank was forced to accept longstanding criticisms that its staff 'had been too optimistic' about the ability of countries to repay under HIPC, and that projections of export earnings were extremely inaccurate, leading to failure by half the HIPC countries to reach their completion points.[15] Although HIPC had been endorsed by NGO campaigners such as Jubilee Plus, it was a mirage from the outset. The London lobby group conceded, 'According to the original HIPC schedule, 21 countries should have fully passed through the HIPC initiative and received total debt cancellation of approximately $34.7 billion in net present value terms. In fact, only eight countries have passed Completion Point, between them receiving debt cancellation of $11.8 billion.'[16]

Add a few other countries' partial relief via the Paris Club ($14 billion) and it appears that the grand total of debt relief from the 1996–2003 exercise was just $26.13 billion. There remained more than $2 trillion of Third World debt that should be cancelled, including not just HIPC countries but also Nigeria, Argentina, Brazil, South Africa and other major debtors not considered highly-indebted or poor in the mainstream discourse. The more radical Jubilee South

network, with strong leadership from groups in Argentina, Nicaragua, the Philippines and South Africa, rejects Jubilee Plus ideas about how much debt is 'sustainable' and 'repayable', arguing for full cancellation, Third World repudiation and G8-country reparations.

The lack of financial provision for HIPC in Western capitals reflects deep resistance to debt relief and, probably, the realisation that there are merits to using debt as a means of maintaining control over Third World economies. An 'enhanced HIPC' was introduced to maintain control and give the *appearance* of concern. Thus at Evian in 2003, the G8 agreed with Mbeki's plea to relook at the programme, but no fundamental changes or substantial new funds were mooted.

Poverty 'Reduction' Strategy Papers

A reason for Africa's lack of progress on debt was that the underlying basis for Bretton Woods interventions – hard-core neoliberalism – was never really challenged by Mbeki or his NEPAD colleagues. HIPC began in 1996, and in late 1999 was accompanied by a renaming of the structural adjustment philosophy: Poverty Reduction Strategy Papers (PRSPs).

More than two years later, at Monterrey, Manuel told fellow finance ministers that PRSPs were 'an important tool for developing countries to reduce their debt burdens . . . a thorough and useful PRSP requires time, resources and technical capacity'. He suggested the Bretton Woods Institutions *increase* their role, to 'provide more technical assistance to meet those particular challenges'.[17] The advice should have been laughed out of Monterrey, and was probably the source of amusement deep within the bowels of the Bretton Woods Institutions. Bank staff in the Middle East and North Africa section had, after all, complained two years earlier in a leaked and well-publicised memo to James Wolfensohn:

> The list of fiduciary tasks is being constantly enlarged with increasing requirements that are burdensome on our borrowers and staff. The list has grown from environment and resettlement a few years ago, to now also include social assessment, financial management . . . and so on. While no one can question the importance of these issues, staff have been put in a straight jacket in how they must approach these issues through detailed 'guidelines' enforced by an army of 'reviewers' . . .
>
> The World Bank is increasingly being drawn into activities which are politically sensitive (participatory processes, involvement of civil society, corruption and so on). There is no doubt about

the importance and relevance of these for development and success of World Bank assistance, but staff are not well prepared to handle these issues which creates more anxiety and stress.[18]

Participation or co-option?

In contrast to Manuel's desire for PRSP expansion, civil society resistance to structural adjustment increased across the Third World, including Manuel's home continent, sometimes in the form of 'IMF riots'. Annual reports in the World Development Movement's *States of Unrest* series include dozens of countries and hundreds of IMF riots. In Africa, as an example, anti-neoliberal protests were called by students, lecturers and nurses in Angola; public sector workers in Benin; farmers, electricity workers and teachers in Kenya; municipal workers in Morocco; healthworkers in Niger; the main trade union federation, including police and municipal workers, in Nigeria; community groups and organised labour in South Africa; and bank customers and trade unionists in Zambia. As the World Development Movement found, the new version of structural adjustment did not fool the victims: 'PRSPs have failed to deviate from the IMF's free market orthodoxy.' The report covering 2002 showed:

> The protesters in developing countries come from across the social spectrum. They are not always the poorest of the poor . . . they are also the newly emerging middle-classes: teachers, civil servants, priests, doctors, public-sector workers, trade-union activists and owners of small businesses. This broad based movement clearly indicates how policies promoted by the IMF and World Bank are not only keeping the poor in poverty, but are also impoverishing sectors of society generally relied upon for wealth creation, economic development and civil society leadership. Policies intended to promote economic development and poverty reduction in the emerging and fragile economies of developing countries are not only failing, but are actually leading to economic stagnation, which is felt across the social spectrum.[19]

In the same critical spirit some months earlier, a Jubilee South conference of the main African social movements in Kampala concluded:
- The PRSPs are not based on real people's participation and ownership, or decision-making. To the contrary, there is no intention of taking civil society perspectives seriously, but to keep participation to mere public relations legitimisation.

- The lack of genuine commitment to participation is further manifested in the failure to provide full and timeous access to all necessary information, limiting the capacity of civil society to make meaningful contributions.
- The PRSPs have been introduced according to pre-set external schedules which in most countries has resulted in an altogether inadequate time period for an effective participatory process.
- In addition to the constraints placed on governments and civil society organisations in formulating PRSPs, the World Bank and IMF retain the right to veto the final programs. This reflects the ultimate mockery of the threadbare claim that the PRSPs are based on 'national ownership'.
- An additional serious concern is the way in which PRSPs are being used by the World Bank and IMF, directly and indirectly, to co-opt NGOs to 'monitor' their own governments on behalf of these institutions.[20]

The latter gambit had begun to fail by the time the FFD convened in Monterrey. Even the World Bank's best African case, Uganda, heard its National NGO Forum report: 'Among civil society organisations there is growing concern that perhaps their participation in the endeavour has amounted to little more than a way for the World Bank and IMF to co-opt the activist community and civil society in Uganda into supporting the same traditional policies.'[21]

Other NGO, funding agency and academic studies of PRSPs were highly critical.[22] The Harare-based debt-cancellation advocacy network, Afrodad, studied the experiences in Burkina Faso, Mauritania, Mozambique, Tanzania and Uganda, the first African countries to undergo PRSPs. Afrodad noted that in each of these countries, there were processes with varying degrees of participation that preceded the PRSPs:

> Mozambique's government policies and strategies since the late 1980s had been expressed in the Plano de Acção para Redução da Pobreza Absoluta, Tanzania adopted a National Poverty Eradication Strategy in 1997, Uganda had a Poverty Eradication Action Plan, Burkina Faso established its priorities under Cadre Strategique da Lutte Contra la Pauvrete, and Mauritania had a series of National Reference Documents encompassing social, economic and other national issues. The World Bank and IMF insisted that these processes should be refashioned to fit the PRSP mould. The PRSPs thus, rather than introducing participation into poverty and

development concerns, interfered to lesser or greater degrees with existing processes. The relationship is still one of 'if you want what we have to offer, you must do things our way.' At the global level, this reflects well entrenched power relations rather than anything that could be called 'participatory.'[23]

A report by a Sussex University academic found a 'broad consensus among our civil society sources in Ghana, Malawi, Mozambique, Tanzania and Zambia that their coalitions have been unable to influence macro-economic policy or even engage governments in dialogue about it'.[24]

Health systems under strain

Were PRSPs working at all by that stage, perhaps at least by redirecting funds to essential state services such as healthcare? By March 2002, the Bank and IMF had only received data on PRSP-defined poverty reduction spending for 2000 from four countries (Burkina Faso, Honduras, Mozambique and Uganda). They conceded that health spending as a percentage of GDP *declined* after the introduction of PRSPs, and increased only fractionally as a percentage of total government spending.

Health ministries were left with the option of reallocating existing budgets to reflect the health sector priorities raised in the PRSPs. The Kenyan PRSP set itself an objective to 'enhance equity, quality, accessibility and affordability of health care'. The means to meet this objective were 'an application of rational, transparent and poverty focused resource allocation criteria and weights for the Government of Kenya Ministry of Health budget for districts; criteria and weights to be gradually phased in beginning with FY 2001/2002 budget'. Its first three commitments were:

- reduction of the budget allocation for the Kenyatta National Hospital, as a share of the total Ministry of Health recurrent budget, from approximately 15% in FY 1999/2000 to 10% by FY 2004;
- establish an acceptable maximum recurrent budget allocation for provincial hospitals; and
- create maximum recurrent ceilings for district hospitals as a percentage of total district health recurrent budget.

The first notable impact of the PRSP on the health sector was a financial squeeze on hospitals. South Africa underwent a similar experience in the latter half of the 1990s, with devastating consequences. Several major tertiary health centres, such as Hillbrow hospital and some in the Western Cape, were shut down. It is fair to say that the first round of healthcare rationalisations were debilitating to the big hospitals and to their lower-income wards who, because of weaknesses elsewhere in the health system, relied on the facilities as basic suppliers of primary clinic healthcare.[25]

There was also a qualitative, not merely quantitative problem, as even the World Health Organisation, often a Bretton Woods ally on healthcare commodification, recognised a few weeks before Monterrey:

> PRSPs characterise health as an outcome of development, rather than a means of achieving it. Most PRSPs contain several strands, one or more on increasing the rate of economic growth and/or maintaining macroeconomic stability, and one strand on improving human capabilities. The 'growth' strand covers sectors traditionally considered 'productive' (business, tourism, manufacturing, etc.) while the 'human capabilities' strand covers the provision of basic services, including health.
>
> This division creates obstacles to improving health status, and limits the potential of improved health to positively benefit other sectors. For example, improved health is key to worker productivity, to creating and sustaining rural livelihoods, and to educational achievement. Similarly, employment, agriculture, the environment and other sectors all have an impact on health status. Most PRSPs fail to make these links . . .
>
> PRSPs reflect traditional definitions of health as a social sector, and health spending as consumption rather than investment. This suggests that within the PRSP framework health will remain under-resourced and marginalised and that opportunities to reduce poverty through improving health will be missed.[26]

This statement was an important recognition of a major defeat in an unending institutional turf war. According to public health authorities David Werner and David Sanders, 'it is an ominous sign when a giant financial institution with such strong ties to big government and big business bullies its way into health care. Yet according to *The Lancet*, the World Bank is now moving into first place as the global agency most influencing health policy, leaving the World Health Organisation a weak second.'[27]

Policy coherence

Ignoring such information, the underlying objective of those who authored the Monterrey Consensus was to grant more power to the Bank, Fund and WTO. In contrast, the WHO, International Labour

Organisation, UN Conference on Trade and Development and UN Research Institute for Social Development were too centrist, or even leftist, to be integrated into Monterrey's neoliberal framework. When Monterrey requested states to 'encourage policy and programme coordination of international institutions and coherence at the operational and international levels', some institutions were more coherent than others. Co-ordination would come between the Bretton Woods Institutions and WTO first, and was a dangerous new mode of introducing cross-conditionality. Although opposed by many Third World negotiators at the WTO, such coherence was one of Manuel's only explicit Monterrey ambitions reported back home: 'ensuring that international institutions effectively consider the extent of overlapping agendas . . . [because] conflicting policies serve no one, especially not the poor.'[28]

On the contrary, it should be obvious that the world's poor *would have* been served if there *had been* conflicting policies between the institutions of the embryonic world-state, for example, if the World Bank had taken former chief economist Joseph Stiglitz's advice seriously, or if conflict simply led to gridlock between the global economic institutions. As critics in the main progressive agriculture think-tanks explained in May 2003, 'Over the decades, loan conditions of the IMF/World Bank have forced developing countries to lower their trade barriers, cut subsidies for their domestic food producers, and eliminate government programmes aimed to enhance rural agriculture. However, no such conditions are imposed on wealthy industrial countries.' Instead, the WTO explicitly permits the dumping of 'surplus foods at prices below the cost of production, driving out rural production in developing countries and expanding markets for the large transnational exporting companies. It also prohibits developing countries from introducing new programmes that may help their local agriculture producers. As a result the agriculture sectors in developing countries, key for rural poverty reduction, have been devastated.' Similar NGO complaints were made about the 'coherence agenda' on water privatisation, regulation of foreign investors, and governance of the multilateral institutions.[29]

Democratic governance?

Manuel and Erwin would no doubt reply that the problems in agricultural markets – especially dumping and northern subsidies – could be resolved, but only if momentum increased to *reform* the institutions to more democratically reflect the needs of southern countries instead of northern voting power. Yet the Monterrey

Consensus offered only timid suggestions for global governance reforms. The Bank and IMF took nearly a full year to come forward with a plan, which, as it turned out, was an insult to the concept of democratic global governance.

The Monterrey final report merely recognised 'the need to broaden and strengthen the participation of developing countries in international economic decision-making and norm-setting . . . We encourage the following actions [from the International Monetary Fund and World Bank]: to continue to enhance participation of all developing countries and countries with economies in transition in their decision-making.'[30]

Manuel did not appear particularly concerned.[31] His Monterrey plenary speech as IMF/Bank Development Committee chair, included only a vague and predictable statement, with no concrete demands to add muscle: 'Reform of international financial governance is critical to [ensure] that developing countries benefit from globalisation through participation. The consensus on enhanced partnership, which would entail clearly defined responsibilities for all stakeholders, cannot be met by a reluctance to change the *status quo* regarding international financial governance.'[32]

The charge of 'global political apartheid' certainly applied to the Bretton Woods Institutions, where nearly fifty Sub-Saharan African countries were represented by just two directors, while eight rich countries enjoyed a director each and the US maintained veto power by holding more than 15% of the votes. There is no transparency as to which board members take what positions on key votes. The leaders of the Bank and IMF are chosen from, respectively, the US and EU, with the US treasury secretary holding the power of hiring or firing.[33] No doubt people of the same ideological orientation from the Third World (such as Manuel) could get seats on a restructured Bretton Woods board of executive directors.

Some reformist gestures were needed for the sake of appearance.[34] Nevertheless, the *Financial Times* reported that the 2003 Bank/Fund strategy emanating from Manuel's Development Committee offered only 'narrow technocratic changes', such as adding *one* additional representative from the south to the 24-member board.[35] Details emerged in mid-2003 when a leaked World Bank paper proposed raising developing country voting power from 39% to 44% and adding one new African executive director. But IMF governance, Bank/IMF board transparency or Bank/IMF senior management selection were all neglected in the June 2003 proposals.[36] For the US, even those milquetoast reforms were too much, and the Bush regime's executive director to the Bank, Carol Brooking, opposed reforms and suggested a new fund for extra research capacity aimed at the two institutions' Third World directors.[37]

Frustration about African impotence in Washington occasionally boiled over, and Manuel sometimes publicly criticised the lack of democracy at the Bretton Woods Institutions. In mid-2003, for instance, he chaired a United Nations Economic Commission for Africa meeting in Addis Ababa, where he complained about an IMF proposal to split the continent in half for internal organisational purposes: 'Will it be along colonial lines, or into north and south? We don't know. What we do know is that Europe is not being divided, nor is America . . . We should be stressing repeatedly; nothing about us, without us.'[38]

Although Manuel's efforts are often reduced to polishing global apartheid's financial chains, after several years of high-profile lobbying for governance reform and insider attempts at change from positions of real influence, he has come to accept this with a certain grace. As he put it at a press conference during the September 2003 IMF/Bank annual meeting in Dubai, when asked why no progress was made on Bretton Woods democratisation, 'I don't think that you can ripen this tomato by squeezing it.'[39]

Indeed, much more than intra-organisational positioning is at stake. The Bank and IMF are central cogs in the wheel of US imperialism. Nothing said at Monterrey prevented the Bank, for example, from reinvigorating its push towards state services privatisation in the 2004 *World Development Report*. According to London School of Economics professor Robert Wade:

> The US has steered the World Bank – through congressional conditions on the replenishment of the International Development Association (IDA), the soft-loan facility – to launch its biggest refocusing in a decade, a 'private sector development' agenda devoted to the same end of accelerating the private (and non-governmental organisation) provision of basic services on a commercial basis. The World Bank has made no evaluation of its earlier efforts to support private participation in social sectors. Its new private sector development thrust, especially in the social sectors, owes almost everything to intense US pressure.[40]

These examples reflect the frivolous nature of the Monterrey mandate for reform of the Bretton Woods Institutions. As Jubilee South Africa's Neville Gabriel commented, 'Monterrey bowed to the *status quo* in international power relations by glossing over the need for more representative global governance mechanisms.' Yet, reported Gabriel,

'Halfway through the conference, German government representatives and IMF and World Bank officials declared a new era in global development thinking, marked by a shift from the Washington Consensus to a new Monterrey Consensus.' The underlying power bloc – which Gabriel accurately described as 'a dictatorship of nameless, faceless, and unaccountable technocrats, obsessed with private market-driven growth that sees the masses of impoverished people as incidental to the wealth creation project' – was undisturbed.[41]

Transparency

Decision making at the Bretton Woods Institutions is opaque, notwithstanding some minor gains on the 'transparency' front. A 2001 commitment to greater transparency by the World Bank was viewed with disdain by the main NGO watchdogs, including the Washington-based Bank Information Center: 'The finished product frustrates the key process of citizen participation in the Bank's activities by keeping confidential many important documents, applying inappropriate timelines for information release, and failing to provide for translation of many key documents.' Even the Bank's own Ombudsman admitted in a report that 'many sources complained about the difficulty of accessing project information, the available information lacked sufficient detail, and business confidentiality concerns (were) inappropriately extended to the social and environmental dimensions of projects.'[42]

A few months after Monterrey, a modicum of change occurred. The London-based NGO Bretton Woods Project noted, 'in September 2002, the Fund's board made a number of decisions such as publishing board minutes after 10 years, and extending the deletions policy to include highly market-sensitive performance criteria and structural benchmarks (conditionalities). Progress on other fronts has been delayed or rejected, for example on grounds that publishing draft Letters of Intent early would "pre-empt approval".' Bretton Woods secrecy is compounded by Third World elite paranoia: 'The apparent reluctance of borrowing countries to disclose more information on their relations with the IMF can be explained by a willingness to prevent closer scrutiny and potential "interference" in sometimes difficult negotiations with the institutions.'[43]

Transparent or not, the dictatorial orientation of Washington financial technocrats and their allied donor governments is no secret in most African capitals.[44] Princeton-based Survey Research Associates was commissioned by the Bank in 2002 to poll leading opinion-makers across the world, and found that in addition to complaints of 'arrogance' and excessive bureaucracy, 'The Bank's recommended reforms were often said to do more harm than good, with more than 60% of respondents in South Asia and Latin America saying they were unhelpful.'[45] The Swedish government commissioned an academic study on Bretton Woods reform that concluded, 'The World Bank continues to be dominant as the main purveyor of development ideas. Although its policy prescriptions change significantly over time, a "the Bank can never be wrong" mentality still prevails in much of the institution's thoughts and actions.'[46]

Yet Western governments (including Sweden) are not only generous funders of the neoliberal agenda via periodic Bank/IMF recapitalisations, they are also often part of the cross-conditionality that makes this dogmatic power so formidable. The Kenyan minister of finance exposed the pressures felt during a Nairobi PRSP process in 2001. One of the country's newspapers reported,

> Letters confirming Kenya's commitment to reform – supposedly written by top government officials – were actually drafted by the donors and handed to him (the Minister of Finance) to sign. Mr Okemo said the arrangement was 'an open secret' and that the minister was told 'to sign along the dotted line as an ultimatum.' He asked: 'Is this not coercion?'[47]

Okemo was removed from office shortly after going public with his complaints.

Coercion by the Bank and IMF on behalf of Washington's geopolitical agenda is another long-standing complaint. The Bretton Woods twins typically argue that their's is an apolitical role, even to the extent of lending to the apartheid regime in 1966, after the United Nations General Assembly passed a resolution against such activity. The Bank's lawyer replied that 'the Bank's articles provide that the Bank and its officers shall not interfere in the political affairs of any member, and that they shall not be influenced in their decisions by the political character of the member or members concerned.'[48] Yet, the Bretton Woods Institutions' political role is so notorious that in mid-2003, other members had to caution against further irrational lending to Turkey, a step justified only by Washington's political calculus.

Power relations associated with financial flows (including aid), and a failure to grapple with contradictions intrinsic to orthodox development financing systems, created underlying problems in the Monterrey Consensus. These contradictions included hard-currency liabilities and Washington's opposition to cross-subsidisation of public goods. They are profound flaws, and the sabotage of reform at

Monterrey reflects how little influence Manuel exerted in a leadership position.

Failing to fix global finance

A final example, perhaps the most crucial, showing how Monterrey amplified the self-destructive tendencies of international finance, was the conference recognition that 'measures that mitigate the impact of excessive volatility of short-term capital flows are important and must be considered'. But in reality, the final document calls for the opposite, 'liberalising capital flows in an orderly and well sequenced process', as if there can be such a process.[49]

This is not a new problem. Manuel was very active in the G20 group of leading finance ministers, where since 1998, discussions were held with the alleged objectives of strengthening financial systems, advancing transparency and accountability, and preventing and managing international financial crises. However, it is unclear whether these led to any behavioural changes or institutional strengthening aside from a larger bailout function for the US Treasury and Bretton Woods Institutions. The underlying premise of the G20 reports was, after all, that the East Asian crisis was one of inaccurate market signalling due to poor information and crony capitalism.[50] Manuel also played a role in the Financial Stability Forum, founded in 1999 and located at the Bank for International Settlements in Basle, which exchanges information and promotes central bank co-operation.[51]

In many such venues, Manuel continually pushes for more rapid – and by implication, *inevitably* disorderly and poorly sequenced – financial liberalisation at home, e.g., via a 'NEPAD Financial Market Integration Task Force', 'to fast-track financial market integration through the establishment of an internationally competitive legislative and regulatory framework', as he promised the Commonwealth Business Council in mid-2002.[52]

Whose agenda was this? Financial liberalisation, according to Wade, remains a crucial tool of US imperialism: 'This is the paradox of economic globalisation, it looks like "powerless" expansion of markets but works to enhance the ability of the United States to harness the rest of the world to its own economic rhythms and structure, to fortify its empire-like power status.'[53]

To illustrate: the Asian crisis stalled the persistent armtwisting efforts of US treasury secretary, Larry Summers, to force through an amendment to the IMF articles of agreement which would end all exchange controls everywhere. Nevertheless, when Ethiopian prime minister Meles Zenawi resisted in 1997, according to both Wade (then inside the Bank) and Stiglitz, the IMF cut off the cheaper loans it had earlier made available. Cross-conditionality also made Ethiopia ineligible for other low-interest loans and grants from the World Bank, the European Community, and aid from bilaterals.[54] Stiglitz waged war within the Bank and Clinton regime, finally winning concessions, but he learned a lesson: 'There was clear evidence the IMF was wrong about financial market liberalisation and Ethiopia's macroeconomic position, but the IMF had to have its way.'[55]

It was not just Ethiopia that would witness a renewed attack on exchange controls. In the immediate wake of the Asian crisis, in 1999, then IMF managing director Camdessus argued, 'I believe it is time for momentum to be re-established . . . Full liberalisation of capital movement should be promoted in a prudent and well-sequenced fashion.'[56] Such an obvious case of crisis-amnesia, in the context of global financial apartheid, should have been grounds for radical governance reforms. Despite Manuel's brief June 2003 outburst against ongoing IMF control of Africa, Zenawi was left to poignantly implore, 'While we will not be at the high table of the IMF, we should at least be in the room where decisions are made.'[57]

Were Manuel and Zenawi reduced to serving as the international equivalents of South Africa's apartheid-era bantustan leaders? Was their function merely begging the new global version of the hated apartheid state for a few crumbs and a little dignity, while promising to obey the rules of the game, and even endorsing the language of financial liberalisation, so very damaging to their constituents, as homegrown policy? It seemed so, for shortly after Monterrey, Manuel testified to the Myburgh Commission of Inquiry into the Rapid Depreciation of the Exchange Rate that 'the government has chosen to follow a flexible exchange rate to act as a shock absorber against global developments.'[58] This was an obvious *non sequitur*, since the March 1995 lifting of the financial rand exchange control (approved by Manuel) made South Africa *more* vulnerable to hot money inflows and outflows. As finance minister from March 1996, Manuel oversaw 30%-plus currency crashes that accompanied his appointment, and again in mid-1998 and 2000–01 – and still had no response other than to approve massive interest rate increases that debilitated the economy and debtors.[59]

Instead of learning some logical lessons, especially the need for tighter exchange controls, Manuel parroted the Washington Consensus in his dangerous September 2002 promise to Commonwealth business tycoons that he would 'fast-track financial market integration'.[60] At the same time, he effectively confessed that Monterrey was actually a

failure (though he did not use the word), because of 'our collective unwillingness to recognise financial disequilibria . . . This speculation reaches such proportions that its bursting wreaks havoc on markets and economies across the globe. We do not have the multilateral financial architecture to address them – and that means that high levels of risk aversion and investor uncertainty will remain features of the global environment for some time to come.'[61]

The reform agenda, in other words, was dead.

The damage of free finance

The durable 'collective unwillingness' of the *verkrampte* defenders of global financial apartheid withstood a serious blow from a surprising source a few months later. In March 2003, leading IMF researchers – including chief economist Kenneth Rogoff, whose juvenile mid-2002 attack on Stiglitz was posted on the IMF website – finally recognised the damage of financial liberalisation over the years. Rogoff and his colleagues, Eswar Prasad, Shang-Jin Wei and M. Ayhan Kose, admitted 'sobering' conclusions:

> A systematic examination of the evidence suggests that it is difficult to establish a robust causal relationship between the

degree of financial integration and output growth performance ... There is little evidence that financial integration has helped developing countries to better stabilise fluctuations ... While there is no proof in the data that financial globalisation has benefitted growth, there is evidence that some countries may have experienced greater consumption volatility as a result ... Recent crises in some more financially integrated countries suggest that financial integration may have increased volatility.[62]

In other words, a liberalised financial system, which Pretoria endorsed by abolishing the financial rand in 1995 and permitting the offshore listing of the largest firms in 1998–2000, does not necessarily bring the benefits that Manuel and Reserve Bank governor Tito Mboweni anticipated. Such a strategy can cause financial turbulence, including massive interest rate increases and job-shedding, of the sort South Africans witnessed in 1996, 1998 and 2000–01.

A few examples from the IMF paper are striking. With negative 13.7% per person growth from 1980–2000, according to the IMF, South Africa had one of the world's slowest growing economies, and yet was also one of the most financially integrated countries. In contrast, China gained a 392% increase in per capita growth over the same period while being, the IMF researchers admitted, only 'partially integrated'.[63] Much closer to home, the IMF conceded, 'Mauritius

(146% per capita growth) and Botswana (135% per capita growth) managed to achieve very strong growth rates during the period, although they are relatively closed to financial flows.'[64]

Recognising the fallacy of relying upon financial globalisation for growth was one thing, but fixing the problem of subsequent crises was another. This was evident in the mid-2003 demise of a debt arbitration mechanism proposed by a Bush regime appointee as deputy director of the IMF, Anne Krueger, who was formerly a World Bank chief economist.

As the *The Guardian*'s Larry Elliott explained:

> Gordon Brown and his fellow finance ministers told the IMF to draw up a plan that would give bankruptcy protection to countries. The idea was to give states the same rights as companies if they went belly-up, avoiding the expensive bail-outs that have accompanied the big financial crises of the past decade. The IMF was given six months to come up with a blueprint, but when it reported back last month the idea was dead in the water. Billions of dollars from the bail-outs ended up in the coffers of the big finance houses of New York and George Bush was told not to meddle with welfare for Wall Street. The message was understood: the US used its voting power at the IMF to strangle the bankruptcy code at birth.[65]

Manuel's muddle

Realistic as Manuel's retrospective defeatism was in the context of such power relations, it is fair to ask whether despondency about global financial apartheid is an inevitable conclusion. Might the frustration of reform also have reflected Manuel's decision not to cause a fuss at Monterrey or to lobby for meaningful, systemic change? Did his softly-softly approach divulge, in the words of a mid-2003 *Business Day* report, that Manuel had been considering other 'international posts – perhaps at the World Bank or IMF,' allegedly, 'for ages. The rationale is that he . . . is seeking new challenges. A few other reasons have been put forward, but a desire by the well-respected finance minister to move on to the global stage seems most plausible.'[66]

It is not necessary to endorse a conspiracy theory to explain Manuel's spinelessness in defending South Africa's rand and hard currency reserves, or in fighting for a fair international financial system. His patriotism is not an issue; his ideology of financial liberalisation *is*. As for Manuel's inertia in Monterrey, Washington and

Pretoria, it is sufficient to note the coziness of a system in which, as Stiglitz explained in relation to former IMF acting managing director Stanley Fischer (subsequently vicechair of the world's largest bank, Citibank), 'These individuals see the world through the eyes of the financial community.'[67]

Regardless of the reasons, Manuel was apparently quite committed to lubricating global financial apartheid where it mattered: whether increasing South Africa's vulnerability to currency volatility or in international conferences that underscored the world elite's 'collective unwillingness to recognise financial disequilibria', as Manuel admitted. It was up to civil society critics, including Canadian financial-democracy activist Robin Round of the Halifax Initiative, to take the critique forward:

> After five long years of preparatory work, the UN Financing for Development conference is a diplomatic disaster. This conference was to find new ways to wipe out poverty and narrow the growing gap between rich and poor. Intense US pressure, however, gutted the process, reducing the final conference statement to a set of vague principles and generalities. Shamefully, Canada became the echo in the room whenever the US spoke.
>
> Governments eliminated or weakened commitments that could have delivered real reform to global finance and trade systems that by their very nature keep the poor poor. They left out commitments to review trade policies that block access to markets in rich countries. How can you develop, when you can't sell your goods abroad?
>
> They overlooked the urgent need to cancel the crippling debt of developing countries. How can you develop, when you must pay the International Monetary Fund before you inoculate children?
>
> They refused to examine how the World Bank and IMF manipulate developing countries' economic, fiscal, and social policies. How can you develop, when you're not allowed to govern your own country?[68]

Notes

1. For more background to contemporary international financial power relations, see Armijo, L. (2001), 'The Political Geography of Financial Reform: Who Wants What and Why?', *Global Governance*, 7, 4; Lee, S. (2002), 'Global Monitor: The International Monetary Fund', *New Political Economy*, 7, 2; Gowan, P. (1999), *The Global Gamble: Washington's Faustian Bid for Global Dominance*, London, Verso; Soederberg, S. (2001), 'The Emperor's

New Suit: The New International Financial Architecture as a Reinvention of the Washington Consensus', *Global Governance*, 7, 4; and Soederberg, S. (2002), 'The New International Financial Architecture: Imposed Leadership and Emerging Markets', in L. Panitch and C. Leys (eds), *Socialist Register 2002*, London, Merlin Press. Background to Monterrey is provided in Focus on the Global South (2002), 'The Road to Monterrey Passes through Washington', *Focus on Trade*, 75, March; Soederberg, S. (2004), 'Recasting Neoliberal Dominance in the South? A Critique of the Monterrey Consensus', forthcoming in *Alternatives*; and Soederburg, S. (2004), *The Politics of the New International Financial Architecture: Reimposing Neoliberal Dominance in the South*, London, Zed Books.
2. In retirement, Camdessus remained an active agent of the Washington Consensus. In 2001 he served as an advisor to Pope John Paul II. In 2002–03 he was head of a World Water Forum infrastructure financing panel that was extremely controversial. In June 2003 he was chosen as the G8's special liaison for Africa.
3. *Business Day*, 15 January 2002.
4. Manuel's own world view is difficult to pin down, for he is an exceptionally flexible politician. Yet he is careful not to step outside the box of conventional wisdom. Thus, in September 2003 he commented in the International Monetary Fund's house journal, *Finance and Development*, 'Macroeconomic stabilisation is critical for growth, but it is not clear that privatisation is. Moreover, privatisation and deregulation simply do not apply to African countries in the same way that they may in Latin American countries . . . It is not clear that rigorous pursuit of the Washington Consensus reforms in African countries would have delivered the outcomes expected from their application in Latin America.' There are several areas in which Manuel's double-talk reveals a *status quo* commitment, even setting aside the fact that Latin America – a macroeconomic disaster zone – was not a particularly good model for Africans to emulate. Macroeconomic 'stabilisation' combines three central factors: fiscal austerity, the cause of many an African 'IMF Riot' the last two decades and enormous unhappiness in Manuel's own political party; the highest real interest rates in Africa's modern history; and the removal of exchange controls and other regulations on investment which in turn led to financial turbulence and allowed vast African capital flight (far more than its foreign debt). In South Africa, Manuel is proceeding with an ambitious privatisation strategy.
5. The appointment was made in November 2001 at the annual meeting of the Bank and Fund. One former chair of the Joint Ministerial Committee on the Transfer of Real Resources to Developing Countries, was Zimbabwean finance minister Bernard Chidzero (1986–89). During his term, the transfer of net financial resources from s*outh to north* soared from nothing in 1987 to in excess of US$50 billion in 1989. (For Chidzero's unauthorised biography, see Bond, P. (1998), *Uneven Zimbabwe: A Study of Finance, Development and Underdevelopment*, Trenton, Africa World Press, Chapter Seven.)
6. United Nations (2002), 'Report of the International Conference on Financing for Development', A/CONF.198/11, Monterrey, Mexico, 22 March, Statement by Mike Moore, Director-General, World Trade Organisation. The IMF and Bank tend to underestimate the recurrent costs associated with most basic-

needs goods, because the institutions generally insist on cost-recovery and self-financing.
7. I had lunch with him and recall Unisa economist Philip Mohr briefing Williamson on how much hard work had transpired to ideologically panel-beat ANC economists into accepting neoliberalism.
8. Manuel, 'Address to the Seminar on South Africa's Relations and Creation of National Wealth and Social Welfare'.
9. Cited in Mann, *Durban Dispatches*, pp. 62–63.
10. Manuel, T. (2002), 'Remarks to the International Business Forum at the International Conference on Financing for Development', Monterrey, 18 March.
11. See Bond, P. (ed.) (2002), *Fanon's Warning: A Civil Society Reader on the New Partnership for Africa's Development*, Trenton, Africa World Press and AIDC, pp. 141–142 for a discussion of the primary pilots and their failings.
12. The citations are from United Nations, 'Report of the International Conference on Financing for Development', paragraphs 2, 4, 25, 39, 41, 49, 52, 54, 71.
13. For a critique of NEPAD's pro-HIPC financing arguments, see Bond, *Fanon's Warning*, pp. 183–192. NEPAD only adds that more resources are required and a few more countries added to those eligible for relief.
14. The quote by Manuel demonstrated a smug analysis of HIPC and a surprisingly unambitious reform agenda (Manuel, T. (2002), 'Mobilizing International Investment Flows: The New Global Outlook', Speech to the Commonwealth Business Council, 24 September). Ironically however, while in Monterrey, Manuel began to admit the programme design flaws: 'We also need to ask: will the debt relief provided by the HIPC Initiative lead to sustainable debt levels? If the answer is no we would need to look at ways to address the areas of concern of the HIPC framework' (Manuel, 'Remarks to the International Conference on Financing for Development'). Such talk was cheap, for in neither the Monterrey Consensus nor NEPAD, nor any initiative of Manuel's, was HIPC's failed framework substantively addressed.
15. *Financial Times*, 27 February 2003. This possibility, often stated at the programme's outset by civil society critics, was only hinted at in Monterrey's main source of official information: International Monetary Fund and International Development Association (2001), 'The Impact of Debt Reduction under the HIPC Initiative on External Debt Service and Social Expenditures', Washington, 16 November. The Bank, paradoxically, blamed failure upon 'political pressure' to cut debt further as the key reason repayments were still not 'sustainable'.
16. Jubilee Plus (2003), 'Real Progress Report on HIPC', London, September.
17. Manuel, T. (2002), 'Remarks at the Finance Minister's Retreat', International Conference on Financing for Development, Monterrey, Mexico, 19 March.
18. Cited in Verheul, E. and G. Cooper, (2001), 'Poverty Reduction Strategy Papers (PRSP): What is at Stake for Health?', Amsterdam, Wemos, September.
19. Ellis-Jones, M. (2003), 'States of Unrest III: Resistance to IMF and World Bank Policies in Poor Countries', London, World Development Movement, April, p. 3.
20. Jubilee South (2001), 'Pan-African Declaration on PRSPs', Kampala, 12 May. The document serves as Appendix Four to Bond and Manyanya, *Zimbabwe's Plunge*.
21. Nyamugasira, W. and R. Rowden (2002), 'New Strategies, Old Loan Conditions:

Do the IMF and World Bank Loans support Countries' Poverty Reduction Strategies? The Case of Uganda', Uganda National NGO Forum and RESULTS Educational Fund, Kampala, April.
22. Anonymous (2001), 'Angolan Civil Society Debates Way Forward', *World Bank Watch SA? SA Watch WB!*, December; Bendaña, A. (2002), 'Byebye Poverty Reduction Strategy Papers, and Hello Good Governance', Unpublished paper, Managua; Cafod, Oxfam, Christian Aid and Eurodad (2002), 'A Joint Submission to the World Bank and IMF Review of HIPC and Debt Sustainability', London, Oxford and Brussels, August; Cheru, F. (2001), *The Highly Indebted Poor Countries Initiative: A Human Rights Assessment of the Poverty Reduction Strategy Papers*, Report submitted to the United Nations Economic and Social Council, New York, January; Costello, A., F. Watson and D. Woodward (1994), *Human Face or Human Facade? Adjustment and the Health of Mothers and Children*, London, Centre for International Child Health; Gomes, R.P., S. Lakhani and J. Woodman (2002), 'Economic Policy Empowerment Programme', Brussels, Eurodad; Malawi Economic Justice Network (2001), 'Civil Society PRSP Briefing', Issue 8, December 21, Lilongwe; McCandless, E. and E. Pajibo (2003), 'Can Participation Advance Poverty Reduction? PRSP Process and Content in Four Countries', Afrodad PRSP Series, Harare, January; Ong'wen, 'O (2001), 'The PRSP in Kenya', *World Bank Watch SA? SA Watch WB!*, December; Panos (2002), 'Reducing Poverty: Is the World Bank's Strategy Working?', London, September; Tanzanian Feminist Activism Coalition (2001), 'Position Paper', Dar es Salaam, 6 September; Wilks, A. and F. Lefrançois (2002), 'Blinding with Science or Encouraging Debate?: How World Bank Analysis Determines PRSP Policies', London, Bretton Woods Project.
23. Afrodad (2001), 'Civil Society Participation in the Poverty Reduction Strategy Paper Process: A Synthesis of Five Studies conducted in Burkina Faso, Mauritania, Mozambique, Tanzania and Uganda', Harare, April.
24. McGee, R. (2002), 'Assessing Participation in Poverty Reduction Strategy Papers: A Desk-Based Synthesis of Experience in Sub-Saharan Africa', Sussex, University of Sussex Institute for Development Studies.
25. See Bond, P. and G. Dor (2003), 'Uneven Health Outcomes and Political Resistance under Residual Neoliberalism in Africa', *International Journal of Health Services*, 33, 3; and Bond, P. and G. Dor (2003), 'The Residual Dominance of Neoliberalism in Africa', in A.Osmanovic (ed.), *Transforming South Africa*, Hamburg, Institute of African Affairs.
26. World Health Organisation (2001), 'Health in PRSPs: WHO Submission to World Bank/IMF Review of PRSPs', Department of Health and Development, Geneva, December.
27. Werner, D. and D. Sanders (1997), *Questioning the Solution: The Politics of Primary Health Care and Child Survival*, California, Healthwrights.
28. *Business Day*, 20 March 2002.
29. Center of Concern, International Gender and Trade Network and Institute for Agriculture and Trade Policy (2003), 'IMF-World Bank-WTO Close Ranks Around Flawed Economic Policies', Washington, Geneva and Minneapolis, http://www.coc.org/resources/articles/ display.html?ID=484. See also reports of the 13 May 2003 meeting between the WTO and Bretton Woods Institution leaders. According to the Bretton Woods Project, a progressive

London NGO, 'The Bank, in its trade agenda for the coming year, admitted that it is "concerned with a possible trade-off of liberalisation policies with increases in inequality . . . and a rise in unemployment for specific groups in the short-term." Rather than question the policy prescription, the response is to ensure the "appropriate design of compensation mechanisms" ' (http://www.brettonwoods.project.org).

30. United Nations, 'Report of the International Conference on Financing for Development', Final Resolution, pp. 62–63.
31. See Bond, *Against Global Apartheid*, Chapter Seven.
32. Manuel, 'Remarks to the International Conference on Financing for Development'.
33. A reformed IMF International Monetary and Financial Committee opens the door for greater Third World inputs, but this has not changed power relations.
34. Weak governance reform proposals can be found in Pincus, J. and J. Winters (eds) (2002), *Re-inventing the World Bank*, Ithaca, Cornell University Press; United Nations Development Programme (2002), *Deepening Democracy in a Fragmented World*, New York, July; United Nations University World Institute for Development Economics Research (2002), *Governing Globalisation: Issues and Institutions*, Helskinki, October; Varma, S. (2002), 'Improving Global Economic Governance', Geneva, South Centre, August; Griffith-Jones, S. (2002), 'Suggestions on Reforming the Governance of the World Bank', Sussex, University of Sussex Institute of Development Studies, http://www.gapresearch.org.
35. *Financial Times*, 13 February 2003.
36. World Bank (2003), 'Issues Note: Enhancing the Voice of Developing and Transition Countries at the World Bank', Washington, 9 June, http://www.brettonwoodsproject.org/topic/governance/WBgovissuesnote.pdf.
37. http://www.brettonwoodsproject.org.
38. The latter phrase is the slogan of Jubilee South. *Business Day*, 2 June 2003.
39. World Bank (2003), 'Proceedings of Press Conference', Dubai, http://www.worldbank.org, 22 September.
40. Wade, R. (2003), 'The Invisible Hand of the American Empire', *Open Democracy*, 13, 3.
41. Gabriel, N. (2002), 'Monterrey: Spinning the Washington Consensus All the Way to Johannesburg', Pretoria, Southern African Catholic Bishops' Conference, p. 2.
42. http://www.brettonwoodsproject.org, May 2003.
43. http://www.brettonwoodsproject.org, May 2003.
44. Recent African examples are assembled in Friends of the Earth and Halifax Initiative (2002), *Marketing the Earth: The World Bank and Sustainable Development*, Washington, DC and Ottawa, August.
45. *Financial Times*, 5 June 2003. The survey found that although performance 'improved' under Wolfensohn and the Bank was seen as generally 'useful', all was not well on the governance front: 'Overall, the bank is seen as doing a barely average job in helping developing countries reduce corruption.' At a June 2003 meeting of the Bank's executive board, there was 'surprise at the negative attitudes still expressed about the Bank, along with irritation that the Bank's management had not shown them the results earlier'.

46. Institute of Development Studies (2002), 'A Foresight and Policy Study of Multilateral Development Banks', Prepared for the Swedish Ministry of Foreign Affairs, Stockholm, November.
47. *Daily Nation*, 26 October 2001.
48. IBRD President Woods (1966), 'Statement to Executive Directors', Washington, 29 March, cited in Darrow, M. (2003), *Between Light and Shadow: The World Bank, International Monetary Fund and International Human Rights Law*, Portland, Hart Publishing, p.151.
49. United Nations, 'Report of the International Conference on Financing for Development', Final Resolution.
50. See, for example, three G22 reports: (1998), *Report of the Working Group on Transparency and Accountability*, *Report of the Working Group on Strengthening Financial Systems*, and *Report of the Working Group on International Financial Crises*, Washington, www.imf.org/external/np/g22/index.htm.
51. See, for example, Financial Stability Forum (2001), *International Standards and Codes to Strengthen Financial Systems*, Basle, www.fsforum.org/Standards/Reiscfs.html.
52. Manuel, 'Mobilizing International Investment Flows'.
53. Wade, 'The Invisible Hand of the American Empire'.
54. Wade, R. (2001), 'Capital and Revenge: The IMF and Ethiopia', *Challenge*, September/October.
55. Stiglitz, J. (2002), *Globalisation and its Discontents*, London, Penguin, p. 35.
56. Cited in Wade, 'The Invisible Hand of the American Empire'.
57. *Business Day*, 2 June 2003.
58. Myburgh Commission (2002), *Commission of Inquiry into the Rapid Depreciation of the Exchange Rate of the Rand and Related Matters*, Pretoria, 30 June, Evidence of Manuel, National Treasury Bundle, 1, pp. 83–84.
59. Bond, *Against Global Apartheid*, Afterword.
60. Manuel, 'Mobilizing International Investment Flows'.
61. Manuel, 'Mobilizing International Investment Flows'. While the reforms he suggested are stronger, there is no evidence that Manuel had embarked upon a strategy to push them to fruition, hence the weakness of Washington's proposals in February 2003:
    - Increase the representation of systemically important developing countries in key international forums, including the Financial Stability Forum.
    - Increase the representation of developing countries in the governance structure of the IMF and Bank by raising the number of and importance of basic votes.
    - Reform the method of determining quotas to reflect sound policy, progress in policy reform and openness, not just GDP per capita.
    - Improve the Contingent Credit Line to increase the attractiveness and automaticity of the facility.
    - The establishment of a formalised debt-restructuring framework.
    - Greater co-ordination in national macroeconomic policies (cross-regional annual meetings, say G8 + Latin America, G8 + Africa, etc.).
    - Better regulation of global financial and capital markets and improved

regulation of domestic financial systems through new proposals by the G20 working with the IMF on appropriate capital account policy and supervision of capital inflows.
Individually or collectively, these proposals cannot be considered serious challenges to the *status quo*, but are polish for the financial chains that strangle the Third World.

62. Prasad, E., K. Rogoff, S.J. Wei and M. Ayhan Kose (2003), 'Effects of Financial Globalisation on Developing Countries: Some Empirical Evidence', Washington, International Monetary Fund, 17 March, pp. 6–7, 37.
63. China's currency is not convertible and tight controls exist on financial flows, even if it is relatively open to foreign direct investment. I would have put China in the relatively closed category, in relation to international financial markets.
64. Prasad et al, 'Effects of Financial Globalisation on Developing Countries', pp. 27–28.
65. *Guardian*, 21 May 2003.
66. *Business Day*, 29 May 2003. My World Bank sources say the job considered most appropriate would be, initially, a vice presidency with responsibility for Africa. The alternative, *Business Day*'s Robyn Chalmers suggested, was the position of South African deputy president in the 2004 election, in view of Manuel's standing as most popular ANC National Executive Committee member (in the December 2002 Stellenbosch conference vote), and the swamp of ethics problems into which competitors Mosiuoa Lekota and Jacob Zuma had fallen.
67. Stiglitz, *Globalisation and its Discontents*, p. 19. Later though (p. 208), Stiglitz also asks, 'Was Fischer being richly rewarded for having faithfully executed what he was told to do?'
68. Round, R. (2002), 'CBC Commentary', 20 March.

6
NEPAD neutered
Tragedy or joke?

Could Africans be allowed to at least pretend to govern their continent? The problem was stated forcefully by Alec Erwin at the same time that Robert Mutable was stealing a presidential election in Zimbabwe in early 2002: 'The West should not hold the NEPAD hostage because of mistakes in Zimbabwe. If NEPAD is not owned and implemented by Africa it will fail, we cannot be held hostage to the political whims of the G8 or any other groups.'[1]

And yet only seven African presidents showed up at the 2003 Heads of State Implementation Committee meeting. Mbeki commented a few weeks later at the World Economic Forum Durban meeting: 'We must insist that our fellow heads of state attend the meetings.'[2] At the next gathering, in Maputo, July 2003, the pro-Mbeki *Sunday Times* headlined, 'The George Dubya of Africa: Even as he relinquishes the reins of the African Union, Thabo Mbeki is regarded with suspicion by other African leaders.'[3]

The application of the Washington Consensus to Africa, known in its first phase (1980–2000) as 'structural adjustment', was a multifaceted tragedy; in its second phase, as NEPAD (2000–), it would become a farce, and conceded as such by its own secretariat management.

Whose NEPAD?

Washington and the rest of the West had no problems with NEPAD's neoliberalism. *Institutional Investor* magazine quoted the Bush administration's chief Africa bureaucrat, Walter Kansteiner: 'The US will focus on those emerging markets doing the right thing in terms of private sector development, economic freedom and liberty.'[4] An IMF *Working Paper on the New Partnership for Africa's Development* termed NEPAD 'visionary', and promoted 'the active selling of reforms' through national marketing and advice centres, such as the African Regional Technical Assistance Centre in Dar es Salaam. It said African governments should 'use PRSPs to translate NEPAD's framework into operational blueprints'.[5]

Critics on the left alleged that NEPAD was a subimperial project, influenced by an elite team of 'partners' who helped craft it in 2000–01. NEPAD surfaced only after extensive consultations with:
- the World Bank president and IMF managing director (November 2000 and February 2001);
- major transnational corporate executives and associated government leaders (at the Davos World Economic Forum in January 2001);
- G8 rulers at Tokyo in July 2000 and Genoa in July 2001; and
- the European Union president and individual Northern heads of state (2000–01).

In late 2001 and early 2002, virtually every major African civil society organisation, network and progressive personality attacked NEPAD's process, form and content.[6] Until April 2002, *no* trade union, civil society organisation whether linked to a church, women's movement, youth, political party, parliamentary, or other potentially democratic, progressive force in Africa was consulted by politicians or technocrats about giving input into the structure and form of NEPAD.[7]

At the World Economic Forum (WEF) Southern Africa regional meeting in June 2002, NEPAD's commitment to participation was unveiled as meaningless. Ashwin Desai reports how, at the Durban International Convention Centre,

> police arrived with a massive show of force and drove protesters away from the building with batons and charging horses. One of

the organisers of the WEF was approached by an incredulous member of the foreign media and asked about the right to protest in the 'new South Africa'. The organiser pulled out the programme and, with a wry smile, pointed to an upcoming session entitled, 'Taking NEPAD to the People'. He said he could not understand the protests because the 'people' have been accommodated.[8]

Tough critiques of the 67-page base document soon emerged from intellectuals associated with the Council for Development and Social Research in Africa.[9] By the time of the July 2002 Durban launch of the African Union, more than 200 opponents of NEPAD from human rights, debt and trade advocacy groups from the Democratic Republic of Congo, Kenya, South Africa, Tanzania and Zimbabwe were sufficiently organised to hold a militant demonstration at the opening ceremony.[10]

Reacting to growing pressure from the political left, Mbeki began holding civil society consultations in mid-2002, with the assistance of a loyalist faction of the South African Council of Churches and the Africa Institute.[11] As Mbeki prepared to present at the Kananaskis G8 meeting, *Business Day*'s Jonathan Katzenellenbogen and Vuyo Mvoko reported:

> NEPAD is under fire from African experts . . . The group, which met in Pretoria recently and was addressed by Mbeki, panned several aspects of the blueprint for Africa's economic recovery, referring to Mbeki and members of NEPAD's steering committee as 'a small group of political elites' and saying the nature of NEPAD would . . . 'perpetuate and reinforce the subjugation of Africa in the international global system, the enclavity of African economies and the marginalisation of Africa's people.' Responding to the criticism, Mbeki's spokesman, Bheki Khumalo, said: 'Ideology and slogans don't feed people. That has been the problem in the past.'[12]

In an unconvincing letter to the editor, Africa Institute director Eddie Maloka replied to the reporters' alleged 'serious distortion and sensationalisation'. He wrote: 'Your article is based on a selective citation of our report to support your afropessimistic negativity and alarmist reporting of the Group of Eight's meeting with African leaders.'[13]

NEPAD's defenders eventually did find some civil society allies. At the Durban African Union (AU) African summit, trade unions met with Mbeki and repeated the criticism that NEPAD, as a 'paradigm and

model, does not depart fundamentally from previous programmes designed by the World Bank and the International Monetary Fund'. Mbeki offered union leaders resources to establish a corporatist structure that would allow ruling parties 'to hold formal talks with African trade unions and business about NEPAD'. Cosatu suggested that this structure 'could possibly be along the lines of the National Economic Development and Labour Council of South Africa', the very organisation which repeatedly failed to persuade Erwin to honour the tripartite Social Clause agreement in trade negotiations.[14]

In Nigeria, a similarly corporatist faction of civil society was organised by an NGO, the Shelter Rights Initiative, in October 2002 to take advantage of NEPAD. The group denounced the lack of activity by Mbeki's main NEPAD co-promoter, Obasanjo: 'There appears to be no high-ranking, middle-level or articulate support staff or bureaucracy to support their work. The situation creates doubt as to whether NEPAD will outlive the present government.'[15]

Africa's trade and finance traps

Doubt was created not just in the consultation process, but also by the economics and politics of NEPAD. We can consider each in turn, beginning with Africa's experience with international trade and finance, and move to NEPAD's grand hopes for democratisation. The two central premises of NEPAD are, after all, that deeper integration into the world economy will benefit the continent, and that the enlightened proponents of NEPAD will discipline Africa's ubiquitous dictators.

Both premises were flawed. Africa's *share* of world trade declined over the past quarter century, while the *volume* of exports increased. 'Marginalisation' of Africa occurred not because of *lack* of integration, but because other areas of the world, especially East Asia, moved to the export of manufactured goods. Africa's industrial potential declined thanks to excessive deregulation associated with structural adjustment.[16] In the process, rapid trade-related integration caused social inequality, a point conceded by some World Bank staff. According to the institution's main econometrician of inequality, Branco Milanovic, 'at very low average income levels, it is the rich who benefit from openness... It seems that openness makes income distribution worse before making it better.'[17]

Moreover, Africa's debt crisis worsened as globalisation intensified. As shown in Chapter One (Figures 5 and 6), from 1980–2000, sub-Saharan Africa's total foreign debt rose from $60 billion to $206 billion, and the ratio of debt to GDP rose from 23% to 66%. Africa now repays more than it receives. In 1980, loan inflows of $9.6 billion were higher than the debt repayment outflow of $3.2 billion. By 2000, only $3.2 billion came in, and $9.8 billion was repaid, leaving a net financial flows deficit of $6.2 billion.[18] Meanwhile, donor aid was down 40% from 1990 levels.

There is convincing documentation that the tearing of safety nets under structural adjustment worsens the vulnerability of women, children, the elderly and disabled people. They are expected to survive with less social subsidy and greater pressure on the fabric of the family during economic crisis, which makes women more vulnerable to sexual pressures and, therefore, HIV/AIDS.[19]

The other source of outflows that must be reversed, if Africa is to overcome its systematic underdevelopment within the circuits of international finance, is capital flight. James Boyce and Léonce Ndikumana argue that a core group of sub-Saharan African countries, with a joint foreign debt of $178 billion, suffered a quarter century of capital flight by elites that totalled more than $285 billion, including imputed interest earnings. 'Taking capital flight as a measure of private external assets, and calculating net external assets as private external assets, minus public external debts, sub-Saharan Africa appears to be a net creditor vis-à-vis the rest of the world.'[20] Capital flight by African elites is not taken seriously in NEPAD. A crackdown would conflict with the programme's commitment to further financial liberalisation on a 'fast-track' basis, as suggested by Manuel.

Political NEPAD

At first blush, the most hopeful political intervention from the African Union and NEPAD was a set of peace-keeping efforts in West African hotspots and the Great Lakes region. However, the particularly difficult Burundi and DRC terrains of war were riven with deep-seated rivalries and socio-economic desperation, which Pretoria did not comprehend, much less resolve. In 2003, prominent South African officials (Mandela – who was chief mediator in Burundi, Mbeki, Dlamini-Zuma and deputy president, Jacob Zuma) facilitated two power-sharing peace deals in these countries, but left the underlying contradictions intact.

The papering-over efforts did not halt the massacre of hundreds in the northeast of the DRC the day of the celebrated Sun City peace deal. Nor did it succeed in bringing key Burundian rebel leaders to the table for many months. By year-end 2003, reported Jean-Jacques Cornish in the *Mail & Guardian,* 'war-weary Burundians continue to be denied their peace dividend' because the National Liberation Front was not included in Pretoria's deal. This left 1 500 South African troops in that war zone along with 2 000 other African peace-keepers. The UN Security Council expressed unease at the lack of reform and disarmament in the DRC.[21]

Millions have died in the DRC, and hundreds of thousands in Burundi. One can only hope that Pretoria's peace deals will stick. Yet the interventions were characterised by top-down decisions from the

presidency, and apparently neglected consultation with the South African National Defence Force or Foreign Affairs, much less African parliaments and societies.

Trying to police the global capitalist periphery required more common sense in relation to the root causes of conflict, because without making provision for total debt cancellation in Burundi, for example, the massive drain on that country's resources creates the conditions in which conflict thrives. In 1998, as strife became endemic, Burundi spent nearly 40% of its export earnings on debt repayment – in the same league as only two other countries, Brazil and Zimbabwe. In Brazil, the people's anger at the economic oppression associated with this level of debt repayment saw the Workers' Party assume political power five years later. In Zimbabwe, the state turned to brutal repression. Burundi, meanwhile, was led, slowly and painfully, first by Julius Nyerere and then Mandela, toward a power-sharing deal that was meant to sort out ethnic divisions, but that could exacerbate the crisis because of the lack of root-cause problem solving.

There was, nevertheless, hope that the good-governance rhetoric in the NEPAD base document might do some good: 'With NEPAD, Africa undertakes to respect the global standards of democracy, which core components include . . . fair, open, free and democratic elections periodically organised to enable the populace choose their leaders freely.'[22]

While South Africa under Mbeki's rule permits free and fair elections (after all, the ANC wins easily), the other main NEPAD leader, Nigeria's Obasanjo, does not. This was apparent during the April 2003 presidential poll, which resulted in what a United Nations press agency termed 'the threshold of total one-party dominance' by the ruling People's Democratic Party. As one example, according to official records, a near 100% turnout occurred in the southern Rivers State, with 2.1 million of 2.2 million registered voters supporting president Obasanjo. Yet electoral observers reported a low turnout.[23] In Obasanjo's home state of Ogun, the president won 1 360 170 votes against his main opponent's 680. The number of votes cast in a simultaneous race in the same geographical area was just 747 296. Obasanjo's explanation, by way of denigrating European Union electoral observers, was that 'certain communities in this country make up their minds to act as one in political matters . . . They probably don't have that kind of culture in most European countries.' International observers found 'serious irregularities throughout the country and fraud in at least 11 of 36 states'.[24]

According to Chima Ubani of the Civil Liberties Organisation, 'it's not the actual wish of the electorate but some machinery that has churned out unbelievable outcomes. We've seen a landslide that does not seem sufficiently explained by any available factor.' The opposition All Nigeria People's Party called the vote, 'the most flagrantly rigged in Nigeria's history'. Complaints also came from the Transition Monitoring Group and the Catholic Church's Justice Development and Peace Commission, which together had 40 000 monitors documenting abuse.[25] In contrast, Mbeki's weekly ANC internet *ANC Today* letter proclaimed, 'Nigeria has just completed a series of elections, culminating in the re-election of president Olusegun Obasanjo into his second and last term. Naturally, we have already sent our congratulations to him.' Mbeki registered, but then dismissed, the obvious: 'It is clear that there were instances of irregularities in some parts of the country. However, it also seems clear that by and large the elections were well conducted.'[26]

NEPAD's Zimbabwe test

A similar lack of respect for democracy was evident in Zimbabwe.[27] Ironically, after opposing NEPAD at the AU meeting in Durban, Mugabe and foreign minister Stan Mudenge were visited by a humble Dlamini-Zuma in October 2002. A few days later, finance minister Herbert Murerwa used his budget speech to parliament to proclaim

that it was 'critical that Zimbabwe remains part of this [NEPAD] process'.²⁸ An increasingly cozy relationship between Pretoria and Harare alienated Zimbabwe's democratic opposition. Morgan Tsvangirai, leader of the Movement for Democratic Change, concluded that Mbeki had 'embarked on an international safari to campaign for Mugabe's regime. Pretoria is free to pursue its own agenda. But it must realise that Zimbabweans can never be fooled anymore.'²⁹ Tsvangirai was framed on a ludicrous treason charge in early 2002, which two years later was still plodding on in the courts.

According to Tsvangirai, the February 2003 gambit by Mbeki and Obasanjo to readmit Zimbabwe to the Commonwealth represented

> the disreputable end game of a long-term Obasanjo-Mbeki strategy designed to infiltrate and subvert not only the Commonwealth effort but, all other international efforts intended to rein in Mugabe's violent and illegitimate regime. Through this diabolical act of fellowship and solidarity with a murderous dictatorship, General Obasanjo and Mr Mbeki have now openly joined Mugabe as he continues to wage a relentless war against the people of Zimbabwe. They are now self-confessed fellow travellers on a road littered with violence, destruction and death.³⁰

Most in Zimbabwean civil society shared that cynicism. In a foreword to a 2003 booklet titled, *Why the New Partnership for Africa's*

Development is Already Failing, Zimbabwe Coalition on Debt and Development chairperson Jonah Gokova wrote of the

> profound rejection of NEPAD by Zimbabweans from important social movements, trade unions and NGOs within our increasingly vibrant civil society . . . we now call on Africans to rally around an African People's Consensus, inspired by a vision of the development of the continent that reflects more genuine African thinking, instead of NEPAD, that 'homegrown' rehashing of the Washington Consensus augmented by transparently false promises of good governance and democracy.[31]

Did Mbeki and Obasanjo deserve such derision? They termed Zimbabwe's 2002 presidential election 'legitimate', and repeatedly opposed punishment of that regime by the Commonwealth and UN Human Rights Commission. In February 2003, Dlamini-Zuma stated, 'We will never criticise Zimbabwe.' The NEPAD secretariat's Dave Malcomson, responsible for international liaison and co-ordination, admitted to a reporter, 'Wherever we go, Zimbabwe is thrown at us as the reason why NEPAD's a joke.'[32]

Later in 2003, the Zimbabwe issue emerged as an international scandal once again. Mbeki had failed in his March 2003 attempt to have Zimbabwe readmitted to the Commonwealth, following the March 2002 election-related suspension. He then tried to ensure

Mugabe would be invited to the December 2003, Abuja meeting of the Commonwealth, hosted by Obasanjo. But the Nigerian head of state was under pressure from London, Canberra and Ottawa, and his fact-finding mission to Harare a few weeks before the Commonwealth summit did not give him sufficient logical ammunition to persuade Commonwealth powerbrokers that political freedom existed in Zimbabwe.

With Obasanjo refusing to invite Mugabe, Mbeki reportedly decided to punish the Commonwealth secretary-general, New Zealander Don McKinnon, who, according to Pretoria, had bent Commonwealth rules. McKinnon's secret 2002–03 consultations concluded a majority of members wanted the Zimbabwe issue decided in December 2003, and not March of that year. Apparently in revenge, Pretoria proposed replacing McKinnon with former Sri Lankan foreign minister Lakshma Kadirgamar. But Mbeki's candidate lost the election by 40–11. The news agency Zwnews.com claimed that Botswana, Cameroon, The Gambia, Ghana, Kenya, Malawi, Mauritius and Sierra Leone voted for McKinnon.

At the Abuja summit, Zimbabwe was suspended indefinitely. Mugabe immediately announced at a ZANU (PF) congress that Zimbabwe would leave the organisation. The real loser, however, was Mbeki, for as University of Pretoria politics professor Hussein

Solomon remarked, 'Mbeki has no credibility as a leader. He is not prepared to stand by the principles espoused in terms of the African renaissance.'[33]

Clearly bitter upon his return home, Mbeki helped craft a statement issued by the Southern African Development Community plus Uganda, complaining that unnamed Commonwealth members were 'dismissive, intolerant and rigid'. Mbeki's next ANC website letter condemned the original March 2002 justification for suspending Zimbabwe, noting that the electoral observation mission Pretoria had reported back with these lines: 'The Mission is, therefore, of the view that the outcome of the elections represents the legitimate voice of the people of Zimbabwe.'

Mbeki then rubbished Zimbabwean democrats:

> In his book *Diplomacy*, Dr Henry Kissinger discusses the place of the issue of human rights in the East-West struggle during the Cold War. He writes that: 'Reagan and his advisers invoked (human rights) to try to undermine the Soviet system.' . . . It is clear that some within Zimbabwe and elsewhere in the world, including our country, are following the example set by 'Reagan and his advisers', to 'treat human rights as a tool' for overthrowing the government of Zimbabwe and rebuilding Zimbabwe as they wish. In modern parlance, this is called regime change.[34]

Zimbabwe Lawyers for Human Rights director, Arnold Tsunga, commented that Mbeki created 'a real danger of human rights defenders being attacked or clamped down upon . . . These remarks are likely to have far reaching and grave consequences on the operating environment of human rights defenders in Zimbabwe.'[35]

To top it off Mbeki visited Mugabe the next week and called on Tsvangirai for the first time, for 25 minutes. The Zimbabwean president once again failed to agree to liberalise the political environment. Mbeki attempted a diplomatic nicety: 'President Mugabe can assist us to confront the problems we have in South Africa, so that we can assist you to solve the problems that face Zimbabwe.' The comment caused a sudden decline in the rand's value, and so former *Sunday Independent* political writer John Battersby, a loyal transmission belt for Pretoria, quoted a 'senior government spokesperson' that the comment was 'to ensure that the Zimbabweans continue listening to us'.[36] But would anyone else?

German chancellor Gerhard Schroeder had a chance in January 2004 during a state visit, when Mbeki announced: 'I'm happy to say that they [ZANU (PF) and the MDC] have agreed that they will go into formal negotiations.' In reality, Tsvangirai was back in court on the

treason frame-up and the MDC's Harare office was raided by police – hardly auspicious signs. The last formal 'talks about talks' had occurred seven months earlier. MDC secretary-general Welshman Ncube told Mbeki, 'We have heard it all before.' Mugabe's justice minister, Patrick Chinamasa, leader of the government's negotiating team, confirmed that he was 'not aware of any new developments'.[37]

NEPAD's 'peers'

Suspicion towards NEPAD from democratic, progressive forces across Africa appeared validated when, in October 2002, political-governance peer review was nearly excised from the programme. *Business Day*'s Katzenellenbogen described how NEPAD 'had fallen victim to the realities of African politics . . . Diplomats said that there were indications that SA had succumbed to pressure from other African countries, including Libya and Nigeria, to confine peer review to economic and corporate governance matters.' But, as Katzenellenbogen offhandedly remarked, 'With reports done by the International Monetary Fund, World Bank, African Development Bank, and United Nations Economic Commission for Africa it is unlikely that a great deal of value can be added.'[38]

Canadian prime minister Jean Chretien reportedly called Mbeki to insist that peer review be restored, even though NEPAD's approach was voluntary and, hence, toothless. Mbeki failed to do damage control on 'the stream of contradictory statements [from Pretoria] since deputy foreign minister Aziz Pahad's bombshell [about peer review being dropped] to the press at the Union Buildings,' Katzenellenbogen wrote.[39] Journalists and diplomats sensed that the fiasco was grounded in *realpolitik*, despite Mbeki's insistence that he stood by NEPAD's democratic rhetoric. African elites didn't want that sort of donor aid-gatekeeping leverage located in Pretoria or anywhere else.

Thus, the March 2002 decision by AU leaders in Abuja to adopt the peer review mechanism was only actioned fourteen months later, when a panel of six 'Eminent Persons' was named, just three days before the Evian G8 meeting. The five from outside South Africa were Mozambican Graca Machel, UN children's advocate and wife of former president Mandela; former Kenyan diplomat, Bethuel Kiplegat, a Renamo supporter during that group's mass murder of Mozambicans; Keynesian-oriented Nigerian economist Adebayo Adedeji; Senegal's former UN development official Marie-Angelique Savane; and Dorothy Njeuma from Cameroon.

The South African peer was Chris Stals, the former Reserve Bank governor whose African credentials included concern stated in late 1993 about the 'huge burden' the subregion presented South Africa.[40] *Mail & Guardian* columnist Richard Calland commented, 'NEPAD's Declaration on Democracy, Political, Economic and Corporate Governance says precious little about development and poverty, and even less about socio-economic rights. Given that he must now oversee compliance, it is hard to know whether to laugh or cry at the fact that the declaration is full of the language that Stals will understand and has very little of that which he would not.'[41] During the 1990s, Stals had been embroiled in several serious governance controversies that should have disqualified him from being a 'peer' to any but the most greedy dictators:

- as a member of the exclusive, racist Afrikaner Broederbond, he participated in venal National Party apartheid politics from 1974;
- he lost R33 billion in SA's hard currency reserves one weekend in mid-1998 trying to defend the rand, during one of its periodic crashes and won winning criticism from the IMF for incompetence, a few weeks later;
- he shifted Reserve Bank monetary policy to a tight-money, deregulatory financial regime, which put real interest rates on SA government bonds at more than 10% by the mid-1990s, compared to less than 5% in Britain and Germany, and approximately 3% in the US, Japan and Australia;

- he assisted with the National Party project of making the Reserve Bank 'independent' in the 1993 Constitution, so that his job would not be subject to influence from parliament or any democratic forum;
- he was Reserve Bank governor during several bank failure scandals, including the 1992 Cape Investment Bank and Commuter Corporation pension fund bankruptcies, and the 1993 Masterbond crash, as well as other bank closures in which depositors lost their savings, with no Reserve Bank deposit insurance as proposed by consumer advocates;
- he bailed out failing large Afrikaans banks, subsequently merged as ABSA, in the early 1990s with an extremely generous, low-interest loan, which cost taxpayers more than a billion rand;
- his reign as Reserve Bank governor included the early 1990s onset of bank redlining against black neighbourhoods and the dramatic 1993 relaxation of the Usury Act which increased interest rates to loan-shark levels for small borrowers.

How, then, was Stals chosen? A similar question was asked in 1994, when Mandela reappointed him Reserve Bank governor, until his retirement in 1999, when he was succeeded by Tito Mboweni. The terms of a December 1993 IMF loan to South Africa, kept secret until leaked to the press in March 1994, included intense pressure on the ANC to reappoint both apartheid finance minister Derek Keys and Stals. A visit by Camdessus in early 1994 sealed the arrangement, and was publicly resented by Mboweni.[42] Before the 2003 Evian summit, in time to influence the Abuja peer review selection process, Camdessus was named G8-host France's 'Africa personal representative', and he enthusiastically endorsed the 'speed' at which the NEPAD peer reviewers were chosen.

The G8 and Africa

As a result of such shenanigans, who could blame observers, including the G8, for a cautious and also disdainful attitude toward Africa? When Pretoria's delegation flew to the G8 meeting at Kananaskis, Canada, in June 2002, expectations had been high, not least because of a front-page *Time* feature on 'Mbeki's mission': 'He has finally faced up to the AIDS crisis and is now leading the charge for a new African development plan.'[43]

Institutional Investor magazine reported that the G8's 'misleadingly named' Africa Action Plan represented merely 'grudging' support for the main donor countries with 'only an additional $1 billion for debt relief. (The G8) failed altogether to reduce their domestic

agricultural subsidies (which hurt African farm exports) and – most disappointing of all to the Africans – neglected to provide any further aid to the continent.'[44] South Africa's *Sunday Times* confirmed that 'the leaders of the world's richest nations refused to play ball.' Mbeki's comment was thus surprising: 'I think they have addressed adequately all the matters that were put to them.' Kananaskis, he said, was 'a defining moment in the . . . evolution of Africa and the birth of a more equitable system of international relations . . . it signifies the end of the epoch of colonialism and neocolonialism.'[45]

The epoch of neocolonialism continued. At the January 2003 World Economic Forum in Davos, Manuel angrily told journalists, 'Africa didn't really shine here. There is a complete dearth of panels on Africa.' A wire service report revealed, 'Among the many snubs Africa received here was the decision by former US president Bill Clinton to cancel his presence at a press conference on Africa today to discuss NEPAD. Forum officials said Clinton did not give reasons for not attending.'[46]

By the time of the 2003, G8 meeting in Evian, France, world elites were aware of NEPAD's lack of street credibility. *Institutional Investor* captured the tone: 'Like other far-reaching African initiatives made over the years, this one promptly rolled off the track and into the

ditch... Almost two years after NEPAD's launch, it has little to show in aid or investment. Only a handful of projects have fallen within the plan's framework.'[47]

Evian provided paltry concessions on the UN Global Fund for health, as well as what the *Financial Times* termed 'year-old pledges to provide an extra $6 billion a year in aid to Africa', a fraction of the amount spent on the Iraq war a few weeks earlier.[48] An estimated 120 000 activists protested against the G8 in the Swiss cities of Geneva and Lausanne. Civil society leaders from six African social movements meeting nearby were scathing: 'The outcome of the 2003 Summit of the G8 reveals that the political will of the eight most powerful nations to meet their obligations to Africa has simply dried up... One or two drops of aid out of Evian amounts to a small patch for the haemorrhaging economies of Africa.'[49]

Mbeki had, a few weeks earlier, offered a righteous condemnation of the protesters, especially Jubilee Africa and the Africa Trade Network:

> What is happening at the precise moment when our continent is taking bold steps to determine its future. I am told that there are some Africans who describe themselves as members of African civil society, who have decided to fly to Evian in France to demonstrate against NEPAD... Strange to say, Africans will fly to France to demand that nothing should be done to help our

continent to move forward on these matters, on the basis of programmes conceived and elaborated by us as Africans. I think the most sensible thing for these Africans to do, if they were inspired to oppose African liberation and development, would have been to demonstrate at the headquarters of the African Union in Addis Ababa, rather than at a place in France closely associated with the high cost that France imposed on the Algerian people as they fought for their independence.[50]

Northern NGOs were also surprised at the lack of progress at Evian. Oxfam complained: 'Not only are there no firm commitments, even their rhetoric is watered down compared with last year.' The health advocacy group, Medicins sans Frontiers, put the G8's failure in geopolitical terms: 'To get a pat on the back from Bush, Chirac has sacrificed the right for millions of people to have access to medicines they need to survive. He abandoned his widely publicised commitment to improving access to life-saving medicines, and the rest of the G8 are merrily going along for the ride.'[51]

Mbeki's response was to spindoctor the supposed gains from Evian: 'I think we have bitten off more than we can chew. If we had tried to take a bigger bite . . . we would not have been able to absorb it . . . we would produce disappointments. With all these resources committed, [people would ask] what are these Africans doing now? They are not using it.'[52]

But the game was given away by Africa's finance ministers, who issued a joint statement after Evian expressing 'deep concern that negotiations on the key elements of the Doha development round have achieved little'.[53] Another Evian visitor, Brazilian president Lula da Silva, declared that the G8's 'incoherence between words and acts cannot but breed skepticism and distrust'.[54] He remarked: 'I noted that the presidents of the poorer countries spend their whole time complaining that the United States does not give us that to which we think we have a right... It does not help to keep crying to the European Union for it to reduce the subsidies it pays to its agriculturalists. No one respects a negotiator who cries or who walks around with his head low.'[55]

Anti-globalisation strategist Dennis Brutus wrote that Mbeki and his African colleagues were 'apparently intent on selling out the continent under the rubric of a plan crafted by the same technocrats who wrote Pretoria's failed Growth, Employment and Redistribution economic programme, under the guidance of Washington and the corporate leaders of Davos... It is past time for us to insist that President Thabo Mbeki rise off his kneepad and assume the dignity of an African leader, or face ridicule.'[56]

Notes
1. Cited in Taylor, I. (2002), 'Obstacles to change in Africa: NEPAD, Zimbabwe, and Elites', Foreign Policy in Focus Commentary, http://www.fpif.org/outside/commentary/2002/0204NEPAD.html.
2. SA Institute of International Affairs (2003), 'NEPAD and WEF', *eAfrica*, July, p. 11.
3. *Sunday Times*, 13 July 2003. According to the article, Mbeki is 'viewed by other African leaders as too powerful, and they privately accuse him of wanting to impose his will on others... In the corridors they call him the George Bush of Africa, leading the most powerful nation in the neighbourhood and using his financial and military muscle to further his own agenda.'
4. Gopinath, 'Doubt of Africa'.
5. http://www.brettonwoodsproject.org, May 2003.
6. See Bond, *Fanon's Warning*; Bond, P. (2003), 'Can the New Partnership for Africa's Development Work?', in K. Wohlmuth (ed.), *African Development Perspective Yearbook: African Entrepreneurship and Private Sector Development*, Bremen, Institute for World Economics and International Management; and Bond, P. and T. Ngwane (2003), 'African Anti-Capitalism', in R. Neumann and A. Hsiao (eds), *Anti-Capitalism: A Field Guide to the Global Justice Movement*, New York, New Press. And the discussion of 'subimperial partnership' in Bond, *Unsustainable South Africa*, pp. 368–375.

7. I was fortunate to attend the first consultation where Wiseman Nkuhlu, head of the NEPAD secretariat, apologised to the Congress of South African Trade Unions for having been 'too busy' beforehand. Alec Erwin and Pretoria's main public relations bureaucrat and a leading intellectual, Joel Netshitenzhe, warded off critiques from Cosatu. I asked Netshitenzhe if there was any chance the base document could be edited to reflect the hostility to neoliberalism so evident there and in all the other commentaries from civil society. He replied, 'No.' The only copy available of NEPAD for the 80 trade union leaders present was the rough draft I circulated of *Fanon's Warning* which contains a point-by-point critique of the base document, available at http://www.aidc.org.za.
8. Desai, A. (2003), 'Neoliberalism and Resistance in South Africa', *Monthly Review*, January.
9. The most rigorous studies in 2002 were conducted by experienced political economists: Adedeji, A. (2002), 'From the Lagos Plan of Action to the New Partnership for Africa's Development, and from the Final Act of Lagos to the Constitutive Act: Whither Africa?' Keynote Address for the African Forum for Envisioning Africa, Nairobi, 26–29 April; Adesina, J. (2002), 'Development and the Challenge of Poverty: NEPAD, Post-Washington Consensus and Beyond', Paper presented to the Codesria/TWN Conference on Africa and the Challenge of the 21st Century, Accra, 23–26 April; Anyang'Nyong'o, P. et al (eds) (2002), *NEPAD: A New Path?*, Nairobi, Heinrich Böll Foundation; Nabudere, D. (2002), 'NEPAD: Historical Background and its Prospects', in P. Anyang'Nyong'o, et al (eds), *NEPAD: A New Path?* Nairobi, Heinrich Böll Foundation; Olukoshi, A. (2002), 'Governing the African Political Space for Sustainable Development: A Reflection on NEPAD', Paper for the African Forum for Envisioning Africa, Nairobi, 26–29 April.
10. *Business Day*, 9 July 2002.
11. Several churchpeople told me how upset they were that, in spite of efforts by some in the SACC to circulate a powerful critique of NEPAD, the presence of Mbeki in the room seemed to shake the more conservative forces into a patriotic pro-NEPAD fervor.
12. *Business Day*, 27 June 2002.
13. *Business Day*, 4 July 2002. Revealing the weakness of his case, Maloka could merely cite the intellectuals' agreement on an 'all-Africa academy of arts and sciences' to advance 'intra-African academic partnership as a civil society component of NEPAD'.
14. *Business Day*, 3 July 2002.
15. *Business Day*, 23 October 2002.
16. Arrighi, G. (2002), 'The African Crisis: World Systemic and Regional Aspects', *New Left Review* 2, 15; Saul, J. and C. Leys (1999), 'Sub-Saharan Africa in Global Capitalism', *Monthly Review*, July.
17. Milanovic, B. (2002), 'Can we Discern the Effect of Globalisation on Income Distribution? Evidence from Household Budget Surveys', World Bank Policy Research Working Paper 2876, April.
18. World Bank (2002), *Global Finance Tables*, Washington.
19. See, for example, Elson, D. (1991), 'The Impact of Structural Adjustment on Women: Concepts and Issues', in B. Onimode (ed.), *The IMF, the World Bank and the African Debt,* London, Zed Books; Longwe, S. (1991), 'The

Evaporation of Policies for Women's Advancement', in N. Heyzer et al (eds), *A Commitment to the Worlds Women*, New York, UNIFEM; Mahmoud, F. (1996), 'Building a Pan-African Women's Movement', in T. Abdul-Raheem (ed.), *Pan-Africanism: Politics, Economy and Social Change in the 21st Century*, Trenton, Africa World Press; and Tskikata, D. and J. Kerr (eds) (2002), *Demanding Dignity: Women Confronting Economic Reforms in Africa*, Ottawa, The North-South Institute and Accra, Third World Network-Africa.

20. Boyce, J. and L. Ndikumana (2000), 'Is Africa a Net Creditor? New Estimates of Capital Flight from Severely Indebted Sub-Saharan African Countries, 1970–1996', Occasional Paper, University of Massachusetts/Amherst Political Economy Research Institute.
21. *Mail & Guardian*, 19 December 2003.
22. NEPAD, paragraph 79.
23. IRIN news service, 12 May 2003.
24. *Mail & Guardian*, 26 April 2003.
25. IRIN news service, 12 May 2003.
26. http://www.anc.org.za, 25 April 2003.
27. The story of Pretoria's bizarre relationship with the Zanu (PF) regime is told in Bond, P. and M. Manyanya (2003), *Zimbabwe's Plunge*.
28. Murerwa, H. (2002), 'The 2003 National Budget Statement', Parliament, Harare, 14 November.
29. Tsvangirai, M. (2002), 'President of the MDC's Speech to MDC Parliamentarians', Harare, 18 December.
30. Cited in Manyanya, M. (ed.) (2003), *NEPAD's Zimbabwe Test: Why the New Partnership for Africa's Development is Already Failing*, Harare, Zimbabwe Coalition on Debt and Development, Foreword. For reasons that are unclear, Tsvangirai, in December 2003, 'encouraged' Mbeki's constructive engagement. At the time, the MDC was hoping to gain admittance to the Socialist International whose other main African member was the ANC.
31. Manyanya, *NEPAD's Zimbabwe Test*, Foreword.
32. *Business Day*, 28 March 2003.
33. *Business Day*, 9 December 2003.
34. Mbeki, T. (2003), 'We Will Resist the Upside-Down View of Africa', *ANC Today* 49, http://www.anc.org.za, 12 December. Notably, Mbeki failed to use the Commonwealth as a venue to criticise the illegal invasion and occupation of Iraq by Britain and Australia.
35. Tsunga, A. (2003), 'The Legal Profession and the Judiciary as Human Rights Defenders in Zimbabwe', Mutare, 24 December, p. 1.
36. *Sunday Independent*, 21 December 2003.
37. *London Times*, 23 January 2004.
38. *Business Day*, 31 October 2002.
39. *Business Day*, 31 October 2002.
40. Bond, P. (1993), 'If and When the New South Africa Looks North', *Financial Gazette*, 22 November.
41. *Mail & Guardian*, 27 June 2003.
42. Reported in the *Cape Times*, 5 May 1994; *Business Day*, 24 January and 24 March 1994.
43. *Time*, 10 June 2002.

44. Gopinath, 'Doubt of Africa'.
45. *Sunday Times*, 30 June 2002; *Business Day*, 28 June 2002.
46. InterPress Service, 28 January 2003. *Johannesburg Star* senior editor, Peter Sullivan, described his Davos experience for *Sunday Independent* (2 February 2003) readers thus: 'The SA contingent worked hard to get investment but partied equally hard: a real "jol" was had by all with great jiving from Kader Asmal, Trevor Manuel and Alec Irwin (sic), while Bertie Lubner and his wife boogied the night away. We also drank a few bottles of KWV's best red.' (Too many, apparently, to spell trade minister Erwin's name correctly.)
47. Gopinath, 'Doubt of Africa'.
48. *Financial Times*, 2 June 2003. According to Reuters (2 June 2003), 'Ismaila Usman, an executive director of the IMF and former Nigerian finance minister, said late on Saturday some creditors are obstructing debt-relief efforts by selling poor countries' debts to litigious third parties rather than forgiving them.'
49. African Women's Communication and Development Network et al, 'Joint Statement'.
50. Mbeki, T. (2003), 'Address at the SA National Editors Forum Conference on the Media, the AU and Democracy', Johannesburg, 12 April.
51. *Guardian*, 4 June 2003.
52. *Business Day*, 4 June 2003.
53. *Business Report*, 8 June 2003.
54. *Le Figaro*, 4 June 2003.
55. Agencia Folha, Alto Araguaia (translation T. Oppermann), 7 June 2003.
56. Brutus, D. (2002), 'Global Agendas are Set by the Usual Suspects', *Business Day*, 27 June.

7
The 'W$$D'
Pretoria meets its match

Monthly Review co-editor John Bellamy Foster documented a decade of failure following the 1992 Rio Earth Summit:
- Carbon dioxide levels in the atmosphere are at their highest in the last 420 000 years. CO_2 emissions, excluding other greenhouse gases, increased 9% globally between 1990 and 2000 and in the United States by double that rate. The 14 warmest years, recorded since measurements began in 1866, have all been since 1980, with the 1990s the hottest on record.
- Global consumption of water is doubling every 20 years, much faster than population growth. By the mid-1990s about 40% of world population in some 80 countries were suffering from serious water shortages. The United Nations has projected that by 2025, two-thirds of the world may be suffering from water stress. Water tables are falling under large expanses of agricultural land in China, India, and the United States due to the overpumping of ground water for irrigation.
- The overall species extinction rate is at least a thousand times (and maybe as much as ten thousand times) faster than the normal, or background, rate of extinction. Habitat destruction, particularly of tropical forests, threatens as many as half the world's species over the course of this century. Coral reefs, second only to forests in biological wealth, are being degraded at an alarming rate. Over a quarter of coral reefs have been lost, up from 10% in 1992. The share to be lost is expected to rise to 40% by 2010.
- Genetically modified crops pose once again the issue of the sorcerer's apprentice, as agribusiness alters the bases of life and our food supply, in ways radically at variance with evolutionary processes. Commercial technologies are altering the genetic and chemical composition of what we eat, with very little consideration of consequences beyond questions of profitability.
- Where development is concerned, there have been no appreciable gains in the relative position of the Global South, which is falling

further behind the rich countries. Income inequality has been rapidly increasing within countries and between countries over the last two decades. Fifty-two countries experienced negative growth over the 1990s.[1]

Mark Weisbrot of the Center for Economic Policy Research takes the analysis of 'development' back a decade, to the point at which globalisation is often considered to have intensified:

> In Latin America and the Caribbean, gross domestic product grew by 75% per person from 1960 to 1980, (but) by only 7% per person from 1980 to 2000. The collapse of the African economies is well known, although still ignored: GDP in sub-Saharan Africa grew by about 34% per person from 1960 to 1980; in the past two decades, per capita income actually *fell* by about 15 percent. Even if we include the fast-growing economies of East Asia and South Asia, the past two decades fare miserably. For the entire set of low- and middle-income countries, per capita GDP growth was less than half its average for the previous 20 years . . . The past two decades have brought significantly reduced progress for major social indicators such as life expectancy, infant and child mortality, litreacy, and education for the vast majority of low- and middle-income countries.[2]

These forms of global apartheid were evident to progressive South African activists, who from 1996 began blaming Pretoria's orthodox economic policies for neoliberalism's negative local manifestations. It is important to record how activists, gathered under the banner of a 'Social Movements Indaba' (SMI) coalition, used the WSSD process for local and global outreach and issue-linkage. There is no question that the 'foreign policy' of the South African movements contributed to their radicalisation.[3]

Indeed, a sensibility emerged within Johannesburg's leading social movements and NGOs during August to September 2002, not dissimilar to that of the World Social Forum. The 2001 to 2003 Porto Alegre meetings in Brazil, followed by Mumbai, India in 2004, attracted increasing numbers of South Africans aiming to network internationally.[4] The more they strengthened their understanding of neoliberalism, and the stronger their critique of the WSSD content became, the more militant they felt. Perhaps this was the mirror image of the situation in Pretoria, where sometimes radical rhetoric veiled increasing conservatism. The more Mbeki and his colleagues gained international prominence, the more they formed partnerships with the G8, multilateral financial agencies and transnational corporations. And the more that community activists felt that these partnerships threatened socio-economic and environmental rights, the more they established a resistance culture, notwithstanding increasingly serious state repression.

Freedom of expression sputters

At sunset on 24 August, Soweto leader Trevor Ngwane addressed a University of the Witwatersrand conference of the International Forum on Globalisation (IFG), also attended by the mass cadreship of the radical coalition, the Social Movements Indaba. He called on the gathering to march to 'John Vorster-Thabo Mbeki Square' (the SMI's new name for Johannesburg Central Police Station) in solidarity with hundreds of people who had been arrested by police in pre-WSSD intimidation raids. A crowd of around 700 grabbed candles and followed.

Little more than 200 m from the academic setting, however, the group was confronted by riot police and dispersed with eight stun grenades. Dennis Brutus, Njoki Njehu, Maude Barlow, Tony Clarke, Naomi Klein, Anuradha Mittal, John Saul and other global justice movement luminaries were on the front line. After extended toyi-toyiing, the marchers dispersed peacefully once police vans arrived to make mass arrests, which the activists reckoned they could not then afford. BBC television ran the ambush at Wits as a lead story for 14 hours on 24–25 August. The subsequent *Mail & Guardian* newspaper carried an unprecedented semi-apology from the South African National Intelligence Agency for police 'overreaction', but severe damage had been done to Mbeki's image as a democrat.[5] Activists across the world demonstrated at South African government consulates in solidarity.[6]

Tensions rose as the SMI planned another march, this time from Alexandra, the impoverished black township enclave close to the conference venue in Sandton. The *Mail & Guardian* reported that the SMI application was 'refused under an apartheid-era law'. According to Ngwane,

> The government suggested that it would only allow a strictly controlled march in a pre-determined route on a 1.8 km stretch in Sandton. Initially, the ANC decided that no one must march from Alexandra because that is where the working class that Mbeki betrays lives. The minister of police (and SACP chairperson), Charles Nqakula, appeared on national TV banging his fist on the table saying the police would clamp down on those who posed a security risk to international guests and heads of state. Everyone wondered why the marchers had to be kept away from Alexandra but allowed to Sandton where the VIPs were going to be. The SMI coalition insisted that it would march from Alexandra to Sandton with or without the authorities' permission.[7]

Ngwane insisted, 'Our Constitution allows us freedom of assembly, freedom of association ... The only option for us is to defy the criminalisation of our march.' Pretoria finally backed down on 28 August. The *Mail & Guardian* reported that it was thanks to 'massive pressure from the political left and behind-the-scenes intervention by, among others, trade union leader Zwelinzima Vavi and the National Intelligence Agency'. The latter agency's second-ranking bureaucrat at the time, Barry Gilder (who later became head of the Department of Home Affairs), admitted that Pretoria 'may have erred on the side of caution'.[8]

Pretoria's caution regarding basic political rights was, unfortunately, quite durable. On the following Monday afternoon at Wits University's education campus in Parktown, with Israeli foreign minister Shimon Peres due to speak nearby, students who looked Muslim were told to leave the vicinity. Palestinian Solidarity Committee leader Salim Vally was accosted by a security official of the Jewish Board of Deputies and then arrested by the police, while walking to his office in the same complex. He later remarked, 'The velvet glove slips, the iron fist is revealed.'[9]

According to Anti-Privatisation Forum publicity officer Dale McKinley, 'Police employed tactics reminiscent of the days of apartheid to deal with the demonstrators, particularly their use of racial slurs while beating and arresting protesters.'[10] Police used water cannons and rubber bullets against those who demonstrated against the arrest of Vally, two people were hospitalised as a result.

The clampdown over the WSSD period generated significant consternation. Freedom of Expression Institute representative Simon Kimani observed that the Regulation of Gatherings Act allowed Pretoria 'to construe the right to assembly in the most restrictive and conservative way possible'.[11] His colleague Jane Duncan added, 'The repression of dissent during the WSSD period was not a flash in the pan. Censorship has a political economy: the political economy of neoliberalism. The theory and practice of repression and dissent in recent years in South Africa and beyond should tell us that the WSSD was a taste of things to come.'[12]

In some regards, though, the new movements of the independent left had the last laugh. At the 31 August march from Alexandra to Sandton, the fall guy was Mbeki's hatchet man, minister Essop Pahad, formerly editor of the East Bloc's *World Marxist Review*. When early in the week it appeared that media sympathy had swung to activists Ngwane and Dennis Brutus, Pahad wrote a snide letter to the country's largest newspaper, the *Sowetan*, ending in these lines:

> Brutus disappeared without trace from the anti-apartheid struggle many years before 1994, and re-emerged in the last few years to hurl invective at the democratic government and programmes for Africa's recovery. However, to the extent that on some issues such as eradicating global inequality, we may agree, perhaps there is hope for co-operation. Welcome home Dennis the Menace! Hope this time you will stay, the better to appreciate that we cannot allow our modest achievements to be wrecked through anarchy. Opponents of democracy seek such destruction. But if you intend once more to leave for demonstrations elsewhere, we can only retort: et tu Brute! Good luck.[13]

The spirit of demonstrations elsewhere, which Brutus has graced as an inspirational poet and strategist, came home with him to Johannesburg. The 78-year-old former Robben Island political prisoner helped unleash voices of dissent that sang cheeky songs about global capitalism, the World Bank, IMF and WTO, NEPAD and US imperialism. Hence when at 4 pm on 31 August, Pahad appeared at the rally at Sandton's 'Speaker's Corner' to receive a memorandum addressed solely to Mbeki (no substitutes allowed), community activist Virginia Setshedi drew him onto the stage and asked the crowd of thousands, 'Do we want to hear from comrade Pahad?' The response: 'Phansi!' (Down! Away!). The next day's *Sowetan/Sunday World* newspaper carried a full front-page photo of Pahad with a screaming headline: 'Voetsek!'

Marching on Sandton

Alexandra township, the oldest black suburb of Johannesburg was first settled by black people in 1912. It sat as an uncomfortable enclave of mostly freehold land during apartheid, and was often a sign of significant anti-apartheid protest, particularly during the 1950s bus boycotts and 1980s anti-apartheid rebellion. However, repression under successive states of emergency beginning in the mid-1980s was so intense that major demonstrations were not only risky, but also always resulted in mass arrests. And so it was that the long-delayed break out from the slum to a district that represented capitalist hedonism, Sandton, was even sweeter. On 31 August, at least 20 000 supporters of the SMI and the landless toyi-toyied along a 12 km route to the site of the WSSD.

From 9 am, crowds gathered for the march of what was known, for just one day, as 'United Social Movements'. The Landless People's Movement had been hampered by internal conflicts, so they waited until last minute interventions were made by their Latin American and Asian comrades before signing up as co-sponsors of the march. Red and green, urban and rural, local and global, autonomist and socialist mixed happily. Across the valley was the glistening Sandton skyline, mainly constructed during the 1990s flight of capital from the Johannesburg central business district. The Convention Centre where 6 000 WSSD delegates were working was in the midst of a high-rent, opulent shopping and hotel area.

Materially, very little had changed in Alexandra since democracy arrived in 1994, aside from new but tiny houses on the township's eastern hill, some new community centres, pavements and traffic lights. A slum-clearance programme began in February 2001, along the filthy Jukskei River, when city officials used a cholera outbreak, which killed four residents, as an excuse for apartheid-style displacement. The country's leading elite paper, the *Sunday Indepenent,* protested those actions as 'bureaucratic know-it-allism and disregard for individuals and indeed communities. Sadly the events in Alex have all the elements of the worst of apartheid-style thinking and action.'[14]

Moving people did not make for a cleaner river. Life-threatening E. coli bacterial counts in the Jukskei soared from 2.4 million parts per 100 ml in August 2002 to 21 million a year later. Water minister Ronnie Kasrils denied a report that he had promised to drink a glass of untreated Jukskei water in 2005 to show his confidence in the clean-up strategy.[15]

Municipal bureaucrats and the mercenary 'Red Ants,' of the outsourced Wozani Security company repeated the forced removals countless other times in Johannesburg townships and inner-city ghettoes. In the first four months of 2002, there were more than 90 000 cut offs of electricity and water in the area serviced by the Johannesburg metropole – a high percentage were disconnections to the poor in inner-city Johannesburg, Soweto and Alexandra. This inspired the city's leading Democratic Alliance politician, Mike Moriarity, to applaud: 'The cutoffs are good but council has to be ruthless and unforgiving against people who don't pay their bills, or those who reconnect their electricity illegally.'[16]

The 'Igoli 2002' programme of corporatisation and privatisation of water, electricity, solid waste removal, and many other functions were designed, in part, by the World Bank. And the main water supply to Johannesburg came from an unnecessary World Bank dam in Lesotho, riven with corruption and eco-social displacement, with overpriced water too expensive for low-income communities.[17] Alexandra residents who tried to complain to the Bank's Inspection

Panel watchdog in 1998 were simply rebuffed.[18] The main beneficiary of Igoli 2002 was French water privatisation company, Suez, which was facing protests across the world for high prices, poor service and disconnections. In all these ways, activists made the global-local connections.

Just as important as the symbolic route of the march were the battles of numbers and of passion: the independent left surprised itself by drawing out mass-based organisations to the march. The Global Civil Society Forum, supported by Cosatu, the South African Council of Churches and the ANC, attracted roughly 5 000 to the Alexandra soccer stadium to hear Mbeki, in spite of the fact that the ANC advertised the possible participation of Fidel Castro and Yassir Arafat (neither of whom made it to the WSSD in the end). At stake in this contest of the marchers was the ability of government officials to disguise dissent. The South African NGO Coalition pulled out of the Forum march at the last moment, declaring that the ANC was manipulating the gathering. Fewer than 1 000 Civil Society Forum marchers left the stadium for the long trek to Sandton.

In a township which had been relatively unorganised during the past decade, due to myriad splits in community politics, the attraction of Alexandra residents to the radical social movements instead of the pro-government group was revealing. The Social Movements Indaba core group had claimed the week before, 'we will take Sandton!' – but the unspoken question was, who would win the hearts and minds of Alexandra?

On the eve of the march, Mbeki's weekly column in the e-zine *ANC Today* included the following analysis:

> So great is the divide that even as many are battling in the WSSD negotiations for a meaningful outcome that will benefit the billions of poor people in our country, Africa and the rest of the world, there are others, who claim to represent the same masses, who say they have taken it upon themselves to act in a manner that will ensure the collapse of the Summit. These do not want any discussion and negotiations.
>
> For this reason, they have decided to oppose and defeat the UN, all the governments of the world, the inter-governmental organisations, the major organisations of civil society participating in the Summit and the world of business, all of which are engaged in processes not different from those that take place regularly in our statutory four-chamber Nedlac, which includes government, business, labour and non-governmental organisations. Those who hold these views, which they regularly express freely in our

country, without any hindrance, also have their own economic views. As with all other ideas and views about the central question of the future of human society, we have to consider and respond to them rationally, whatever is happening in the streets of Johannesburg, for the benefit of the global mass media.[19]

'Without any hindrance?' Hundreds had been jailed for non-violent protest in preceding weeks: the Anti-Privatisation Forum's 'Kensington 87' were shot at and arrested when they demonstrated outside the Johannesburg mayor's house; 100 from a landless group in the Mpumalanga town of Ermelo; 77 from the Landless People's Movement demonstrating outside the Gauteng premier's office; and nearly 100 from the Soldiers' Forum, an Anti-Privatisation Forum affiliate of ex-ANC armed forces treated badly in the post-apartheid army. They would have disputed Mbeki's claim that they could express themselves freely. All were later released *without being convicted,* indicating that Pretoria's fear for the security of world leaders was unfounded.

On 31 August, police and army overkill was evident. 'One would have thought that South Africa had gone to war during the Summit,' commented Human Rights Foundation director, Yasmin Sooka. 'It was almost unbelievable to watch the heavily armed police and soldiers lining every inch of the route with guns pointed at the marchers.'[20] Defending the police action, Johannesburg metro police executive Chris Ngcobo made this leap:

> A massive international event of this kind had the potential to attract acts of terror and incidents of violent protests. In this sense, it would have been grossly irresponsible on the part of police and security agencies in the country to think that the summit was free of such dangers. One only needed to be reminded about the violent events that occurred in Seattle in 1999 and Genoa in 2001 to understand the sort of situation that confronted the country's security organs. Nevertheless, the Johannesburg Metro Police Department is very proud . . .[21]

Needless to say, authorities in Seattle and Genoa found their security forces guilty of using excessive force during those police riots. In the event, with more than 20 times as many people on the anti-WSSD march, and with a mostly empty stadium as his audience, Mbeki was not convincing in this critique of the new movements. Ironically, the 'benefit of the global mass media' was a factor in favour of Mbeki's opponents – as his ANC colleagues later complained. Indeed, international attention was partly responsible for the massive public pressure required to even gain police permission for the protest march.

A new movement?

The social movements march gathered together the Landless People's Movement and the SMI's main membership: the Anti-Privatisation Forum, Jubilee SA, the Environmental Justice Networking Forum, the Soweto Electricity Crisis Committee, the Rural Development Services Network, Friends of the Earth, First People, Indymedia and the Palestinian Solidarity Committee, as well as international allies and local unaffiliated activists. Ngwane called this 'the coming of age of the new anti-capitalist movements in South Africa'. He linked it to 'the international mobilisations such as those that took place in Seattle and Genoa. Some have honored the event by calling it the A31 mobilisation. The red march revealed Mbeki's Achilles Heel: his lack of support at home. Can he speak for Africa when social movements in his own country march against him? How is NEPAD good for Africa when South Africans do not support it?'[22]

By no means, however, was the new alliance of left social movements without internal contradictions, and not only between those emphasising 'green' environmental values and those committed to 'red' social justice. For example, at the opening of the final rally at Speaker's Corner, a spokesperson from the Landless People's Movement

called out, 'Viva Robert Mugabe, Viva! Viva ZANU (PF), Viva!', to applause from the large rural delegation. South Africa's landless leaders had attracted thousands from across the country. They had creatively transformed their convergence centre near Nasrec, close to Soweto, from an abandoned, surreal 1980s entertainment centre to a site where debates raged and small workshops were provided for rural folk.

Still, as witnessed by the landless leaders' support for Mugabe's repressive regime, the rural movement had promise but also pitfalls. Ngwane took the microphone soon after the Zimbabwean ruler's name was uttered: 'While we are happy to have unity with the landless, we respectfully disagree on the matter of Mugabe. He is a dictator and he has killed many Zimbabweans.' Roars of approval followed from, among others, the Zimbabwe Coalition on Debt and Development which had travelled a full day by bus to attend.

Notwithstanding deep division on a matter of such great importance, the SMI could rightfully claim victory in front of the low-income black constituencies over which civil society fights most vigorously for hearts and minds. The failure of the liberation movement's left flank in the SACP and Cosatu to anticipate and outrun the new social movements' radicalism was codified by the events of A31. 'The new movements have arrived,' Ngwane announced.[23] It was time, he might have added, to think-globally, act-locally and act-globally. With Pretoria's most active economic officials emerging as the loudest Third World voices for reforming global apartheid, there arose a necessity to forge unity with the many international activists who felt that the WSSD failed to represent progress.

Pretoria's 'lack of transparency and procedure'

The ordinary South African could be forgiven for not understanding the WSSD's flaws. Johannesburg's largest suburban newspaper, *The Star*, reported it as 'one of the greatest international conferences ever' and 'an inspiration for our children'.[24] The assessment from the world's credible civil society voices was nearly entirely negative.
- Vandana Shiva described the outcome simply: 'What happened in Jo'burg amounts to a privatisation of the Earth, an auction house in which the rights of the poor were given away.'
- Friends of the Earth cited backsliding on the Convention on Biological Diversity.
- The NGO Energy and Climate Caucus concluded: 'The agreement on energy is an outright disaster, with the dropping of all targets and timetables.'

- The Gaia Foundation called the final summit document 'an incredibly weak agreement'.
- Even centrist Oxfam called the WSSD 'a triumph for greed and self-interest, a tragedy for the poor and environment'.²⁵

In the key fields of water, energy and healthcare, the WTO considers essential state services to be commodities, and the WSSD's new 'Type 2' Agreements codified public-private partnerships, as a replacement for intergovernmental agreements and actions, which have been extremely scarce in any case since the Rio Earth Summit in 1992.

Monthly Review's Foster, asked why the WSSD went 'down in history as an absolute failure', answered:

> The first reason is perhaps the most obvious, at least to environmentalists. The decade between Rio and Johannesburg has seen the almost complete failure of the Rio Earth Summit and its Agenda 21 to produce meaningful results. This has highlighted the weaknesses of global environmental summitry.
> Second, the US refusal to ratify the Kyoto Protocol and the Convention on Biological Diversity – the two main conventions evolving out of Rio – has raised questions about the capacity of capitalism to address the world environmental crisis. The United States, as the hegemonic power of the capitalist system, further

signaled its rejection of global environmental reform by announcing that President Bush would not be attending the Johannesburg summit.

Third, both the rapid globalisation of the neoliberal agenda in the 1990s and the emergence of a massive antiglobalisation movement in Seattle in November 1999 highlighted the system's antagonism toward all attempts to promote economic and environmental justice.

Fourth, the capitalist world economy as a whole is experiencing global recession. Hardest hit are the countries of the Global South, which – thanks to neoliberal globalisation – are caught in worsening economic crises over which they have less and less control.

Fifth, we are witnessing the growth of a new virulent wave of imperialism as the United States has begun a world war on terrorism in response to the events of September 11, 2001. This is taking the form of US military interventions not only in Afghanistan, but also potentially against Iraq, along with stepped-up US military activities in locations throughout the third world. Under these circumstances, war is likely to trump the environment.

Sixth, South Africa, which nearly ten years ago became a symbol of human freedom with the overthrow of apartheid, was chosen mainly for that reason as the site of the second earth summit. It has now come to symbolise, for many, something quite

different: the rapacious growth of neoliberalism and the refusal to address major environmental and social crises.[26]

And so, in a sense, failure was assured. But Pretoria's own role should not be excused, including the repeated attempts to stifle protest.

In the policy magazine *New Agenda*, the ANC's Ben Turok interviewed environment minister Valli Moosa in a cover story on 'The battle for the WSSD'. Asked about the 'Wits (*sic*) exercise to shut down the conference,' Moosa replied, 'They did not make any impact. To their discredit they were completely incoherent . . . Frankly, it was theatrics because there was no content.' Alternatively, Moosa had not been paying attention to the critics:

> What was their problem with sustainable development or with the manner in which sustainable development was being dealt with? Were they saying, we need to fight against the adverse effects of globalisation? But they heard our president say at the opening ceremony, we are going to fight global apartheid. That was a very strong word to use. If they were saying that, I think they should have tried to strengthen our hand in the fight against a unipolar world, unilateralism, undemocratic global governance, unfair international trade.[27]

Moosa claimed that Mbeki bent over backwards to accommodate civil society concerns about process and content issues. In 'the broader NGO world . . . all the major groups' did want to work with Pretoria, and met Mbeki twice during the WSSD, according to Moosa:

> The international director of the World Wildlife Federation, in his introductory remarks said he wanted us to know that when he addressed the global forum he had told them that never before at any international conference had the president of the host country taken the time to sit down with the leaders of civil society and listen to them. He said this was unique, 'You have a new benchmark.' They were full of praise. The president took detailed notes, I was sitting next to him, and at the end of all the inputs he said he more or less agreed with everything they had said and there was no need for a discussion because these are the issues that were agreed.[28]

Perceptions about 'agreement' and process were different among the less compromising NGOs.[29] The handling of the WSSD was 'way out of line with the normal procedure of UN conferences', according to

Third World Network director Martin Khor, and *not* in a way that favoured civil society inputs. 'The extended six-hour final plenary was held up halfway as delegates haggled over a second draft of the political declaration that was released only after the plenary had started.' As a result, wrote Khor, 'a great deal of disquiet was expressed by many delegations on the utter lack of transparency and procedure of the political declaration process, and some delegates, familiar with the WTO, remarked in frustration that the infamous WTO Green Room process had now crossed over to the usually open and participatory UN system.' He concluded, 'with such small results ... it will be quite a long time before a convincing case is made for another world summit of this type.'[30]

The same conclusion was reached by Venezuelan president Hugo Chavez, speaking for the Group of 77 countries and China: 'We have to have a radical change in the formats of these summits ... We just read a speech ... There is no proper dialogue, it seems to be a dialogue of the deaf. Some people go from summit to summit. Our people go from abyss to abyss.'[31]

Still, even if the WSSD failed to catch up with, much less advance beyond, the Rio Agenda, the event was a useful exercise for the global justice movements. It also helped to reawaken the left in South Africa, after a period of eight years of relative and socio-economic decline after liberation from apartheid.

The strongest single commitment from the WSSD was that donor governments would more actively promote water and sanitation. Was there any basis for the hope that the fight against global water apartheid would be joined by Pretoria, this time on the side of social justice and ecology?

Notes
1. Foster, J. (2003), 'A Planetary Defeat: The Failure of Global Environmental Reform', *Monthly Review*, January.
2. Weisbrot, M. (2002), 'Progress Postponed: The Economic Failure of the Last Two Decades of the Twentieth Century', Washington, http://www.cepr.org.
3. Many networks were built through highly specialised sectoral groups. These were manifested in the local NGO 'groundWork' co-hosting a Corporate Accountability workshop in Sandton the week before the WSSD. Several other sector-specific meetings occurred which allowed local groups to meet international delegations of fisherfolk, farmers, community forestry activists and indigenous peoples, among others. A variety of SA groups were involved in the four main organised parallel summits: Global Peoples Forum (Nasrec), Landless Summit (Shareworld), IUCN Environmental Centre (Sandton), and the People's Environment Summit (St Stithians School). For more information, see Bond, *Unsustainable South Africa*, pp. 357–365; Bond, P. and T. Guliwe (2003), 'Contesting "Sustainable Development": South African Civil Society Critiques and Advocacy', in O. Edigheji and G. Mhone (eds), *Governance in the New South Africa: The Challenges of Globalisation*, Cape Town, University of Cape Town Press; and especially Munnik, V. and J. Wilson (2003), *The World Comes to One Country*, Berlin and Johannesburg, Heinrich Boell Stiftung.
4. Cock, J. (2003), 'A Better or Worse World? Report on the Third World Social Forum, Porto Alegre 2003', University of the Witwatersrand Department of Sociology, paper for the University of Natal Centre for Civil Society (http://www.nu.ac.za/ccs), Durban, February. See also Bond, P. (2003), 'Battle of the Trevors', *Sowetan*, 7 February.
5. *Mail & Guardian*, 30 August 2002.
6. Reminiscent of the old days, international solidarity quickly materialised. SABC reported in its nightly news a few days later that 'a group called Global Resistance would protest outside the South African embassy in London, while a couple of hundred protesters would picket the South African embassy in Paris. In Buenos Aires, Argentina, an unemployed workers movement plans to protest in solidarity with the arrested South African activists and against the summit. In Canada, a small group organised by the Ontario Coalition Against Poverty would protest outside the South African embassy in Toronto.' SABC News (2002), 'SA Govt faces "Global Protest" over WSSD', Johannesburg, 27 August.
7. Ngwane, T. (2003), 'A Tale of Two WSSD Demos', forthcoming in R. Neumann and A. Hsiao (eds), *Anti-Capitalism: A Field Guide to the Global Justice Movement*, New York, New Press. Nqakula said anyone who marched would 'fall foul of the law and will be acted against'.

8. *Mail & Guardian*, 30 August 2002.
9. Vally's analysis of the nature of the state is valuable: Vally, S. (2003), 'The Political Economy of State Repression in South Africa', in S. Kimani (ed.), *The Right to Dissent: Freedom of Expression, Assembly and Demonstration in the New South Africa*, Johannesburg, Freedom of Expression Institute, p. 66.
10. McKinley, D. (2003), 'Trying to "Kill" the Messenger, and Failing: Experiences of the Anti-Privatisation Forum during the WSSD', in S. Kimani (ed.), *The Right to Dissent: Freedom of Expression, Assembly and Demonstration in the New South Africa*, Johannesburg, Freedom of Expression Institute, p. 99.
11. Kimani, S. (2003), 'South Africa at the Crossroads: Dissent and the New Political Agenda', in S. Kimani (ed.), *The Right to Dissent: Freedom of Expression, Assembly and Demonstration in the New South Africa*, Johannesburg, Freedom of Expression Institute, pp. 15, 17.
12. Duncan, J. (2003), 'A Flash in the Pan? The Relevance of the WSSD for Freedom of Expression', in S. Kimani (ed.), *The Right to Dissent: Freedom of Expression, Assembly and Demonstration in the New South Africa*, Johannesburg, Freedom of Expression Institute, p. 108.
13. *Sowetan*, 28 August 2002.
14. *Sunday Independent*, 18 February 2001.
15. *Johannesburg Star*, 8 October 2003.
16. *Sunday Times Gauteng Metro*, 19 May 2002.
17. For updates on corruption and resettlement/compensation problems, see http://www.irn.org, especially Mopheme/The Survivor (Maseru), 9 April 2003.
18. The story is told in Bond, *Against Global Apartheid*, Chapter Three; and *Unsustainable South Africa*, Chapters Three–Six.
19. http://www.anc.org.za, 30 August 2002.
20. Sooka, Y. (2003), 'Defining the Constitutional Right to Freedom of Expression, Assembly and Demonstration', in S. Kimani (ed.), *The Right to Dissent: Freedom of Expression, Assembly and Demonstration in the New South Africa*, Johannesburg, Freedom of Expression Institute, p. 58.
21. Ngcobo, C. (2003), 'Local Authorities and the Regulation of Assemblies and Demonstrations', in S. Kimani (ed.), *The Right to Dissent: Freedom of Expression, Assembly and Demonstration in the New South Africa*, Johannesburg, Freedom of Expression Institute, p. 58.
22. Ngwane, 'A Tale of Two WSSD Demos'.
23. The exception, as noted above, was Moosa (*New Agenda*, 8, 2002).
24. *Star*, 5 September 2002.
25. Various wire reports, cited in Bond, P. (2002), 'Globalisation hits the Poor', *City Press*, 8 September.
26. Foster, 'Planetary Defeat'.
27. *New Agenda*, 8, 2002. The strange reference to Wits University is based on the International Forum on Globalisation conference of 24–25 August, described below.
28. *New Agenda*, 8, 2002.
29. For a critique of WWF and other big green groups, see Cockburn, A. and K. Silverstein (1996), *Washington Babylon*, London, Verso, Chapter Six.

30. Khor, M. (2002), 'A Disappointing Summit,' *Third World Resurgence*, December 2002. Khor provides a detailed account of a combination that many civil society critics charge is typical of Pretoria's overall strategy and accomplishments: namely, skullduggery associated with text manipulation, leading to a meaningless outcome that reinforces the *status quo:* 'The last preparatory meeting at Bali ended without a draft declaration, and the Preparatory Committee chairman, Emil Salim of Indonesia, issued a draft of elements paper under his own authority after the Bali meeting. Even that document was not discussed in Johannesburg. There was no process or meeting held at Jo'burg on the declaration. The host country, South Africa, distributed a first draft only on the night of 1 September, three days before the Summit was to conclude. That draft was received with a lot of criticism from many countries. No meeting was held to discuss it. On the night of 3 September, when the Main Committee met to discuss the Implementation Plan, a few delegations led by Malta asked what had happened to the declaration process and when a meeting would be held to discuss it. South African foreign minister, Nkosazana Dlamini-Zuma, replied that there were as many proposals for amendments to the first draft as there were people in the hall (about 300 delegates). She said a second draft would be ready on 4 September. WSSD secretary-general Nitin Desai indicated that a meeting of the Main Committee would be called that morning to discuss it. However, when pressed by delegates, neither could answer when the meeting would be convened.

'On the Summit's last day, 4 September, delegations were eagerly awaiting the new declaration draft and the opportunity to discuss it, neither the draft nor the meeting materialised. The final official plenary chaired by President Mbeki started after 3 pm without delegates having had the chance to see the new draft for a declaration. It was circulated after the plenary started, with the heading, "Draft political declaration submitted by the President of the Summit".

'With several delegations, and NGOs, informally indicating their displeasure at the new draft . . . Mbeki announced the meeting would be suspended for ten minutes. But the break stretched to almost two hours as several delegations were seen in intense discussion among themselves and with senior South African and UN officials. After the plenary resumed, a document with four new points or amendments was circulated, and the Johannesburg Declaration on Sustainable Development was adopted.

'The manner in which the declaration was introduced . . . was way out of line with the normal procedure of UN conferences, in which many drafts of such an important document would have gone through months of negotiations at various stages of the preparatory committee and at the Summit.'
31. Sapa, 5 September 2002; *Guardian*, 6 September 2002.

8
Water wars

Dams, privatisation and pre-paid meters, from Johannesburg to Kyoto and back

The global fight for water rights came of age in The Hague in February 2000, at a summit of a formerly closed establishment grouping called the World Water Forum, and intensified at a December 2001 session in Bonn. In August 2002, the battleground moved to the Johannesburg Waterdome, a vast indoor-stadium exhibition (in the MTN Sundome) hosted by the Department of Water Affairs during the WSSD. It then moved to the Kyoto World Water Forum eight months later. Meanwhile, grassroots and labour battles against privatisers in numerous settings forced the big French and British water firms to begin a strategic withdrawal. Former high-profile privatisation pilot projects from Buenos Aires to Manila (with several South African towns in between) revealed that selling as essential a commodity as water to low-income people was becoming impossible, due simply to unaffordability and protest.

While the main issue under debate at these international fora was water commodification, a variety of related struggles were playing out in South Africa and internationally.[1] Together, the numerous water-sector manifestations of social deprivation and ecological destruction attained a high profile in part because of the WSSD, but also because for millions of South Africans, access to a basic human need, water, had worsened after 1994, notwithstanding Pretoria's self-congratulatory rhetoric.

It was not long before some of the world's leading journalists picked up on the contradictions between Pretoria's leftist talk and neoliberal water walk. In just six months, between December 2002 and May 2003, a series of critical articles about South African water policy, particularly the huge flaws in commercialised urban and rural systems, appeared in the *New York Times, Washington Post, Le Monde Diplomatique, London Observer, Boston Globe, Houston Chronicle, Mother Jones, L'Humanite* and outlets supplied by the

International Consortium of Investigative Journalists.[2] South Africa's SABC Special Assignment, Canadian Broadcasting Corporation radio, BBC radio, Dutch national television, Korean Christian radio and several other outlets also aired thoughtful stories in subsequent weeks. By early 2004, updated televised documentaries about South African water inequities were shown in the US and Canada.

Destroy the meter, enjoy the water!

The combined impact of popular action, with slogans like 'Destroy the meter, enjoy the water!', and high-profile media exposure helped shift policy. Technocratic advice, inputs by parliamentarians and mild-mannered 'advocacy' was largely ignored.

To illustrate, on the eve of the WSSD, Kasrils invited the South African Civil Society Water Caucus to discuss issues associated with his policy, programmes and projects. The Caucus was formed in July 2002 explicitly for the WSSD, and drew from 40 water advocacy organisations. Its steering committee included representatives from: Earthlife Africa, Environmental Monitoring Group, Network for Advocacy on Water in Southern Africa, the Anti-Eviction Campaign, Rural Development Support Services, Mvula Trust, the Youth Caucus and the South African Municipal Workers Union. The Caucus addressed a variety of issues in its statement of objectives: sanitation, ecosystems, human rights, privatisation and commodification of water, anti-evictions and water cut-offs, rural water supply, urban water, large dams, water conservation and demand management, regional and transboundary water issues, labour and the promotion of public services.

At the August 2002 meeting at Department of Water Affairs and Forestry (Dwaf) headquarters with Kasrils, the Caucus Points of Consensus were presented:

- Water and sanitation are human rights. All are entitled to access to water to meet their basic human needs, and rural communities are entitled to water for productive use to sustain their livelihoods.
- Water management must be accountable to communities at a local level.
- We respect the integrity of ecosystems as the basis for all life, with an emphasis on maintaining river ecosystems and groundwater resources.
- We reject the commodification and privatisation of water services and sanitation, and water resources.
- We reject the role of the USA, the other G8 countries and Trans-National Corporations for their role in pushing privatisation and commodification.

- We reject the UN WSSD process and outcomes so far, as nothing more than structural adjustment of the south. We resolve to work together with social movements to realise an alternative vision.
- We reject NEPAD and (its) plans for water... as not being sustainable. It is structural adjustment by Africa for Africa. In particular, we reject the privatisation of water and the hydropower focus. We commit ourselves to building a mass movement for the reconstruction and sustainable development of Africa.
- We undertake to educate and raise awareness and to mobilise communities towards the WSSD.

Kasrils gracefully received this list of grievances and other harshly critical comments about Dwaf. He was affable and humble, conceding that social movement and environmental concerns were generally valid. Kasrils was unwilling to give ground on critiques of big dams, however. He said that the point of the meeting was *not* to simply show a surface-level consultation with NGOs in the days prior to the WSSD. The Caucus issued a press statement designed to ensure he kept his word: 'Of particular importance are the issues of NEPAD, water cut-offs and evictions, and it is expected that a number of meetings will be held with the Ministry in the near future to resolve these issues. While the civil society representatives that were present at this meeting were happy with the spirit of openness, there is some concern that this should be the beginning of an ongoing dialogue and not just a short-term strategy to appease civil society before the Summit.'[3]

Over the previous eight years, those who would later form the Water Caucus had raised similar concerns. From the outset of democracy in 1994, the first water minister, Kader Asmal, adopted several controversial policies which quickly came under fire:
- The South African Municipal Workers Union opposed the private-sector and NGO-oriented rural water programme and the promotion of public-private partnerships in municipal water delivery;
- Some community organisations, social movements and NGOs, mainly affiliated to the National Land Committee and Rural Development Services Network, complained that most taps installed after 1994 quickly broke and that millions of South Africans remained without water. They said Dwaf did not take seriously the RDP promise of 50 litres per person per day of free water;
- Environmentalists in the Group for Environmental Monitoring, Environmental Monitoring Group, Earthlife and the Soweto and Alexandra civic associations complained that Pretoria championed unnecessary Lesotho dams (it has built two – Mohale and Katse –

and contracted another four, although whether they get built is in question);
- Many civic groups protested intensifying municipal water cut-offs, with fierce demonstrations in the townships of Gauteng, Durban, Cape Town and several smaller towns;
- Criticism continued against low infrastructure standards, such as mass pit latrines in urban areas.

By August 2002, the various South African water groups were sufficiently confident to attack Kasrils for failing to apply his mind to a variety of long-standing grievances (see Table 3). The groups' sophistication on these issues, in identifying local, catchment-area, national, regional and international problems, and potential solutions was matched by an anger that reflected durable tensions with Pretoria.

Protest at the Waterdome

Parallel to organising the Social Movements Indaba, many Caucus members, joined by the Anti-Privatisation Forum and displaced Basotho people called Survivors of the Lesotho Dams (SOLD) planned a protest at the Waterdome. On 3 September, the final day of WSSD deliberations, at the outset of a session promoting for-profit water deals with more than a hundred representatives of water corporations, states and international agencies, 70 Caucus activists chanted slogans for ten minutes.[4] As the SMI press statement recorded,

> Demonstrators chose a presentation by Kasrils to drive home the point that millions of South Africans, and close to two billion people worldwide, still have no access to water. The message was clear, there can be no sustainable development as long as capitalist market forces dominate the ownership and distribution of water. Water is a human right, not a capitalist privilege to be enjoyed only by those who can afford to pay. Minister Kasrils chose to ignore the legitimate issues raised by the activists, instead labelling the activists, 'thugs' and 'anti-democratic' ... The simple fact is that the voices of the poor have been marginalised, replaced by those who simply see development as a means to make more money and to gain favour with the rich and powerful.
>
> The SMI is not alone in its denunciation and rejection of the corporate agenda of the W$$D. Yesterday, members of the World Coalition against Water Privatisation and Commodification (a

global umbrella body representing many different social movements and progressive NGOs), announced their withdrawal from the W$$D. They noted that, 'the summit has been hijacked by corporate and national interests and market-driven jargon,' and denounced the 'lack of courage and human vision' that has characterised the W$$D.[5]

As an example of the tough international critique, highly-regarded Indian scientist Vandana Shiva condemned a hand washing promotion by Kasrils and other water administrators in South Africa and the Indian province of Kerala, during and after the WSSD:

> One of the outcomes of the recently concluded W$$D was the public-private partnership project, 'Washing Hands,' launched by the World Bank, the London School of Hygiene and Tropical Medicine, US Aid, Unicef, WHO, and soap companies such as Unilever, Procter and Gamble and Colgate Palmolive. The project talks of 'saving lives' through reducing diarrhoeal diseases by half, by doubling hand washing by selling soap . . .
> Kerala has the richest indigenous systems for non-chemical, non-polluting, natural hygiene products from biodiversity such as 'shikakai,' a herbal soap, to natural soap making at the small-scale level. The project is an attempt to destroy indigenous knowledge, indigenous biodiversity and indigenous economies. It is a project to destroy lives, not save lives, by destroying employment in cottage based industries, as well as, introducing polluting chemical based toxic detergents from global corporations. This violent imposition of a colonising project is ironically being launched on 2nd October, Gandhi's birthday, which should celebrate non-violent alternatives to toxic products from global corporations.
> The project is also legitimising water privatisation through private-public partnerships, which are aimed at undermining people's water rights and the state's duties to protect water and people's water rights. The case of Coca Cola destroying water in Kerala by extracting 1.5 million litres per day for its bottling plant, is an example of how private-public partnerships are a recipe for over exploitation of scarce fresh water resources, a threat to people's water rights and a recipe for creating thirst and disease. So-called Type 2 agreements between unaccountable governments, international agencies and global corporations launched at W$$D, such as the Kerala project, are an attempt to privatise the earth's resources and colonise people's every day lives.[6]

Adjusting pro-partnership rhetoric

Dwaf's pro-privatisation position was not as solid as it appeared at first glance. In Johannesburg, *The Star* newspaper reported that the Waterdome protesters 'said they had made their point and left, after which Kasrils told delegates that the anti-privatisation lobby was a minority in South Africa'.[7]

However, it was not long before Kasrils and his colleagues began to adjust their pro-private rhetoric. In the weeks prior to the Kyoto World Water Forum, Dwaf director-general Mike Muller presented a strong anti-privatisation message in a 'Water 2003' speech. Muller conceded, 'We should start by acknowledging key lessons from Johannesburg (the WSSD).' One of these was that 'business as usual will not achieve the goals. We need to acknowledge the constraints and review the paradigms within which we work.'[8] Muller observed that

> the aggressive push by international water and financial interests for private engagement has been working to their detriment. The pendulum is swinging against too great an involvement of private sector. Resistance to private engagement is the result, in part, of the obvious failure of private initiative to address the core challenge of the unserved. There is a vital role for private expertise and resources in providing water services. Unfortunately, if that role is forced down the throats of potential beneficiaries, they often choke.
>
> If we do not want to give credibility to those who describe private sector engagement as neo-imperialist expansion, designed to boost profits of the rich world's service industries, we must demonstrate that it is the product of rational institutional decisions designed to achieve public objectives.[9]

Muller conceded privatisation's 'obvious failure' to serve poor people, but insisted that it remain a 'rational' strategy, worthy of defence against anti-imperialists.

Kasrils used the same tack three years earlier, at an August 2000 Stockholm water symposium:

> The ... World Water Vision, presented by the World Bank at the World Water Forum in The Hague earlier this year ... stated that 'consumers must be charged the full cost of providing water services.' There is acknowledgement that governments may provide subsidies to the poor, but it is proposed that 'subsidies should be delivered directly to people, not to service organisations.'

Table 3: Water and sanitation apartheid, and social movement solutions.[10]

Challenge at Dwaf	Social movements proposal
Failure to enforce the constitutional right to water	Reiterate the ministry's endorsement of right, and prosecute any water supplier, whether state, parastatal, private-sector or NGO, that denies this right to people, or refuses to expand access to all who lack water
Failure to halt water disconnections by municipal and catchment-area water managers	Declare disconnections of water supplies to households to be a 'water emergency', and intervene under the provisions of the National Water Act to immediately reconnect at least the on-site lifeline supply
Lack of delivery on promised free lifeline supply of 50–60 litres per person per day	Establish in policy the minimum free supply to be 50 litres per person per day (not 6 kl/household/month)
Insufficient subsidies to rural water programmes and projects where municipal support is not yet in place	Change scope of Dwaf revenue accounts: increase charges on high-volume retail users and high-volume users of raw water including commercial agriculture, forestry, commerce and industry, to boost direct subsidisation of municipalities which lack revenues for internal cross-subsidisation
Failure to deliver emergency water in cholera-stricken areas through water tanker trucks	Households without water, especially in cholera-risk areas, must immediately be provided trucked supplies of water
Inadequate systems to monitor, regulate and repair rural water projects run on a semi-privatised basis	National monitoring and evaluation of all existing supply schemes must become a high priority
Shortfalls in sanitation due to excessive emphasis on cost recovery and co-payment	End co-payment, and dramatically increase sanitation spending for installation of environmentally sound and hygienic supplies
Roll-overs in annual budget allocations	Identify blockages to delivery, and end bureaucracy that hampers fund flows (e.g., to low-income municipalities)
Failure to consider all eco-social costs of mega-dams (due to pro-dam construction bias, instead of demand-side management)	Prohibit construction of large new dams (e.g., Skuifraam) until full demand-side measures are undertaken
Opposition to World Commission on Dams report	Commit to WCD, with a moratorium on construction of Mohale Dam until all WCD recommendations are carried out
Kasrils' endorsement of China's eco-socially disastrous Three Gorges Dam	Retract endorsement, condemn dam and work with international NGOs and human-rights groups against project
Refusal to investigate companies involved in Lesotho dam corruption and take action. The only investigators are in Lesotho and they are underfunded and slow. Meanwhile, the same SA companies get significant contracts in South Africa	Press for suspension of contracts (including on Mohale Dam) involving companies implicated in LHDA corruption and ensure those companies are debarred from further state construction contracts anywhere in South Africa

Table 3: (cont.)

Challenge at Dwaf	Social movements proposal
Dam safety needs improvement, as shown during Mozambique flooding (2000–01)	Investigate, repair and compensate problems caused by inappropriate SA dam control
Failure to redistribute water resources enjoyed below cost by farmers on land reserved for whites under apartheid	Impose higher charges and incentives to fix leaks on major water users, to cross-subsidise other users and to ensure conservation for the benefit of environments and downstream people, including those in Mozambique, Zimbabwe and Namibia. Educate farmers to adopt less water-intensive cultivation systems.
Insufficient regulation of water use by forestry plantations	Revise pro-plantation and pulp-export policy, including reversal of corruption-tainted privatisation
Unpunished water pollution by TNCs, especially in the mining, metals and agricultural sectors	Withdraw pollution permits to notorious polluters e.g., Iscor and many mining companies, and charge punitive polluter-fines to prevent further despoliation
Failure to implement regulations on municipal water privatisers, even in the wake of publicised crises at Dolphin Coast, Nelspruit and Nkonkobe	Halt municipal water privatisations in lieu of lack of national regulation and risks associated with failed pilots and begin process of remunicipalisation
Erratic leadership against global water commodification	Endorse the Blue Planet Project's Treaty Initiative to Share and Protect the Global Water Commons

This formulation and its assumptions about the role of government were unacceptable to me and many of my colleagues from developing countries.[11]

However, reflecting Kasrils' simultaneous drive to privatise, the same speech raised this canard: 'If even Cuba can use private-sector providers to help manage Havana's water supply, why should there be an objection to such an approach in South Africa?'[12] The objections are numerous, of course, and the comparison invalid.

The use and abuse of Cuban water

Muller made the same point in mid-2003, during a brief intervention on a water-rights email listserve: 'Cuba has two concession contracts with Agbar – a subsidiary of Lyonnaise – one for approximately 50% of Havana. I believe it would be useful for critics of privatisation to consider the Cuban case and the background to their decision to choose this route, to develop a better understanding of the challenges that face *public* service providers in all countries.'[13]

What *is* the background, and how does it compare to South Africa?
- The Cuban economy is firmly under state control, while South Africa has left white monopoly capital virtually untouched. Pretoria has been part-privatising state-owned assets since the dying days of apartheid: the main iron and steel firm in 1989, several long-term water concessions in the early 1990s, telecommunications in 1997 and electricity, and the transport sector throughout. The results have been disastrous in terms of job cuts and disconnections of service to low-income people.
- Egalitarianism marks Cuban life, despite threats of dollarisation, based upon a grassroots-driven, revolutionary adoption of new social policies that eradicated the inequality so pervasive in the Third World. From the time the ANC was elected to government in 1994, it began entrenching inequality by imposing neoliberal policies, including the 1994 Water and Sanitation White Paper.
- Water-system regulations are rigorous in Cuba. Pretoria's regulations are so weak that the world's biggest water firms failed to provide water to the poor in small towns like Dolphin Coast, Nkonkobe and Nelspruit, all meant to be model private participation pilot projects. This led, in Nkonkobe, to Suez being tossed out. At Dolphin Coast, Saur insisted on a contract rewrite to assure higher profits. In Nelspruit, Biwater threatened to withdraw because of consumer dissatisfaction. These problems emerged without any supportive pro-municipal interventions from Pretoria.
- Cuba's state finances are desperate because the decades-old US embargo forced the economy to depend upon the East Bloc. When those regimes fell during the early 1990s, trade and barter arrangements ended. Cuba experienced a 75% loss in export earnings from 1991 to 1993. In contrast, after anti-apartheid sanctions were lifted in a newly-liberated South Africa, export earnings flourished. Nevertheless, Pretoria's 1995 relaxation of most exchange controls and 1998–99 permission for large Johannesburg firms to relocate their financial headquarters to London, led to massive capital flight. South Africa's economic bleeding was caused not by factors beyond control as in Cuba's case, but by ideologically-driven financial suicide.
- Cuba's financial deficits are exacerbated because cross-subsidisation from big water users, for example, cane fields and forestry, adversely affect the scarce inflows of hard currency. Possibilities for harmonising the social and ecological aspects of the hydrological cycle are limited. In contrast, South African water apartheid is

severe and Muller's water department has done little to discipline hedonistic users of water, or provide incentives to fix leaks. As for fiscal priorities, Pretoria was happy to authorise more than R43 billion to buy offensive high-tech weaponry, despite a lack of clean water and sanitation for most South Africans.
- Cuba does not disconnect people from their water supplies. In contrast, even after millions of water disconnections, there are still municipal officials, like an official in Durban, who brags about disconnecting water supplies to 1 000 families in his jurisdiction every day, notwithstanding periodic cholera outbreaks and persistent diarrhoea problems in Durban's black townships.[14]

More mea culpas

Muller concluded his Water 2003 argument by suggesting

> two initiatives that might help. The first would be for donors and lending agencies to cease making private sector involvement a pre-condition for water sector support. Respect the fact that most governments and communities are seeking to meet their water service needs and help them to make sound choices, their own choices. In particular, we should allow them to make their own decisions on service provision options. Given a strong focus on basic water and sanitation needs, we may well create conditions in which more appropriate – and more successful – private intervention can be developed.
>
> Related to this, the second initiative would be for the OECD countries, their companies, preferably both, to call for water services to be taken off the table in the General Agreement on Trade in Services and related trade negotiations. This would help to make the point that we are serious about achieving the global objectives and not just pursuing our trade objectives under a benevolent guise.[15]

The World Bank, IMF, WTO, European Union, and United States government apparently did not agree with either suggestion, for pressure continued despite an apparent retreat by water companies.

In his 2003 statement, Muller addressed more specific social movement concerns about Pretoria's own policies, and here, the influence of the critique was more nuanced, characterised more by excuses and 'passing the buck'. For example, Muller conceded, 'Sanitation progress has been much slower, reflecting in part the low perceived priority of sanitation provision which hardly featured in pre-1994 surveys of community aspirations and expectations of government.'[16] Critics replied that the low take-up on the Dwaf policy of installing pit latrines reflected not the 'low priority' but poverty and the insensitivity of Dwaf in requiring expensive co-payments. Dwaf traditionally charged R700 or more as part-payment for installation of pit latrines – the equivalent of a monthly pension payout. Hence, only a few tens of thousands were actually constructed prior to the WSSD.

Muller continued, 'A cholera outbreak in KwaZulu-Natal in 2000 highlighted the importance of improved sanitation if the health benefits of water supply are to be fully realised. Sanitation is now a national political priority.'[17] Critics claim that the cholera outbreak reflects the fact that water cut-offs, which in a just South Africa would be declared unconstitutional, as Kasrils acknowledges, were at the epicentre of the epidemic. Moreover, a focus on pit latrines instead of higher-quality sanitation has adverse health and environmental impacts.[18]

As for the problem of high water costs reflected in 10 million water disconnections during the late 1990s, Muller insisted that 'the major challenge is to establish social consensus around free basic services and the corollary of payment for higher levels of service'.[19] In reality, social movement critics argue, the major challenge is to stop systemic bureaucratic sabotage of free water, including halting the ongoing epidemic of water disconnections, and to restructure South Africa's urban tariff system.

Massive inequality and poverty and an upsurge of anti-privatisation protests around the world has made profits from water sales difficult. By 2003, Suez was recording serious problems not just in Johannesburg, but in Atlanta (USA), Argentina, the Philippines and Puerto Rico. As British journalist Nick Mathiason reported at the outset of the Kyoto world water meeting, 'many of the biggest private sector water companies' were in retreat:

> Suez, the biggest water company in the world, is reducing its exposure in developing countries by a third. It had plans to reduce costs by 340 million euros this year and a further 68 million euros next year and now intends to cut deeper. Not surprisingly, in a harsh macro-economic climate, the company now favours 'currency risk-exempt financing,' having had its fingers burnt in Argentina and the Philippines . . .
>
> Likewise, Saur – the third biggest water firm – has in the last two years withdrawn from a contract in Mozambique while Vivendi, the second biggest player in the world, has expressed

concern about the financial viability of servicing the poor in developing countries, preferring locations where customers or governments can guarantee payment.[20]

According to David Hall of the Public Services International Research Unit in London, Suez suffered protests and criticism in Casablanca and Jakarta. In December 2002 massive losses forced it to pull out of Manila and in January 2003 it was pushed out of Atlanta, the largest water commercialisation in the USA. The company's chief executive, Gerard Mestrallet, committed to 'reduce investments' in the Third World. In the event of further failure, as witnessed in Manila and Argentina, of nations paying agreed profits in hard currency, Suez would 'prepare to depart'.[21]

World Bank records of private sector investment in Third World utilities show a collapse in 2001, to half the $120 billion level of 1997. 'We have agreed to take the commercial risk, but it is the political risks that kill you,' admits Mike Curtin of Bechtel Group which suffered large losses in the April 2000 anti-privatisation revolts in Bolivia. 'My fear is that the private sector is being driven out of the water sector.'[22]

The reports are the same in South Africa. According to the closing paragraphs in an International Consortium for Investigative Journalism study by Jacques Pauw, privatisation has run out of steam:

> Sitting in his office outside Johannesburg Development Bank building, James Leigland – the man who brokered the privatisation deal in Nelspruit – is convinced that the process has ground to a halt.
>
> 'Further privatisation of water? It's not going to happen in the near future. There will be no new Nelspruits or Dolphin Coasts. There is too much of a downside,' he said.
>
> Leigland represents the Municipal Infrastructure Investment Unit, which the government created in 1997 to 'encourage and optimise private sector investments in local authority services.' He praised the local achievements of Biwater and Greater Nelspruit Utility Company as numerous and said that bringing water to the poor in Nelspruit has been very successful. 'This would not have been possible without privatisation. We couldn't have done it without Biwater.' But he acknowledged the concession is 'very fragile.' Private companies were anxious to get a foothold in the country, Leigland explained. 'They are still very eager, and I don't think they have been totally discouraged. But there is a lot of mistrust towards them.'
>
> Indeed, the foreign multinationals appear to be reassessing their position in southern Africa. Saur has withdrawn from

Mozambique and Zimbabwe. Suez has not appealed the cancellation of its Nkonkobe contract in the Eastern Cape. Biwater says it is committed to Nelspruit, but is not seeking any further concessions. Thames Water has no presence in the country. Vivendi's one executive seems wary of the situation.

'To be very honest, the municipal market is not ready,' said Picaud, the managing director of Vivendi Water in South Africa.[23]

The Washington Consensus returns to water

There were also awesome countervailing pressures, including attempts by Kasrils and Muller to obfuscate the issues with political rhetoric. According to a Kyoto report-back by Maj Fiil-Flynn of the Ralph Nader group, Public Citizen,

> South Africa had a huge presence at the World Water Forum. Ronnie Kasrils told the audience on several occasions that he was a freedom fighter who would do no wrong to his people. Mike Muller tried to get everyone to shout 'Viva Water.' After three attempts and NGOs shouting 'Phansi Mike Muller!,' he gave up.
>
> The good news is that the civil society groups/labour broke the corporate consensus on privatisation in the forum by breaking the meetings with in depth questions and details from real life. The bad news is that they probably won't listen.[24]

An emblematic tactic deployed by Muller at Kyoto was to claim that 'NGOs want us to stay poor, not allowing developing countries to build dams'.[25] Indeed, the broader pro-dam and pro-private sector strategy of the 20-person delegation from Pretoria and other South African state bodies coincided with that of the corporate 'water mafia' in several ways.

At least five powerful pro-corporate lobbying groups, and individuals such as Michel Camdessus, had emerged over the previous decade and played major roles at Johannesburg and Kyoto.[26] First, the Global Water Partnership is a Swedish-based group created by the World Bank, UNDP and the Swedish aid agency, SIDA, in 1996. Its members subscribe to the water-commodification principles established at Dublin and Rio. Core constituencies are multilateral development banks and international financial institutions, the bilateral aid community, and private water companies.

Second, the Marseilles-based World Water Council was founded in 1996 by representatives of Suez, the Canadian aid agency CIDA, and the Egyptian government. Its 300 members are largely private companies, government ministries, and international organisations.

Third, the International Private Water Association (IPWA), formed in 1999, was soon supported by 'Advisory Members' that included representatives of the World Bank group, the US Credit Export Agency and Overseas Private Investment Corporation and the European Bank for Reconstruction and Development. According to investigators from the Corporate Europe Observatory,

> IPWA has decided to modify their blunt pro-privatisation rhetoric and embrace the new buzzword engineered by more sophisticated corporate players such as the World Business Council for Sustainable Development, namely 'public-private partnerships.' (IPWA director) Kathy Shandling explains: 'We don't use the word privatisation. Not anymore. We use public-private partnerships. Privatisation is a bad word . . .'
>
> IPWA fails to admit that there are fundamental problems with the private sector record in delivering water, particularly in the South. The disastrous mismanagement by US-based Bechtel Corporation in the Bolivian city, Cochabamba, was merely a 'miscomunication problem.' It was 'a project not as structured as it should have been,' Shandling claims. The many broken promises by Suez (including Manila and Atlanta) are also dismissed as insignificant. On the large price hikes imposed by water TNCs following privatisation with often dramatic social impacts, Shandling cynically comments: 'People who are suddenly getting water bills who didn't get them before are saying, "Water is an act of God. I shouldn't have to pay for it." '[27]

Fourth, the World Bank continued to promote privatisation, even in its 2004 *World Development Report*.[28] A study by the International Consortium of Investigative Journalists in February 2003 found that over a dozen years, the Bank lent $20 billion to water-supply projects and imposed privatisation as a loan condition in a third of the transactions.[29] By late 2003, the Bank had returned to 'high-risk, high-return' mega-project proposals, including big dams, which was quickly criticised as disastrous by three green groups, Environmental Defence, Friends of the Earth and International Rivers Network.[30]

Fifth, the World Panel on Financing Infrastructure that reported to the World Water Forum in Kyoto was chaired by former IMF managing director Camdessus during 2002–03, and brought together the Global Water Partnership, presidents of major multilateral development banks (IADB, ADB, EBRD, WB), representatives of the

IFC, Citibank, Lazard Freres, the US Ex-Im Bank, private water companies (Suez, Thames Water), state elites (from Egypt, France, Ivory Coast, Mexico, and Pakistan) and two NGOs (Transparency International and WaterAid).[31] According to International Rivers Network, 'Most of the 20 panel members are senior officials from the world's major development banks, private lenders and water companies. All 20 panel members are men.'[32]

Camdessus recommended that the World Bank and aid agencies increase guarantees and other public subsidies for private water investors, and 'resume lending' for 'major' dam and water transfer projects. Camdessus called for $180 billion in capital expenditure, even though a sixth would be earmarked for investments aimed at meeting drinking water, sanitation and other hygiene needs. Public Services International, whose union affiliates represent 20 million members, declared that Camdessus had produced

> pretty much what we expected: an attempt to resuscitate the ailing fortunes of the international water corporations ... The bankers' panel pursues the goal of having private corporations manage and profit from delivering the world's water. They want these companies to serve the world's cities, and to build more dams and reservoirs. They present a plan to grab much of the increase in foreign aid promised since the 9-11 disaster, when the link was made between terror and poverty ... (yet) there is no attempt to address the issue of how the international community can effectively cross-subsidise the provision of clean water for the poor ...
>
> The panel's most concrete proposals are to create two new financial mechanisms to protect the water corporations: a 'Devaluation Liquidity Backstopping Facility' (paid for by whom, and how?), to protect the multinational water corporations' from losses due to currency devaluation, so devastating to Ondeo in Manila and Buenos Aires, and problematic for Thames in Jakarta; and a 'Revolving Fund' to pay for the 'large fixed cost of preparing Private Sector Participation contracts and tenders.' This would likely go to international lawyers and consultants to write dense contracts to protect the corporations, which most municipalities will be unable to interpret or enforce.[33]

Camdessus' financing report attracted protest from water advocacy groups at Kyoto. Former water minister Asmal, a patron of the Global Water Partnership, accused Camdessus of 'inadequate research and a lack of guidance', because of the relegation of the 1998–2001 World

Commission on Dams (chaired by Asmal) to a dismissive footnote. Asmal wrote:

> I am astounded and disappointed that the World Panel's report chooses to effectively ignore the framework proposed by the World Commission on Dams . . . For an esteemed panel to effectively write off the WCD, whose core recommendations have been endorsed by many of its member organisations, is quite remarkable and raises concerns about the value of the report. Failing to address this point effectively takes us back many years.[34]

Camdessus claimed that the WSSD 'signified an important change of mood' *in favour* of large dams, and that 'prior to this an opposing view, reached among much controversy, was encapsulated in the [WCD report]'. The Berkeley-based NGO International Rivers Network pointed out that the 'WSSD Plan of Implementation does not contain the word "storage" or "dam" and mentions hydro only once'.[35] Like Camdessus, Dwaf official Mike Muller claimed 'that the pendulum had swung from an anti-dam position to a position where dams are regarded as important for economic development'.[36]

When Kasrils endorsed Camdessus' mission, it was a repeat of conflict with Asmal over interpreting the application of the WCD report to southern Africa. Kasrils explicitly downplayed the WCD guidelines in 2001.[37] Asmal threatened to resign from the Partnership, but no one seemed to pay much notice. Instead, momentum continued swinging back to the Washington Consensus, with an important pro-privatisation backlash recorded at the June 2003 G8 summit in Evian. Agence France Press reported,

> In a town famous for its springs, leaders of the powerful G8 group of nations Monday agreed an action plan promising access to vital water supplies, but it was immediately denounced by aid groups . . .
>
> The plan contains no figures. The commitments are ill-defined. There is no mention of earlier suggestions of doubling development aid. Above all, charged Barry Coates, director of the World Development Movement which has been monitoring the water crisis, 'it is an ideologically driven push for privatization . . .'
>
> The plan was adopted as around 200 anti-G8 protestors demonstrated outside the Geneva headquarters of the World Trade Organisation demanding a halt to privatisation of water supplies. They waved banners declaring 'Our water, our life, not for sale' and 'Free water for all.'[38]

Despite concessions by Kasrils, Muller and the South African government, numerous eco-social grievances remained outstanding in global, regional, national and local settings. The most important were ongoing disconnections, installation of pre-paid water meters, insufficient cross subsidies and a lack of official commitment to demand-side management, instead of expensive supply enhancements.

The international trend towards the commodification of water would remain a significant problem, as reflected in *The Economist* magazine's mid-2003 sector survey, which warmly praised Kasrils: 'Throughout history, and especially over the past century, [water] has been ill-governed and, above all, collossally underpriced.' Identifying this problem naturally begets this solution: 'The best way to deal with water is to price it more sensibly,' for 'although water is special, both its provision and its use will respond to market signals.' In particular, 'Charges should be set, as far as possible, to cover full costs, including environmental ones.' In rural areas where there is competition among farmers for irrigation water, 'the best solution is water trading', and as for the problem of delivering water to the poor, 'the best way of solving it is to treat water pretty much as a business like any other.'[39]

A final instance of public international debate over local water apartheid illustrates how far Pretoria lurched right, while talking left.

The power of international elite opinion

The year 2003 witnessed a barrage of water coverage by the media, most of which exposed the crisis of disconnections. The result was to undo the public relations offensive that Kasrils and Muller had launched at the WSSD and taken through to Kyoto.

Intense grassroots critiques of water disconnections, pre-paid meters and creeping privatisation emerged from many communities. Through South African Indymedia, Francois L'Ecuyer reported on the February 2003 murder of Emily Lengolo, in Johannesburg's distant southern township of Orange Farm:

> The Orange Farm Water Crisis Committee (OWCC) was created by local activists, who started mobilising the community. There were public meetings and mass rallies, but also taxi and church gatherings were used to inform people about the reality of pre-paid meters. And graffiti. Lots of graffiti . . .
>
> When OWCC activists heard that Ronnie Kasrils, the Minister of Water Affairs, was coming to Orange Farm on the 1st of October 2002, to officially launch the installation of pre-paid water meters all over the township, they didn't miss the occasion. Strong from

their mass mobilisation during the W$$D, they organised a mass meeting on Sunday 29th of September, where 3 000 people showed up. The message sent to the ANC councilor, who was almost attacked by the community when he appeared at the meeting, was clear: Orange Farm citizens don't want pre-paid water. 'Free Water for All!' or 'Break the Meter – Enjoy the Water!,' as graffiti says in Orange Farm.

On the 8th of February 2003, 61-year-old OWCC activist Emily Lengolo paid with her life, her fight against water privatisation. At about 1:00 AM, two men broke into her house and shot her twice, killing her instantly. The two men didn't take anything from the house before escaping, neither did they touch four other family members who were present in the house and who heard, just before the fatal shots: 'This is the one we are looking for.'[40]

Local and international reports in subsequent months highlighted the plight of other communities. A front-page *New York Times* report on 29 May 2003 seemed to be the straw that broke Kasrils' back. Reporter Ginger Thompson conducted detailed research in the cholera-ridden township of Shakashead near Dolphin Coast, poorly served by the Paris-based Saur company's 25-year outsourcing contract, as well as in Orange Farm. Excerpts show why Kasrils and Muller had been trying to deceive international audiences:

> Not long after the country's first democratic government came to power in 1994, putting an end to white minority rule, the new government enshrined the right to 'sufficient food and water' in its Constitution, and pledged to make water and sanitation available to every citizen by the end of 2010.
>
> At the same time, the government also began to shift more of the financial burden of those promises to a population in which at least one-third of people live on less than $2 a day. Officials urged municipal water utilities to adopt 'cost recovery' policies that require them at least to break even, if not turn a profit.
>
> Municipalities have begun working to turn debt-ridden and inefficient water utilities into profitable operations that could attract private investment. A handful have already granted long-term management concessions to private multinationals . . .
>
> 'Privatisation is a new kind of apartheid,' said Richard Mokolo, leader of the Crisis Water Committee, which was formed to resist the privatisation effort in a township called Orange Farm, 25 miles south of Johannesburg. 'Apartheid separated whites from blacks. Privatisation separates the rich from the poor.'

South African officials say the change in policies has helped expand water services to 8 million of 13 million people who did not have water when apartheid ended. But the statistics have not added up to progress in many poor communities, which have won their first reliable water services but now struggle to pay for them.

The issue of access to services has become an explosive new cause in the same urban townships and rural squatter camps that were principal battlegrounds in the fight against apartheid. During the World Summit on Sustainable Development last August, thousands marched from the tin shacks of Alexandra past the elegant mansions of Sandton to protest, among other things, water and electricity cutoffs and evictions. Their cry: 'Water for the thirsty. Light for the people. Homes for the homeless . . .'

Leaders in sprawling townships including Soweto, Alexandra and Orange Farm have encouraged people not to pay electricity and water bills. They have organised teams of bootleg plumbers and electricians to reconnect utilities when they are cut off. Political rallies and demonstrations have turned into street fights.

The highest costs to poor communities have come in the form of disease and mass disconnections . . . A survey by the government's Human Sciences Research Council for the independent Municipal Services Project found that up to 10 million people have been affected by water cutoffs since the end of white-minority rule.

David McDonald, co-director of the Municipal Services Project, said the government's own reports have portrayed a 'crisis of serious proportions.' One report, he said, indicated that some 700 000 people were affected by water cutoffs in the final months of 2001. Meanwhile, he said, surveys showed some 1.3 million people had their electricity cut off, including some 20 000 customers each month in Soweto.

In a telephone interview and e-mail exchanges, a high-level water official rebutted the water cutoff estimates, saying they were 'based on a deliberate distortion of very limited survey information.'

Mr McDonald countered: 'As far as I'm concerned, you can cut our estimates of water cutoffs in half. The figures are still a serious indictment of post-apartheid cost recovery policies . . .'

Three years ago, Johannesburg Water signed a more limited management contract with the France-based conglomerate Suez.

Among the newest efforts by Johannesburg Water has been the installation of prepaid water meters in townships around the country's business capital. The first prepaid meters were installed last year in Orange Farm, and led to the formation of the Orange Farm Crisis Water Committee, the group headed by Mr Mokolo.

Under the prepaid system, to begin next month and to be expanded to other Johannesburg townships in the next couple of years, families will only get as much water as they can pay for in advance. Their payments will be recorded on digital discs, about as big as a quarter. The disc fits inside the water meter, and activates the taps.

Jean-Pierre Mas, the operations executive at Johannesburg Water, said prepay meters would allow customers to use only the amount of water they could afford, and help the utility avoid clashes over cutoffs.

'Under the old system, people were billed for far less water than they consumed, and still they were not paying their bills,' Mr. Mas said. 'They had no incentive to lower their consumption. They had no incentives to pay. If we don't do anything about it, it will be an unsustainable setup. We will have a financial disaster.'

On the dirt streets of Orange Farm, where state-of-the-art water meters have been installed in front of lopsided tin shacks, people foresee a human disaster. Because of its location, it is known as the 'deep south.' However, it seems a fitting nickname in other ways.

The township has become a microcosm of the nation's most pressing social problems, including high rates of unemployment, violent crime and HIV-infections.

Officials at Johannesburg Water acknowledged that in communities like these, billing people for water has been like squeezing water from a stone. In addition to the limited resources, a culture of nonpayment lingers from the years when people refused to pay utility bills, usually a flat fee for water and electricity, in support of boycotts against the apartheid regime.

'The problem is not that we do not want to pay for water,' said Hilda Mkwanza, a 45-year-old mother of six who lives in Orange Farm. 'The problem is we cannot pay.'

Interviews with her and other Orange Farm women, who live by doing other people's laundry, said they barely had enough money to pay for food and school fees. Many have prepaid electricity meters in their homes, and they say their families end up in the dark for several days each month.

Mr. Mokolo, a veteran of the anti-apartheid movement, urges people not to pay. 'The government promised us that water is a basic right,' he said. 'But now they are telling us our rights are for sale.'[41]

In a letter to the *Times* the following week, Kasrils replied dishonestly: 'We seek, in a practical, nonideological way, sustainable solutions. We work in partnership with those who can help achieve our objectives. The result is not millions of people cut off.' Yet, a 2001 survey showed an estimated 10 million people experienced cutoffs. He described the pre-paid water meter system as 'an example of how South Africa is harnessing home-grown technology for development'.[42] A dishonest reply, because such meters were introduced *en masse* in Britain during the 1990s, and by the end of the decade had been banned, because they presented a public health risk. This kind of sophistry reveals the pressure Kasrils was under, but that was nothing compared to people like Mokolo, whose life was periodically threatened, and who remained on the front lines of the Jo'burg water war.

Urban entrepreneurialism and water

We return to Kasrils' most urgent challenge: halting the disconnections of water that resulted from people's inability to pay high bills. The sabotage of the ANC's 'free basic water' promise was evident in revised July 2001 water tariffs following the December 2000 municipal elections. Those tariffs provided a very small free lifeline, 6 000 litres per household per month, followed by a very steep, convex curve, such that the next consumption block became unaffordable, leading to even higher rates of water disconnections in many settings. The 6 000 litres represent just two toilet flushes a day for a household of eight, for those lucky enough to have flush toilets. It leaves no additional water to drink, wash with, or clean clothes or the house.

Optimally, a different strategy would provide a larger free lifeline tariff, ideally on a per-person, not per-household basis, and then rise in a concave manner to penalise luxury consumption (Figure 7). Johannesburg's tariff was set by the council with help from Suez, and began in July 2001 with a high price increase for the second block of consumption. Two years later, the price of that second block was raised 32%, with a 10% overall increase, putting an enormous burden on poor households which used more than 6 000 litres each month. The rich got off with relatively small increases and a flat tariff after 40 kl/hh/month, which did nothing to encourage water conservation.

To fully comprehend water apartheid one has to travel from Johannesburg's local circumstances up to the global scale to consider neoliberal capitalism's basic processes, and then back to local struggles. The primary reason for squeezing water supply to the poor is to keep prices for rich people and big business as low as possible.

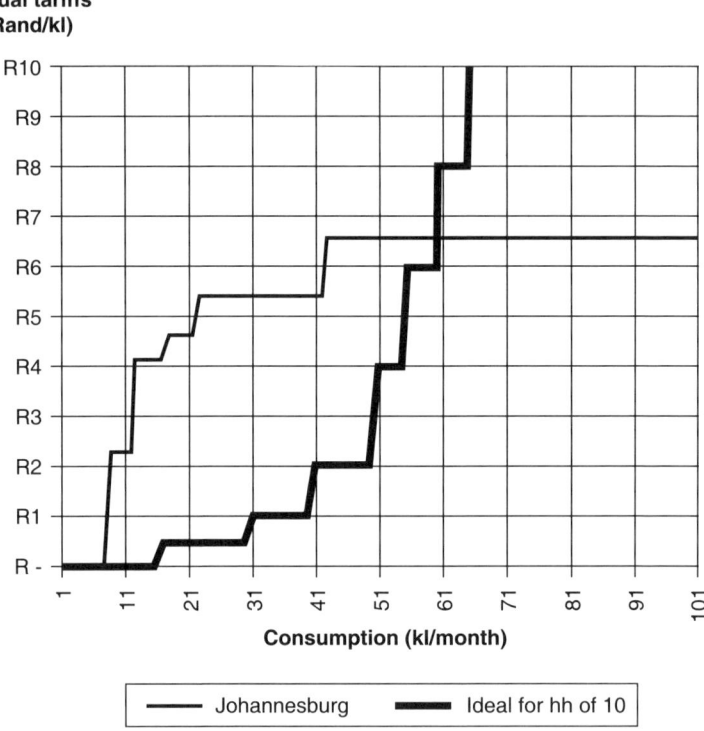

Figure 7: Divergent water pricing strategies, Johannesburg (2001) v. ideal tariff for large household.
Source: Johannesburg Water (thin) and own projection (thick)

In this sense, the logic of the Washington Consensus was superimposed upon the ANC's free water policy.

Official documents reflect the debate: 'The World Bank has worked with the City [of Johannesburg] (CoJ) in recent years to support its efforts in local economic development and improving service delivery,' according to Bank staff and consultants. Early interventions included a 1993 study of services backlogs and the 1994 Municipal Infrastructure Investment Framework. More recently, according to the Bank, Johannesburg's vision strategy document for 2030 'draws largely on the empirical findings of a series of World Bank reports on local economic development produced in partnership with the CoJ during 1999–2002, and places greater emphasis on economic development. It calls for Johannesburg to become *a world-class business location.*' In turn, the Bank insists, businesses, not low-income consumers, should be allowed benefits that might later trickle down: 'The ability of the city to provide services is related to its tax revenue base or growth. *The CoJ does not consider service delivery to be its greatest challenge to becoming a better city*... The city finds further support for its Vision in a survey that suggests that citizens are more concerned about joblessness than socio-economic backlogs.' This fib is addressed below. Bank staff cited 'the World Bank's local economic development methodology developed for the CoJ in 1999', which 'sought to conceptualise an optimal role for *a fiscally decentralised CoJ* in the form of a regulator that would seek to alleviate poverty... through job creation by creating *an enabling business environment for private sector investment* and economic growth in Johannesburg' (emphasis added).[43]

This short-term commitment to what planners term 'urban entrepreneurialism' negates poor people's needs for effective municipal services, paid for through cross-subsidies from business. Johannesburg would become less competitive as a base within global capitalism if higher tariffs were imposed. By December 1996, Chippy Olver, then the government's chief infrastructure official (and later the director-general of environment), told the *Mail & Guardian* why he and Department of Finance officials refused to consider widescale redistributive national tariffs through cross-subsidies mandated in the 1994 Reconstruction and Development Programme: 'If we increase the price of electricity to users like Alusaf, their products will become uncompetitive and that will affect our balance of payments... international capital holds sway as we come to the end of the 20th century.'[44]

To what extent did international capital hold sway in Johannesburg when it came to providing water to the vast majority of the city's residents?

The metropolitan area has a population of 3.2 million, according to the October 2001 census,[45] of whom 72% are black 'Africans', 6.5% 'coloured' people, 3.7% 'Asians' and 17% 'white' people.[46] Thanks to the historic uneven development of Johannesburg, inequality and poverty are reflected in water infrastructure and services. Yet like the Bank, the municipality offers this denial: 'Only 16% of households [receive] services below the minimum statutory standards. Services is not the greatest challenge facing Johannesburg in its drive to become a "better" city.'[47]

Low standards for informal settlements were a conscious municipal policy adopted in the city's 1995 Strategic Initiative, before the first democratic local government elections: 'The service level for this purpose had been set at one standpipe per twenty dwellings for the water supply and one chemical toilet per seven dwellings for sanitation. The emergency measures have not been phased out as anticipated.'[48] The failure to phase out the emergency standard services was conceded in 1999, but by 2003 there was still no change.

Indeed, given not just access but also municipal services quality (e.g., regularity and pressure), many residents argue that services are the 'greatest challenge' to living a decent life in Johannesburg. There is only one recent (2000) official survey that systematically measures citizen satisfaction with water services, and it is not flattering: 'There is a strong indication that residents from all areas are beginning to feel a heightened sense of frustration and decreased sense of control that they have over their communities and the city due to perceptions of the council's decreasing ability to manage the services under their jurisdiction.'[49] Among their top five complaints, residents listed electricity (48%), water (42%) and toilets (33%) as three of the five worst problems. The other two were the city's failure to create jobs and maintain health clinics. For black African Johannesburg residents, the figures were, respectively, 58%, 53% and 45%, ranking as the first, second and fourth worst problems.[50]

Most dissatisfied residents live in low-income townships. The municipality divides Johannesburg's low-income areas into two types, formal and informal. The formal settlements, including Soweto, Alexandra, Ivory Park and Orange Farm have 192 000 dwellings. There are 83 informal settlements in greater Johannesburg, with 189 000 dwellings.[51] Most informal settlements lack piped water or sanitation, electricity and other municipal services such as solid waste removal, stormwater drains, street lights, fire and emergency services, libraries or recreation facilities. Johannesburg's servicing of these areas has followed global-scale processes associated with intensified competitiveness and decentralisation of services.

A key intermediary is Suez affiliate, Johannesburg Water (JW), an arms-length 'private company with limited liability'. It serves as the operating vehicle for both the City of Johannesburg and Suez.[52] JW purchases nearly a billion rands worth of water from the Rand Water Board each year, and records turnover of R2.1 billion. More than 9 500 km of water pipes and 9 000 km of sewers, 86 reservoirs and 33 water towers lead to six treatment plants. The company was established on 1 January 2001, after a sale of assets (R1.6 billion) and debtors books (R573 million). The company pays Johannesburg R60 million interest and R40 million redemption on the purchase loan each year. Capital investment for 2002 was R187 million, but this commitment fell 38% in 2003 to R116 million.

The mandate the company has is 'to provide an efficient and cost effective service for the city to attract economic growth and development. JW must provide sufficient lifeline and subsidised tariffs at the lower level of consumption to maintain social stability among the populace.'[53] JW has 550 000 domestic, commercial and industrial customers, but only takes billing responsibility for the top 15 000 consumers, leaving the rest to the city. The deal with Paris-based Suez lasts until 2006, when it could be renewed for more than two decades.

Advocates of a neoliberal approach to water provision and pricing, ranging from World Bank advisors to JW's management, have introduced several unsound features. JW's pricing strategies fail to incorporate eco-social factors, including public health, gender equity, the environment or economic benefits such as employment generation or stimulation of small-scale enterprises. Johannesburg's narrow financial-rate-of-return policy fragments city services, disengaging civil servants in the water or electricity or waste-removal sectors from those in the health sector, for instance.

Governance deficits have also been serious. JW refused to provide Wits University researcher Ebrahim Harvey and his allies at the Freedom of Expression Institute with information on their contract bid or the controversial Orange Farm pilot projects, a refusal Harvey and the Institute are contesting legally. In addition to the debates over pricing and disconnections, there are three other areas in which problems can be observed: inadequate existing standards of water and sanitation services; installation of pre-paid water meters; and new sanitation systems.

Growing dissatisfaction with water services was recorded in the Johannesburg Metropolitan Council Attitude Survey in 2000. The nearly one million people living in informal settlements continued to experience inequity in the delivery of water: 65% used communal standpipes, 14% yard standpipes and 20% water tankers. For sanitation, 52% had only pit latrines, 45% chemical toilets, 2% communal flush toilets and 1% ablution blocks.[54] The threat of service disconnections due to poverty was severe for those with their own water taps.

Because disconnected water pipes were increasingly (unlawfully) reconnected by the Anti-Privatisation Forum and informal township plumbers, thousands of pre-paid meters were installed in Johannesburg. The R342 million, five-year operation, termed 'Gcin'amanzi', Zulu for 'conserve water', was aimed at 'self-disconnection' as the solution to durable non-payment problems in Soweto, Orange Farm, Ivory Park and Alexandra. Identified as a key Mayoral Strategic Priority, the operation aimed to lower the 'unaccounted for water' rate in Soweto from 62% to the standard 21% water loss for the city's non-township neighbourhoods. Soweto is responsible for a R158 million annual loss, with 68 billion litres of water each year unaccounted for, compared to a total Johannesburg metropolitan area flow-through of 230 billion litres a year.[55] The fight against pre-paid meters began in Orange Farm in 2002 and by 2003 created havoc in the Phiri section of Soweto, where repeated arrests did not succeed in normalising the JW strategy.

Another Gcin'amanzi strategy addressed sanitation. JW's objection to installing full sewage is the ongoing operating expense, the 12 litres per flush of conventional toilets. A somewhat lower capital cost for JW's 'shallow sewer' reflects the lack of water inflow piping. Instead of cisterns, buckets are used for flushes to limit water flow-through. However, in the field of sanitation, money saved in one area may be lost elsewhere. To take one example, the installation of Ventilated Improved Pitlatrines (VIPs) was agreed upon by Johannesburg's Transformation Lekgotla in June 1999 without public participation. But in budgeting R15 million worth of pit latrines from privatisation revenues, instead of water-borne sewage, which would save money for the soon-to-be corporatised JW, city officials failed to factor in the environmental or public health implications of E. coli flooding through the Jukskei River and into the Sandton water table.[56]

Notwithstanding the dangers, according to JW business plans, the company intends to spend R16 million constructing 6 500 VIPs from 2003 to 2006 in several informal settlements. The shallow sewer system is also attractive to the company, because the maintenance costs are transferred to 'condominium' residential units. Residents are instructed on how to clean the system every three months in a manner that threatens public health. The most extraordinary feature is that pipes are regularly blocked with excrement, *not by accident but as a matter of design*. JW provides 'Maintenance Procedure' instructions for the unfortunate residents:

- Open all inspection chambers
- Wear gloves
- Remove all solids and waste from the inspection chambers
- Do a mirror test for each chamber-to-chamber section
- If waste material is found in a section, bring in the tube from the upstream inspection chamber until it comes into contact with the obstruction
- *Block off the outlet from the downstream inspection chamber with a screen that allows water to pass through but not solids* [italics added]
- Push the tube until the material is moved to the downstream inspection chamber
- Wear gloves and remove waste material by hand

- Pour a large quantity of water through the section between the two inspection chambers and check for cleaning
- Repeat the mirror test
- Close the inspection chambers
- Inspection chambers must be kept closed at all times except during cleaning operations.[57]

Controversies over similar features of Johannesburg-style water apartheid are increasingly common in sites of corporatisation and commodification in Latin America, Africa, Asia and even advanced industrial countries. The most fundamental contradiction can now be addressed: the desire to limit water cross-subsidisation by corporations and rich people to low-income consumers. The global-local connection is not merely, as Olver suggested, about the importance of 'competitiveness' for Johannesburg businesses, hence their desire for lower water prices. By buying into the logic of global neoliberalism, Pretoria reproduces and amplifies class apartheid in its municipalities.

The distortion of market prices by cross-subsidy is also a deterrent to further water privatisation, as World Bank water official John Roome was quick to point out in his 1995 advice to then minister Asmal. Roome's power-point slideshow, which he later claimed was 'instrumental' in a 'radical revision' of Asmal's water pricing policy,[58] argued that municipal privatisation contracts 'would be much harder to establish', if poor consumers had the expectation of getting something for nothing. If consumers didn't pay, Roome continued, Asmal needed a 'credible threat of cutting service'.[59]

The logic played out over the subsequent eight years. The 2000–03 move to commodify Johannesburg's water through outsourcing to an international water corporation brought several new profitable techniques: revised tariffs that appeared to provide free water, but did not; pre-paid meters aimed at self-disconnections; and no-flush sanitation of an appallingly low standard.

The consequent eco-social tensions, essentially over whether water services should reflect local values or global aspirations, grew deeper within the city's soul. Binghampton University sociologist Martin Murray wrote: 'The evolving architectural vernacular of Johannesburg has always reflected the self-conscious desire of urban planners, design specialists, and corporate clients to favourably position the city in the vaunted global economy by emulating, and sometimes even crassly imitating, the built environment of the European and American metropolitan core.'[60]

What is new over the past decade or so of intensified global apartheid, is the extent to which not just above-ground architectural form and urban design reflect the influences of international business, or local business with international ambitions, in edge-cities like Sandton – but also, below-ground in townships like Soweto and Alexandra. Infrastructure planning and management have followed Third World patterns at the behest of international financial agencies and multinational corporations.

Will Pretoria keep disconnecting water?

The water sector encapsulates so many aspects of the struggle against global apartheid, including Pretoria's ambiguous role, that the only appropriate way to conclude is with fierce rhetoric, from government and social movements, reflecting how much is at stake. For example, in his June 2003 parliamentary budget speech, Kasrils tackled the 'phony revolutionaries' and 'North American populists' (myself included) with sarcasm and xenophobia:

> Unhappy that their status as the true revolutionary leaders is not recognised by a democratic non-racial South African government, they ally with and encourage forces that would destroy it. Their slogan 'smash the meter, enjoy the water' tells it all. These sad men find company with Afro-cynics in the *New York Times* and the *Observer*, who also know much better than South Africans how to run a country. They accept claims of rampant privatisation, although only five municipalities, 3% of the total, have chosen a private alternative. They accept claims that cost recovery causes cholera, although cholera occurs mainly where people do not have metered services...
>
> The concerted campaign against South Africa reflects our refusal to accept external prescriptions of 'public good, private bad'... In many communities, services are still irregular and unreliable – often because some households draw freely through illegal connections, abetted by the mindless 'anti-privatisation' populists.[61]

Kasrils' outburst needs to be seen in context of the attack on the 'ultraleft', described in the next chapter. It may appear that Kasrils is infuriated by alleged 'Afro-pessimists', who in reality are reputable journalists with no bone to pick with the ANC, as well as international academics. McDonald responded:

> Kasrils demanded that we retract our claims on the number of cutoffs and called us 'phony revolutionaries' for 'misleading

working people.' This very public and bombastic outburst does nothing to alter our original position . . . but it does demand a reply.

First, the statistics. The ten million figure was taken from a representative national survey of approximately 2 500 people in July 2001. Conducted by the Human Sciences Research Council (HSRC), in collaboration with the MSP, one of the questions we asked is whether interviewees had ever experienced water cutoffs due to non-payment of bills. Thirteen percent of respondents said 'yes.'

Water cutoffs affect the entire household, and since large, low-income households are most likely to be affected, we extrapolated the data to get a more realistic picture of the number of people impacted by disconnections. This methodology was explained in our report and has been available to Dwaf for over a year. At no point has Dwaf asked us to discuss or explain these statistics.[62]

If there remains any question about the statistics,[63] it is useful to consider the only other source of national data on water disconnections: the Department of Provincial and Local Government's (DPLG's) 'Project Viability', which requires officials from most municipalities to report every three months on city finances and credit control measures. By late 2003, the latest national disconnection statistics available from DPLG were from the fourth quarter, 2001. That report noted that of 133 000 disconnections, after three months only 50 000 people were able to pay their bills: a very low 38% reconnection rate.[64] Assuming merely five people per low-income household, and 24 quarters from 1997–2002 (the key period of pro-disconnection policy under consideration), this crude extrapolation also derives 10 million total net disconnections.[65] To make matters worse, the DPLG numbers of disconnected households exclude the nine million rural people who were given water under the full cost-recovery regime put in place by Dwaf with World Bank help in 1994. But, a quarter to a half of those people suffer because the projects no longer work.

The debate continued,[66] until Kasrils angrily jibed:

> The international radical careerists are desperately upset by our approach. They hate to see South Africa taking its place as a world leader, without the benefit of their distinguished political advice. So they go out of their way to rubbish us among their lecture tour organisers and publishers in North America and Europe.

> But we cannot allow ourselves to be distracted by these performances. We will continue to focus our energies on the practical programmes and proposals that we are implementing. We intend to complete our extraordinarily successful programme of getting infrastructure in the ground for those rural people who still do not have access to basic water supplies.[67]

Two days later, the 'extraordinarily successful' rural water supply projects were unveiled in *Business Day* as a flop. HSRC researcher David Hemson, whom Kasrils had praised a few weeks earlier in his address to parliament (and who was also associated with the Municipal Services Project), conducted a study of rural water projects in KwaZulu-Natal. Kasrils had commissioned the work and announced it in his 2001 budget speech. Hemson found that 74% of the projects were 'working at one level or another'. However, using the minimalist definition of water access mandated in the Reconstruction and Development Programme, 57% of projects were either 'not working' or 'problematic', because 'water provision was below required RDP levels'.[68] Those minimum levels, 25 litres per person per day within 200 meters of a household, are *short-term* (years unspecified). Using the *medium-term* objective of 50–60 litres per person per day on site, which would be a logical objective after nine years of democracy, it is fair to estimate that fewer than 5% of the projects were working.

This review of the discourses and realities surrounding global and local water inequities reveals intensely competitive ideologies at play, not to mention hard financial calculations. Kasrils and Muller utilised Third World nationalist rhetoric when defending themselves against the exposure of human rights violations, but did not shift from applied neoliberalism: disconnections, pro-business tariff pricing, pre-paid meters and water commercialisation. They adopted a global Post-Washington Consensus *rhetorical* strategy that requested the Bretton Woods Institutions, donor agencies and Paris and London firms to retreat from their full cost-recovery and privatisation mantra.

On the opposing team, water affiliates of the global justice movements discovered that notwithstanding occasional moments of overlapping critique shared with Pretoria, power relations were determined by material struggles. Those struggles were not leading to unity, but instead division, between the Post-Washington, Third World nationalist and global justice advocates. Activist frustration with the World Water Forum, the WSSD Waterdome and other water talk-shops led progressive forces to establish a People's World Water Forum in early 2004, prior to the World Social Forum in Mumbai. It is in the water sector's independent left that the future lies.

Notes

1. For an excellent documentary film version of the WSSD debate see, for example, Cashdan, B. (2002), *Down to Earth: Water*, SABC ChannelAfrica documentary, 6 September. Local issues are covered in Bond, *Unsustainable South Africa*, Chapters Three–Five. Progressive recent international books on water which link supply-side and demand-side issues include Barlow, M. and T. Clarke (2002), *Blue Gold: The Battle Against Corporate Theft of the World's Water*, Toronto, Stoddard; Shiva, V. (2002), *Water Wars: Privatization, Pollution and Profit*, Boston, South End Press; and Petrella, R. (2001), *The Water Manifesto: Arguments for a World Water Contract*, London, Zed Books.
2. For documentation, see http://www.queensu.ca/msp under media, where many of the articles are posted.
3. South African Civil Society Water Caucus (2002), 'Press Release', Pretoria, 5 August.
4. *The Star*, 3 September 2003. The actual number was probably somewhat lower.
5. Social Movements Indaba (2002), 'Anti-Privatisation Activists Expose Corporate Takeover of W$$D at Waterdome', Johannesburg, 3 September.
6. Shiva, V. (2002), 'Savings Lives or Destroying Lives? World Bank sells Synthetic Soap and Cleanliness to Kerala the Land of Health and Hygiene', Water Liberation Movement Press Statement, New Delhi, 17 September.
7. *The Star*, 3 September 2003.
8. Muller, M. (2003), 'Water 2003 – What Should be Done: Lessons from Johannesburg and Pointers for the Future', Pretoria, Department of Water Affairs and Forestry.
9. Muller, 'Water 2003'.
10. Table constructed by author from interviews of Water Caucus participants.
11. Kasrils, R. (2000), 'A Desiccated Vision of Water Delivery', *Business Day*, 22 August.
12. Kasrils, 'A Desiccated Vision'.
13. Right-to-Water listserve, 24 May 2003.
14. Bond, P. (2003), 'Cuba dares to Resist Washington and Resurrect the Ideas of Marx', *ZNet Commentary*, 31 May.
15. Muller, 'Water 2003'.
16. Muller, 'Water 2003'.
17. Muller, 'Water 2003'.
18. Bond, P. (2004), 'The Neoliberal Roots of South Africa's Cholera Epidemic', in M. Fort (ed.), *Globalisation and Health*, Boston, South End Press.
19. Muller, 'Water 2003'.
20. Mathiason, N. (2003), 'Left High and Dry by the Water Companies', *The Observer*, 16 March.
21. Hall, D. (2003), 'Water Multinationals in Retreat', London, Public Services International Research Unit, University of Greenwich. http://www.psiru.org.
22. Bloomberg, 7 March 2003.
23. Pauw, J. (2003), 'Metered to Death: How a Water Experiment Caused Riots and a Cholera Epidemic', International Consortium of Investigative Journalists, Washington, 5 February. The Nelspruit reports were confirmed by SABC's *Special Assignment* investigation on 24 June 2003.

24. Fiil-Flynn, M. (2003), 'Report from Kyoto', e-debate listserve, 27 March.
25. http://www.citizen.org/cmep/Water/humanright, 20 March 2003.
26. International Rivers Network (2003), 'Who's Behind the World Water Forums? A Brief Guide to the World Water Mafia', Berkeley, March.
27. http://www.web.archive.org/web/*/http://www.ipwa.org; see also Corporate Europe Observatory (2003), 'Anti-privatisation Wave Sinks Corporate Lobby Group', Amsterdam.
28. http://www.worldbank.org; for a critique see http://www.servicesforall.org.
29. Logan, M. (2003), 'Multinationals Ride Wave of Water Privatisation', OneWorld US, 4 February.
30. http://www.irn.org/programs/finance/030919.wbgambling.pdf.
31. www.gwpforum.org/gwp/library/WaterReport.pdf.
32. International Rivers Network (2003), 'Some Preliminary Comments on the Camdessus Report', Berkeley, 10 March.
33. Public Services International (2003), 'The Report of the World Panel on Financing Water Infrastructure', Geneva, 12 March.
34. Asmal, K. (2003), 'Report of the World Panel on Financing Infrastructure: Letter to Dr Margaret Catley-Carson', Pretoria, 10 April, p. 2.
35. International Rivers Network, 'Some Preliminary Comments on the Camdessus Report'.
36. Spicer, D. (2003), 'More Resources Expected for African Water Projects', *Engineering News*, 28 March.
37. See Bond, *Unsustainable South Africa*, pp. 171–175.
38. *AFP*, 2 June 2003.
39. *The Economist*, 'Survey of Water', 19 July 2003.
40. http://squat.net/cia/gp/greenpepper.htm, 26 March 2003.
41. Thomson, G. (2003), 'Water Tap Often Shut to South Africa Poor', *New York Times*, 29 May.
42. Kasrils, R. (2003), 'South Africans' Water', *New York Times*, 5 June.
43. World Bank (2002), 'South Africa: Monitoring Service Delivery in Johannesburg.' Washington, pp. 1–9.
44. *Mail and Guardian*, 16 November 1996.
45. Thale, T. (2003), 'Census gives Joburg a Clearer Picture', http://www.johannesburg.org.za, 11 July.
46. Johannesburg (2001), 'Budget 2001–2002: City Development Plan 2001/ 2002', Johannesburg.
47. Johannesburg (2002), *Joburg 2030*, p. 14.
48. Minutes of the Southern Metropolitan Local Council Executive Committee, 21 June 1999.
49. Johannesburg (2001), 'Johannesburg Metropolitan Council Attitude Survey', pp. 8–9.
50. Johannesburg's white households ranked as their main grievances job creation, community litter, emergency services, pollution and parks/public transport. Johannesburg, 'Johannesburg Metropolitan Council Attitude Survey', pp. 14–17.
51. Johannesburg Water (2001), *Business Plan*, p. 26.
52. Johannesburg Water has a performance contract with the city and primary owner, Jowam, a joint venture made up of Northumbrian Water Group plc

(51%), Water and Sanitation Services SA (Pty) Ltd (29%) and Suez Lyonnaise des Eaux (20%). In turn, however, Suez controls 100% of Northumbrian and 49% of Water and Sanitation Services South Africa. For Suez, this appeared a potentially lucrative proposition in the medium term, even though the bid for the initial 'loss-leader' contract called for low returns. The business plan for Johannesburg called for (after-tax) profits to increase from R3.5 million in 2000–01 to R419 million in 2008–09.
53. Johannesburg Water, 2002.
54. Harvey, E. (2003), 'A Critical Analysis of the Decision to Corporatise the Water and Wastewater Services in the City of Johannesburg'. Johannesburg, University of the Witwatersrand Graduate School of Public and Development Management, Masters Dissertation, Jowam data cited in Table 2.
55. Cited in Harvey, 'A Critical Analysis of the Decision to Corporatise the Water and Wastewater Services in the City of Johannesburg', drawing upon JW Business Plans, 2003–05.
56. The World Bank advocated this method of sanitation in South Africa for 20% of all citizens since its late 1994 Urban Infrastructure Investment Framework, on grounds that if people are too poor to pay cost-recovery tariffs for water, they should be denied the opportunity to flush. The 1999/2000 metropolitan budget included R15 million in allocations for construction of VIPs, which was 70% of all spending on wastewater projects. If supplied at R700 per unit, there would have been sufficient funding for more than 20 000 VIPs in the 1999/2000 budget. The R15 million was allocated from the sale of R76 million worth of fixed property, according to the Greater Johannesburg Metropolitan Council Budget Estimates.
57. Cited in Harvey. 'A Critical Analysis of the Decision to Corporatise the Water and Wastewater Services in the City of Johannesburg'.
58. World Bank (1999), *Country Assistance Strategy: South Africa*, Washington DC, Annex C, p. 5. The issue is discussed in detail in Bond, *Unsustainable South Africa*, Part Three.
59. Roome, J. (1995), 'Water Pricing and Management: World Bank Presentation to the SA Water Conservation Conference', unpublished paper, South Africa, 2 October.
60. Murray, M. (forthcoming), *City of Extremes: The Spatial Politics of Johannesburg After Apartheid*, London, Verso, p. 19 of manuscript.
61. Kasrils, R. (2003), 'Report on Water Cut-offs a Case of Sour Grapes among US Populists', *Sunday Independent*, 8 June. Kasrils offered an absurd misreading of a paper by (the then imprisoned) John Pape – the fugitive ex-member of the Symbionese Liberation Army who enjoyed enormous support from progressives in South Africa upon his capture in November 2002 – and was rebutted by Pape's colleague Leonard Gentle in the *Sunday Independent*, 22 June.
62. McDonald, D. (2003), 'Attack the Problem Not the Data', *Sunday Independent*, 15 June.
63. Kasrils' 8 June article alleged that 'the Human Sciences Research Council, which published the report, says that the claim is not justified by the data. CEO Mark Orkin says, "the figure is a misplaced extrapolation by a researcher of an HSRC survey and considerably overestimates the phenomenon".' My own view, backed by several HSRC sources, is that this

reflects pressure placed on Orkin by Muller. Orkin surrendered his principles on a similar occasion, when unemployment statistics were rejigged during his tenure as head of Statistics South Africa. Kasrils conceded that Orkin's letter recorded 'a plausible estimate of the number disconnected at any point during that period would have been less than 2% of all connected households'. That slippery remark allows Kasrils to compare apples and oranges, for the Municipal Services Project analysis estimated disconnections in historical aggregate, not 'at any one time'. (The total *number* of disconnections, instead of the number of people who at any given time have been disconnected, is vast.)

64. Are these assumptions reasonable? There are three 'conservative' and two 'liberal' factors. Firstly, because Project Viability only measures those municipalities which report, the poorer municipalities which have bad record-keeping and are more prone to disconnect are not included. Secondly, 2001 was not a typical year: there was relatively more money available for municipal recurrent expenditures than in previous years via the Treasury's Equitable Share, and 2001 was the year that free water was meant to become available (in July), so in both cases that should have meant *fewer* disconnections in the final quarter than in a typical year. Moreover, the final quarter of any year is atypical because people are getting their 13th cheque or other bonuses in December, which mean that the fourth quarter disconnections would logically be lower than other quarters. Thirdly, there are more than five people per household, especially in low-income households which often have backyard shacks.

As to overestimation bias, the 'net' disconnection implies that people who lose their yard or house connections will never have it re-established through legal methods. It ignores that some people open up new connections under another name, or move residence, so they may have had their water 're'-connected even if doesn't show up in Project Viability, perhaps under a 'new connection'. From 1997–2002, the pace of municipal cut-offs ebbed and flowed. By 1997, municipal water disconnections were common, and by 2000 many of the Dwaf rural schemes – such as cholera epicenter, Ngwelezane – were cutting community supplies due to fiscal stress. In his June 2003 budget speech, Kasrils threatened to 'name and shame' municipalities which disconnected without having an emergency community tap nearby, but by December, in a debate I had with Kasrils' political advisor Dennis Goldberg, it was evident that there were still no plans to do so.

It is reasonable to stand by the allegedly exaggerated numbers, especially because Kasrils' advisors put him in an embarrassing situation of not distinguishing between the number of water disconnections 'at any one time' versus cumulative figures since 1994.

65. The records are net, because those who had their water reconnected within an average of 45 days are not part of the statistical count.
66. See comments by Lenny Gentle, myself and Sue Ruben, *Sunday Independent*, 22 June and 29 June 2003.
67. Kasrils, R. (2003), 'From Myth to Reality in the Great Water Debate', *Sunday Independent*, 29 June 2003.
68. Hemson, D. (2003), 'Rural Poor Play a Role in Water Projects', *Business Day*, 1 July.

PART THREE

POLITICAL ANALYSIS, STRATEGY AND ALLIANCES

9
Pretoria talk
Exhausted Leninism and the 'ultraleft'

A positive outcome of Pretoria's frustrated global reform strategy was a heightened consciousness among South African social movements about issues, alliances, strategies and tactics. This led to a series of attacks by government and the ANC against new 'ultraleft' social movements, or 'left sectarian factions' as Mbeki labelled them.[1] Regrettably, it did not lead to the coherent political conversation so urgently needed in contemporary South Africa.

This was also true north of the Limpopo River, where Mbeki's ally Robert Mugabe and his cadres in the Zimbabwe African National Union (Patriotic Front), better known as 'Zanu', were engaged in radical-sounding oratory, while actively repressing human rights. Talking left while oppressing the poor and working-class meant that Mbeki's project earned the epithet, even within the ANC Alliance,

'Zanufication'. Just before the WSSD began in August 2002, SACP deputy secretary Jeremy Cronin was forced by two heavyweights, ANC president's office spokesman Smuts Ngonyama and Dumisani Makhaye, a regional politician close to Mbeki and prone to race-baiting, to say sorry for revealing the dissent. Still, Cronin is indelibly associated with the political swearword Zanufication.[2]

It was not as if the ANC did not take the subject of global apartheid seriously in its often byzantine discussion papers, characterised by what SACP intellectual Raymond Suttner terms 'Brezhnevite Marxism'. The December 2002 preface to the ANC 'Strategy and Tactics' statement claims, 'The standing of South Africa has been enhanced at the core of the efforts of developing countries and Africa, in particular, to reverse the unequal power relations that define global politics and economics today. In the midst of this, global capitalism has witnessed many crises, exposing its incapacity to address in a lasting and comprehensive way, the plight of the world's poor.'[3]

The implication is that a proud liberation movement attaining power in a country like South Africa, as capitalist crisis gathered across the world, *should* attempt to reverse unequal international power relations, and pose an alternative to 'global capitalism', to meaningfully address poverty and world minority rule.

The ANC did not, unfortunately, approach this potential. Instead, the head of ANC policy and research, Michael Sachs, blamed 'the reality of a unipolar world with the strength of finance capital'. He explained to global justice movement author Paul Kingsnorth: 'You can't just go and redistribute things in this era. Maybe if we had a Soviet Union to defend us we could do that but, frankly, you've got to play the game, you've got to ensure that you don't go on some adventure. You know you *will* be defeated. They were defeated in Chile, they were defeated in Nicaragua.' Sounding like Margaret Thatcher, Sachs continued: 'Should we be out there condemning imperialism? If you do those things, how long will you last? There is no organisational alternative, no real policy alternative to what we're doing.'[4] Southern African scholar-activist John Saul describes this brand of defeatism as quite functional: 'Globalisation made me do it!'

ANC officials were so afraid of being defeated, that instead of *trying* to reverse unequal power relations, they became an *accomplice* to global apartheid. Their reform proposals ('act right') were frustrated, because they were ameliorative, notwithstanding claims to great virtue ('talk left'). This was not just evident in Pretoria's international adventures, but at home, in the form of unnecessary, excessively rapid financial and trade liberalisation, massive tax cuts for the wealthy and big corporates, privatisation, fiscal austerity, monetarism, and other indicators of domestic neoliberalism. At the same time, those South Africans who *were* serious about fighting global apartheid were often attacked by officialdom.

Traditions of the left

Shortly after the WSSD, *Khanya Journal* carried an article by Anti-Privatisation Forum chairperson John Appollis, a leading Gauteng trade unionist, who argued that 'by consistently highlighting the central role of the ANC government in driving the neoliberal agenda many international movements were won over to the side of the SMI.' He continued:

> What was instructive was the use of repression by the ANC government to further its political agenda – a method reminiscent of the apartheid regime . . . The fact that the ANC government had to resort to repressive tactics to block, or reverse, political inroads made by the new movements has dented the image of the ANC as the champion of democracy and the poor.
> Important alliances and connections were made during the WSSD. These laid the basis for broadening the mass base of our struggles. Our struggles in South Africa at this point are largely defensive in nature. They are not yet underscored by a coherent political programme for social change. Organised labour and students are not yet drawn into these struggles. These weaknesses of our struggles could be seen in the march against the WSSD. One of the key challenges facing us is to broaden the mass base of the new movement.[5]

A few months later, SACP general secretary Blade Nzimande offered a respectful counter-analysis: 'The baton of global popular mobilisation and of anti-systemic politics has swung powerfully (and one-sidedly) towards social movement and NGO politics – what is sometimes called the "new left" (but which properly belongs to an old tradition, anarcho-syndicalism, co-operative socialism, etc), as opposed to the so-called "old left" (communism, social democracy, trade unions, and third world national liberation movements).'[6]

Although he conceded the vibrancy of activism to his left, Nzimande warned of 'characteristic negative tendencies' such as 'diffuse pluralism,' a 'negative single-issue ("anti-globalisation")', and an inability 'to advance a positive, strategic programme of transformation'. For Nzimande, the global justice movements' 'tendency to renounce formal politics often means that bourgeois state power is left largely uncontested'. He pointed to the role of 'an "old", sometimes very sectarian, ultraleft. There are many examples where their overall strategic role has been reactionary or negatively divisive'. Nzimande distinguished the disruptive new left from the SACP's position, namely appeals 'for North-South "partnerships" (an important social democratic theme, dating back to at least Willie Brandt and Olaf Palme and in NEPAD), *and* consistent anti-imperialism (a centrepiece of Leninism)'. He argued: 'We need to assert unity between progressive governments (our own in the first place) and progressive social movements.'

Civil society critics could respond that NEPAD is *not* social democratic, but neoliberal, in view of its promotion of the Washington Consensus, privatisation, odious-debt repayment and integration into unreformed international markets. The new left typically finds 'unity' with Pretoria impossible in many sectors, given the many political, economic, social, health, development and security policies that are considered so objectionable.[7]

From its explicitly defensive perspective, the SACP greeted the announcement of protests against the WSSD in July 2002 as 'infantile' and 'irresponsible'.[8] The SACP's critics wondered if the attack on the independent left was meant to distract attention from the direction in which the party was travelling.[9]

A local-global threat

Raging rhetoric also emanated from ANC headquarters in Johannesburg's Luthuli House after the WSSD, and continued to burn after the ruling party's December 2002 national conference. The ANC's Political Education Unit introduced the claim in September 2002 that the independent left sought 'to mobilise other groups, globally, to join in the campaign against the ANC and our government' (not untrue). The tone then turned nasty:

> In the aftermath of the victory of the neoliberal agenda globally, the period of the international domination of the 'Washington Consensus,' loose international coalitions of 'left' groups opposed to neoliberalism gradually emerged. Through its (*sic*) focus on the issue of neoliberalism as its campaign platform, these groups have become identifiable as the 'anti-neoliberal coalition.' This coalition has launched an offensive against the ANC and our government, accusing them of implementing an anti-popular, neoliberal programme in our country . . .
> Interestingly, a significant number of the leaders of this anti-ANC offensive in our country are foreigners. This signifies the importance of this offensive to some international circles. These have determined that the defeat of our government is of strategic importance. In time, we will explain who these South African-based foreign enemies of the ANC and the government are . . .
> The international coalition engaged in this struggle describes itself variously as communist, socialists, anarchists and anarcho-syndicates. It subscribes to the objective of the victory of socialism, loosely defined. It finds this loose definition of socialism very convenient. This is because it helps the members of the coalition to avoid any struggle among themselves about long-term goals. This assists the coalition to build a united front based on tactical cohesion around a programme of action concentrated on immediate issues. Together the coalition represents tendencies that have existed in the global left movement for many decades, [but] it has never been able to act together to achieve a revolutionary, anti-capitalist victory.
> In our country, it is represented by important factions in the SACP and Cosatu, as well as the Anti-Privatisation Forum, the local chapter of Jubilee 2000, and other groups and individuals. All of these maintain links with like-minded counterparts internationally and work to mobilise these to act in solidarity with them in support of the anti-neoliberal campaign in our country.

Together with their international allies, they have determined that the ANC and our government represent the subjective factor in the contemporary expression of the capitalist mode of production in our country . . . there is no substance whatsoever to this statement.'10

Xenophobia and paranoia characterised several such statements. More preposterous was the oft-recited claim that local global justice movement activists were tactically allied with the Washington Consensus:

> Its pursuit of sectarian interest, deceptively clothed in progressive-sounding language, has nothing to do with advancing the interests of the working people of our country. The very fact that they are forever silent about the forces of reaction that are opposed to our movement, that they do not confront these in daily struggle, answers the question definitely – whose interests do they serve!
> So determined is the coalition of anti-neoliberals to act in alliance with the real neoliberals, that it hides these patrons of unbridled capitalism by launching a strident campaign based on outright lies, to attach the neoliberal label on our movement and detach it from the real neoliberals.
> To achieve these objectives, the anti-neoliberal coalition is ready to treat the forces of neoliberalism as its ally . . . to open fire on the ANC and our government. The forces of reaction and repression have tried for many decades to defeat and destroy the ANC and failed. Nevertheless, they have not abandoned this objective. Today they have the anti-neoliberal coalition as their ally.[11]

Dumisani Makhaye alleged in the official ANC web-zine that the independent left 'worked to turn the international forces that worked to defeat the apartheid regime, into opponents of our movement. They do this through a sustained campaign to discredit the efforts of the ANC and the democratic state . . . This confirms the global experience of the progressive movement for a period that extends over a century, that left factionalists end up working as allies of right-wing reaction.'[12]

In a statement to an ANC policy conference, Mbeki demonstrated how deeply he was shaken by the international solidarity and militancy of 31 August 2002:

> Our movement and its policies are also under sustained attack from domestic and foreign left sectarian factions that claim to be

the best representatives of the workers and the poor of our country. They accuse our movement of having abandoned the working people, saying that we have adopted and are implementing neoliberal policies. These factions claim to be pursuing a socialist agenda. They assert that, on the contrary, we are acting as agents of the domestic and international capitalist class and such multilateral organisations as the World Bank and the IMF, against the interests of the working people.[13]

In an October interview with the *Sunday Times* he continued:

One should look at the positions of the ultraleft, globally – not just in South Africa. They define themselves variously, in all that I've read, as anarchists, socialists, fourth international and so on, and they have a common platform which is: let us unite to defeat globalisation and let us unite to defeat neoliberalism, which is a manifestation of that globalisation process.

These are the basic positions and in that context there would be particular matters – for instance neoliberalism would refer to issues of privatisation of state assets, how you handle public finances with regard to issues like budget deficits.

It is actually a global platform. It is not peculiarly South African. What you then get is an interpretation of ANC and government policies which defines them within that context, so when we say 'restructuring of state assets' that is read as 'privatisation,' as implementation of this neoliberal agenda, accommodation with globalisation. So the demand becomes 'change government policies on a whole variety of matters to be consistent with an anti-neoliberalism position, an anti-globalisation position'.[14]

At roughly the same time, an extraordinarily crude pamphlet was issued by Gauteng finance minister Jabu Moleketi and ANC veteran Josiah Jele suggesting that the independent left 'works to mobilise like-minded groups internationally to join the struggle against the democratic movement in our country . . . [It suggests] that, under its leadership, South Africa can and should be transformed into a base to prosecute an anti-capitalist struggle globally. This adventurist and provocative position cannot but result in uniting the global forces interested in denying our people their right to assert their national independence, to defeat the democratic revolution and transform our country into a client state.'[15]

The pamphlet drew repeatedly on Lenin's classic missive, 'Ultra-leftism, an Infantile Disorder', but appeared unaware that the Bolshevik leader was defending a genuine revolutionary project, not an elite transition to neoliberalism. Twisting and turning to spin their argument, Moleketi and Jele rehearsed the slur of a presumed left-right alliance:

> The bourgeoisie and sections of our population that benefited from apartheid and seek to protect their privileges, have identified this faction as their most effective force for deployment against the democratic revolution. Various left sectarian factions elsewhere in the world have joined the domestic faction, domestic and international bourgeoisie groups, including their media spokespersons, together to achieve the defeat of our revolution as a common strategic task.[16]

The problem with the 'left sectarian faction', the authors insisted, was that 'it rejects the fundamental and central characterisation of socialism as being manifested in the dictatorship of the proletariat'.[17] True enough, the independent left had very few such Leninist inclinations, but such bizarre reference to a purist revolutionary discourse reflected scholastic politics learned in the USSR and applied nowhere since. As a result, Moleketi and Jele continued, the SACP 'has an obligation to join the struggle against the counter-revolutionary forces that seek the defeat of the democratic revolution. It has a particular responsibility because groups that project themselves as socialist have set themselves up as the principal opponents of the democratic revolution and movement.'[18]

The response of the three leading Cosatu spokespersons, Oupa Bodibe, Patrick Craven and Vukani Mde, all SACP members, is worth quoting at length because they pinpoint the talk-left, act-right tendency:

> The Moleketi-Jele intervention is an attempt, albeit clumsy, to rationalise the strategic shift that the liberation movement should pursue in the current environment... Moleketi and Jele... caricature the positions of Cosatu and the SACP to support their ultra-left charge. It is as if they do not want to be bothered with facts in their rush to crush the ultra-left. The positions that are being paraded as evidence of the ultra-left within the SACP and Cosatu are mainstream policy positions of the two organisations. For example, it is alleged that the ultra-left has a penchant 'to organise its most destructive mass actions at the precise moments when world progressive forces engage the dominant world groups to achieve forward movements, in the interest of the people'. What could this be referring to other than Cosatu's anti-privatisation strikes?...

The pamphlet's anti-ultra-left crusade resonates with PW Botha's total onslaught strategy and McCarthy's anti-communism. It is simply a modern manifestation of the rooi-gevaar. For example, the apartheid regime believed that the ANC was used by the 'Communists' as a launching pad for world communism . . .

The methodology of the analysis is irredeemably flawed. The authors seem to have three basic strategies: McCarthyism, liberal usage of red herrings, and what can only be described as a religious fundamentalist approach to Marxism-Leninism . . . Throughout the document, issues are confused rather than clarified by inserting long quotations from Marx, Engels and Lenin, that are so selective and ripped out of historical context that they are totally irrelevant to the point the authors are trying to make . . . Marxism is being treated quite shabbily, not as a living body of knowledge and as a tool of analysis, but as a bible of eternal truths to be pulled out of a hat and quoted extensively on any day, to silence the modern heretic . . .

It would have been far better for the authors to openly admit this at the outset and declare that they are opening a debate on the merits of capitalism as opposed to socialism. Or that the only route open to manage a capitalist economy is via conservative macroeconomic policies or trickle-down economics. Then we could have a very real debate within our movement. Why confuse everybody, by wrapping up their argument in pseudo-Marxist mumbo jumbo about 'revolutionary democracy', irrelevant passages from Marx and Lenin and wild conspiracy theories? Why not simply say: 'we believe capitalism is the best policy for the ANC government to adopt', and stop claiming that anyone who disagrees with that or advocates socialist policies is by definition 'ultra-left'?

Clearly the authors lack the courage of their capitalist convictions. The reason is not hard to find. They know full well that within the ANC's membership and constituency there will be very little support for their ideas, and so they have to pretend that their pro-capitalist policies are actually defending and extending the national democratic revolution and fighting for the national liberation of the African people . . .

In Moleketi and Jele's hands Marxism-Leninism is an instrument to pacify the working class and compel them into subjugation under the pretext of advancing the NDR and fighting narrow sectionalism. Socialism itself becomes an opium of the working class – bear the brunt of capitalist exploitation for there is no alternative because in some distant future the world will belong to you. This is capitulation politics par excellence! This is what Fanon warns against in the chapter on the 'Pitfalls of National Consciousness' in his seminal work, *The Wretched of the Earth* . . .

The McCarthyism of Moleketi/Jele could, ironically, have the effect of stirring up the same anti-communist hysteria associated with the apartheid psyche. Already we see the left being treated as one unvaried, dangerous monolith, its entire world of ideas as un-nuanced, counter-revolutionary propaganda. We are treading dangerous ground indeed.

We are in desperate need of an intervention that focuses the movement on the real debate. What economic policies, in South Africa and in the continent, will take forward the struggle for national liberation and will begin to overcome the massive problems that still afflict us. Launching a witch-hunt against the 'ultra-left' is an attempt to avoid facing up to the necessity for such a debate.'[19]

Recounting this lamentable material from late 2002 may be the most appropriate way to move to a tentative conclusion about Pretoria's broader relationship to global apartheid. Tired ANC nationalism in faux-Leninist mode reflected Mbeki's incapacity to address his political problems rationally. The turn to red-baiting became a source of mortification for those who took part in the South African struggle against apartheid believing the Congress tradition was one of progressive internationalism and *enlightenment*. The ANC authors cited above could no longer claim to uphold that heritage.

Notes
1. I take this problem up in more detail in Bond, *Elite Transition*, second edition.
2. http://www.comms.dcu.ie/sheehanh/za/cronin02.htm. For more on what this signifies, see Bond and Manyanya, *Zimbabwe's Plunge* and Bond, *Uneven Zimbabwe*, Chapter Six.
3. African National Congress (2002), 'People's Power in Action: Preface to the Strategy and Tactics of the ANC', 51st National Conference, Stellenbosch, December.
4. Kingsnorth, P. (2003), *One No, Many Yeses: A Journey to the Heart of the Global Resistance Movement*, London, The Free Press, pp. 119–120. Thatcher coined the acronym 'TINA': There Is No Alternative.
5. Appollis, J. (2002), 'The Political Significance of August 31', *Khanya Journal*, 2.
6. Nzimande, B. (2003), 'New Possibilities for a Progressive Global Politics', *Umsebenzi*, www.sacp.org.za, March.
7. The SACP supported the ANC government's 'Growth, Employment and Redistribution' policy in June 1996, although GEAR was not subject to democratic consultation and was substantially drawn up with World Bank staff and econometric modelling support. So much for the merits of partnerships; the SACP rejected GEAR a year later.
8. *Star*, 8 July 2002.
9. Trevor Ngwane noted in his *New Left Review* (July–August 2003) interview, 'When Mbeki attacks the Cosatu leaders and the SACP, calling them "ultra-left" – as he did when he felt threatened by the scale of the anti-privatisation mobilisation around the WSSD summit – he is whipping them into line. And it works. The SACP immediately declared, "This is our government, our ANC. We will defend it." The president of Cosatu, Willie Madisha announced: "We must not let our disagreements overshadow the many areas of agreement." Mbeki needs Cosatu and the SACP to contain the working class and deliver votes. There's no way he wants to break up the Alliance; he just doesn't want them to cross a certain line.'
10. African National Congress Political Education Unit (2002), 'Contribution to the NEC/NWC Response to "Cronin Interviews" on the Issue of Neoliberalism', Johannesburg, September. The charge that the 'ultraleft' included Cosatu and SACP leaders was aimed at a few key individuals. See the rebuttal by Cosatu/SACP activists below.
11. African National Congress Political Education Unit, 'Contribution to the NEC/NWC Response to "Cronin Interviews" on the Issue of Neoliberalism'.
12. Makhaye, D. (2002), 'Left Factionalism and the NDR: The ANC must Respond to Professionals of the "Left" ', ANC Today, http://www.anc.org.za, 29 November.

13. Mbeki, T. (2002), 'Statement of the President of the African National Congress, Thabo Mbeki, at the ANC Policy Conference', Kempton Park, 27 September.
14. *Sunday Times*, 8 October 2002.
15. Moleketi, J. and J. Jele (2002), 'Two Strategies of the National Liberation Movement in the Struggle for the Victory of the National Democratic Revolution', Discussion document distributed by the African National Congress, Johannesburg, October, p. 1.
16. Moleketi and Jele, 'Two Strategies of the National Liberation Movement', p. 2.
17. Moleketi and Jele, 'Two Strategies of the National Liberation Movement', p. 1. For reminding me of this evocative quote, I was grateful that the *Mail & Guardian* editors (19 December 2003) named Moleketi as their 'dream' finance minister for 2014, and moi as their 'nightmare' finance minister. Forward to the dream!
18. Moleketi and Jele, 'Two Strategies of the National Liberation Movement', p. 1.
19. Bodibe, O., P. Craven and V. Mde (2002), 'Black Shadows and Red Herrings: A Rejoinder to the Moleketi-Jele Pamphlet', Johannesburg, personal discussion paper, October, and, 'The Politics of Paranoia', *Mail & Guardian* (1 November 2002). The Cosatu authors observed: 'In the end there is but one solitary statement by an identified advocate of the "ultra-left" views under discussion. That "honour" falls to Patrick Bond, whose views on NEPAD are presented as proof of the "ultra-left" agenda. All the rest of the authors' venom is directed at shadows – unidentified, mysterious "forces" who are so powerful and dangerous that they threaten to derail and roll back the liberation struggle, yet apparently they have produced no manifesto or policy declaration, and operate in such obscurity that no one, including comrades Moleketi and Jele, knows who they are . . . the pamphlet stirs hysteria and paranoia and sets the movement on a witch-hunt to find and defeat the ultra-left. The tone and language makes it impossible to have a rational debate and the authors use blackmail to solicit support.' (Quotes from my work and that of Raj Patel – at http://www.zmag.org – demonstrate the authors' nuanced Internet capacities.)

10
Analysing Washington's agenda
Are there anti-imperial options?

How should we theorise global apartheid, being cognisant of the formidable power relations observed in this review of Pretoria's failed reform initiatives?

A good place to start searching for an answer is in South Africa during the apartheid era.[1] The power relations associated with apartheid were formidable for many decades, and had extremely deep roots. The system of racial oppression perfected in the middle of the 20th century was also, primarily, a system of *gender*-based super-exploitation that made possible migrant labour throughout southern Africa.

South Africa's urban capitalist managers designed a subsidy from the rural areas to lower the cost of workers in the mines and factories. Economic development was, according to the Chamber of Mines, dependent upon this system. A leading mine official testified to a government commission in 1944: 'The ability of the mines to maintain their native labour force by means of tribal natives from the reserves at rates of pay which are adequate for this migratory class of native, but inadequate in practice for the detribalised urban native, is a fundamental factor of the economy of the gold mining industry.'

How did this work? The migrant 'tribal natives' did not require companies to pay parents enough to cover school fees, or pay taxes for government schools to teach workers' children. Sick or disabled workers were often shipped back to their rural homes until ready to work again. When the worker were ready to retire, the employer typically left him a pittance, such as a cheap watch, or a bicycle, not a pension that allowed the elderly to survive in dignity.

From youth through to illness and old age, capitalists were let off the hook. The subsidy covering child-rearing, recuperation and old age was provided by rural African women. The central lesson from this crucial aspect of apartheid was that capitalism systematically looted 'bantustan' areas and exploited women, who formed such a large proportion of workers.

If gender, race and class all contributed to apartheid's super-profits, then these factors are also crucial to global apartheid's uneven prosperity. To generalise from early 20th century South Africa to the world is not impossible, for some of the key insights into the earlier version of global apartheid – simply called 'imperialism' – came from the German revolutionary Rosa Luxemburg.

A new political economy and geopolitics of imperialism?

Let us reconsider Luxemburg's contribution, updated by contemporary writers in the independent left intellectual tradition. Though best known as a German revolutionary killed thanks to collusion between conservatives and her Social Democratic competitors in 1919, Luxemburg's intellectual work was stellar, albeit flawed in some areas. She played a central role in interpreting an earlier version of global apartheid, which she and Lenin, Trotsky, Bukharin, Hilferding, Bernstein and Bauer simply called 'imperialism'.[2]

Luxemburg considered polarisation between the developed and developing worlds to be functional, not irrational, just as the apartheid polarisation between white cities and black rural areas was functional to South African capitalism. This was ultimately the contradictory logic behind uneven global and combined development. In her book *Accumulation of Capital*, Luxemburg wrote of 'the deep and fundamental antagonism between the capacity to consume and the capacity to produce in a capitalist society, a conflict resulting from the very accumulation of capital which periodically bursts out in crises and spurs capital on to a continual extension of the market'.[3]

Luxemburg's thesis was straightforward: 'Capital cannot accumulate without the aid of non-capitalist organisations, nor . . . can it tolerate their continued existence side by side with itself. Only the continuous and progressive disintegration of non-capitalist organisations makes accumulation of capital possible.' She continued, 'the relations between capitalism and the non-capitalist modes of production start making their appearance on the international stage. Its predominant methods are colonial policy, an international loan system – a policy of spheres of interest – and war. Force, fraud, oppression, looting, are openly displayed without any attempt at concealment, and it requires an effort to discover within this tangle of political violence and contests of power the stern laws of the economic process.'[4]

This fine description alerts us to similarities between early 20th and early 21st century global apartheid. Today, the international stage offers us views of a new colonial policy (HIPC, PRSPs, NEPAD, donor aid, the Pentagon and all the other processes that Washington and its allies deploy to maintain control). Today, we have an international loan system that corresponds to spheres of interest writ large, and not only via banking relations on colonial-geographical lines. Today, persistent wars in Africa and around the world reflect the tensions associated with capitalist crisis, interimperialist rivalry and barbarism.

We need reminders of earlier debates before we review opportunities at the global scale, and finally return to ways that people can make a difference in the fight against global apartheid. A grassroots anticapitalism is emerging and linking across the globe to change power relations and fight a mode of capital accumulation that has degenerated via, in Luxemburg's word, 'appropriation'. For Luxemburg and many contemporary critics, capitalist crisis tendencies were translated into an aggressive, systematic geopolitical process, characterised by 'oppressive taxation, war, or squandering and monopolisation of the nation's land, and thus belongs to the spheres of political power and criminal law no less than with economics'.[5]

If diverse forms of underdevelopment are integrated within production and reproduction, how is this managed by international economic managers? David Harvey, a renowned social scientist based at City University of New York, reminds us that 'primitive accumulation'[6] remains one of capitalism's persistent tactics:

> A closer look at Marx's description of primitive accumulation reveals a wide range of processes. These include the

commodification and privatisation of land and the forceful expulsion of peasant populations; conversion of various forms of property rights (common, collective, state, etc.) into exclusive private property rights; suppression of rights to the commons; commodification of labour power and the suppression of alternative (indigenous) forms of production and consumption; colonial, neocolonial and imperial processes of appropriation of assets (including natural resources); monetisation of exchange and taxation (particularly of land); slave trade; and usury, the national debt and ultimately the credit system as radical means of primitive accumulation.[7]

For Harvey, some of the most effective vehicles for capital accumulation via appropriation, or 'dispossession', are financial:

> The credit system and finance capital have, as Lenin, Hilferding and Luxemburg all remarked, been major levers of predation, fraud and thievery. Stock promotions, Ponzi schemes, structured asset destruction through inflation, asset stripping through mergers and acquisitions, the promotion of levels of debt encumbrancy that reduce whole populations, even in the advanced capitalist countries, to debt peonage, to say nothing of corporate fraud, dispossession of assets (the raiding of pension funds and their decimation by stock and corporate collapses) by credit and stock manipulations – all of these are central features of what contemporary capitalism is about.[8]

The financial markets amplify traditional forms of primitive accumulation, which remain relevant to Africa thanks to the rapid spread of commodity under neoliberalism, crippling debt crisis and capital flight. Trade and investment relationships also become systems of dispossession. Harvey notes:

> The emphasis upon intellectual property rights in the WTO negotiations (the so-called TRIPS agreement) points to ways in which the patenting and licensing of genetic materials, seed plasmas, and all manner of products, can now be used against whole populations whose management practices have played a crucial role in the development of those materials. Biopiracy is rampant and the pillaging of the world's stockpile of genetic resources is well under way to the benefit of a few large multinational companies. The escalating depletion of the global environmental commons (land, air, water) and proliferating habitat

degradations that preclude anything but capital intensive modes of agricultural production have resulted from the wholesale commodification of nature in all its forms. The commodification of cultural forms, histories and intellectual creativity entails wholesale dispossessions (the music industry is notorious for the appropriation and exploitation of grassroots culture and creativity). The corporatisation and privatisation of hitherto public assets (like universities) to say nothing of the wave of privatisation (of water, public utilities of all kinds) that has swept the world indicate a new wave of 'enclosing the commons . . .' the power of the state is frequently used to force such processes through – even against popular will.'[9]

Samir Amin, Africa's leading political economist, describes this process as theft: 'The US programme is certainly imperialist in the most brutal sense of that word, but not "imperial" in the sense that Antonio Negri has given the term, since it does not aim to manage the societies of the planet . . . to integrate them into a coherent capitalist system . . . it aims only at looting their resources.'[10]

Princeton economist Paul Krugman argues that this is not just about foreign domination, but reflects US domestic strategy for capital accumulation in favoured sectors:

> George Akerlof, the Nobel laureate in economics, described what's happening to public policy as 'a form of looting.' Some scoffed at the time, but now even publications like *The Economist* . . . are sounding the alarm. To be fair, the looting is a partly bipartisan affair. More than a few Democrats threw their support behind the Medicare bill, the energy bill or both. But the Bush administration and the Republican leadership in Congress are leading the looting party.
>
> What are they thinking? The prevailing theory among grown-up Republicans – yes, they still exist – seems to be that Mr. Bush is doing whatever it takes to win the next election. After that, he'll put the political operatives in their place, bring in the policy experts and finally get down to the business of running the country. But I think they're in denial. Everything suggests that Mr. Bush's people have given as little thought to running America after the election as they gave to running Iraq after the fall of Baghdad. And they will have no idea what to do when things fall apart.[11]

The management of contemporary capitalism entails the parasitic capture of surpluses and subsidies by mainly northern corporations.

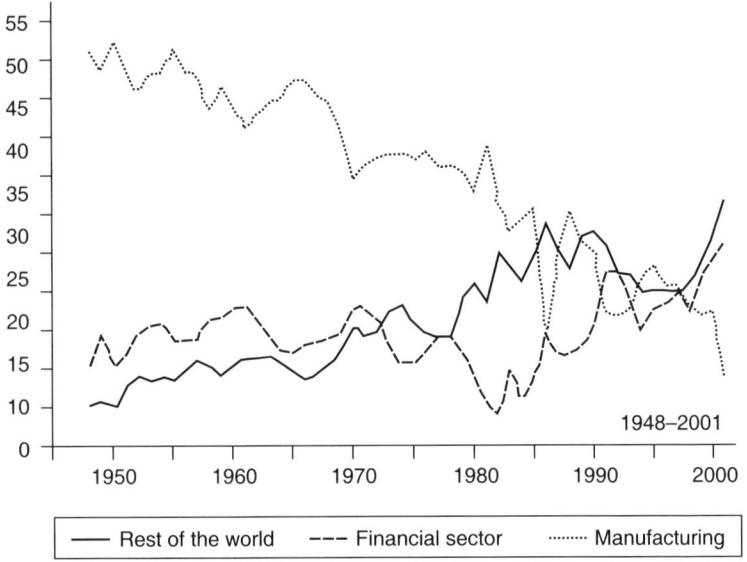

Figure 8: US corporate profits: Percentage breakdown by key components.
Source: Gerard Dumenil and Dominique Levy, Cepremap website

If we observe trends in the US corporate sector, we find that the period of sharply declining profit rates from the late 1960s to mid-1980s was followed by a weak upturn (1985–95), and then a bubble-driven expansion which subsequently collapsed. What is perhaps more important is the composition of capital accumulation for US businesses. Figure 8 shows that manufacturing declined while returns on foreign investments and financial services activities soared from around 1980. These trends appear to indicate that Washington managers were effective at 'shifting and stalling' the crisis, by moving it through geographical displacement, also known as globalisation, and by delaying its impact through credit-induced financial expansion.[12]

If geographical space and financial-delineated time are essential for capitalism's reproduction, what political contradictions might we find to address its vulnerabilities? Accumulation, through dispossession, entails *geopolitics* to establish a coherent strategy.

Two editors of the annual *Socialist Register,* Leo Panitch and Sam Gindin, have traced the post-World War II development of the US state with great insight. Although they do not rely upon the crisis theory adopted by Harvey, Robert Brenner and other Marxists, Panitch and Gindin explain how Washington – i.e., the Washington Consensus and Resurgent Rightwing ideologies and power blocs, in fairly tight alliance – represents an enormous concentration and centralisation of trade, finance and war-making:

> Most important was the immense attention the Treasury and State Department paid during World War II, to planning for relaunching a coordinated liberal trading regime and a rule-based financial order, via manipulating its main allies' debtor status, the complete domination of the dollar as world currency and the fact that 50% of world production was accounted for by the US economy . . . The Bretton Woods conference confirmed . . . the immense managerial capacity the American state had developed . . . With the IMF and World Bank headquarters established at American insistence in Washington, DC, a pattern was set for international economic management among the leading capitalist countries that continues, one in which even when European or Japanese finance ministries and central banks propose, it is the US Treasury and Federal Reserve that dispose . . .
>
> The new integral relationship that developed between American empire and global capitalism could not be reduced to a one-way (let alone solely coercive) imposition. The relationship was often more properly characterised by the phrase 'imperialism by invitation.' But while this often meant the consent of the citizenry of a country, the notion of US *state* (as opposed to cultural or economic) hegemony only adequately captured the relationship that developed among states and ruling classes. Active mass consent to even informal imperial rule was always mediated by the legitimacy that each state integrated within the American imperium could retain for itself and muster for any particular American state project; just as the American state did not take as its responsibility, the incorporation of the needs of subordinate classes or other states within its own construction of informal imperial rule.[13]

Here we find another hint of emerging contradictions within contemporary imperialism as applied to Africa. Panitch and Gindin allow 'the liberalisation of finance enormously strengthened Wall Street through the 1970s and proved crucial to the broader changes that followed [in a] belated recognition on the part of American capital, that the strengthening of finance was an essential, if sometimes painful, cost of reconstituting American economic power.'[14]

This condition represents not only the *strength* of finance capital but also its *vulnerabilities*. For example, more than $7 trillion in savings were wiped off the New York Stock Exchange in 2000–02. The Bush regime faces enormous problems in maintaining the hegemony of the US dollar during a period of sustained deficits, trade, payments, and the government budget, particularly in relation to the Euro and a strenghtening Chinese economy.

Amin gives other areas where US imperialism will meet its match:

> Competition between Ariane rockets and those of NASA, as well as between Airbus and Boeing, testifies to the vulnerability of present American advantages. Faced by European and Japanese competition in high-technology products, and by Chinese, Korean and other Asian and Latin American industrialised countries in competition for manufactured products, as well as by Europe and the southern cone of Latin America in agriculture, the United States probably would not be able to win were it not for the recourse to 'extra-economic' means, violating the principles of liberalism imposed on its competitors . . . the US only benefits from comparative advantages in the armaments sector, because this sector operates outside the rules of the market and benefits from state support.[15]

Amin insists that the US 'lives parasitically to the detriment of its partners in the world system . . . The world produces, and the United States, which has practically no funds in reserve, consumes. The "advantage" of the US is that of a predator whose deficit is covered by loans from others, whether consenting or forced . . . The US cannot give up the asymmetric practice of liberalism, since this is the only way that it can compensate for its deficiencies. American "prosperity" comes at the price of others' stagnation.'[16]

Occasionally, the contradictions associated with the Resurgent Rightwing's asymmetric economic strategy overwhelm even the White House. At the end of 2003, for example, the WTO ruled that the 30% steel import tariffs imposed by Bush in March 2002 were illegal, and that the EU, Asia and Latin America had the right to introduce countervailing penalties against US imports. The EU announced it would begin with surgically chosen products from major US states in which Bush's 2004 electoral campaign was vulnerable. When Bush dropped the tariffs, the United Steelworkers of America trade union complained that 'global overcapacity in steel – which the Bush Administration has done nothing to arrest – will lead to more surges and dumping'.[17] What the episode revealed, observed Lori Wallach of Public Citizen, was the following: 'US trade safeguard laws have been challenged at the WTO 11 times to date, with the US losing nine cases. [The] rollback of steel safeguards, in addition to WTO rulings in the other cases and WTO orders against the Foreign Sales Corporation tax program, the Clean Air Act, the Endangered Species Act and other US policies, should be a wake-up call to Congress about the WTO's erosion of democratic decision-making.'[18]

The Bush regime's protectionist instincts require monitoring and criticism, and are clearly not what Wallach has in mind when citing democratic decision-making. The main lesson to learn from the steel tariffs retreat is that profound economic problems in the US may worsen, if rightwing defence interests continue to conflict with the Washington Consensus. By 2002, the combination of predatory power via dollar hegemony and weakness on the production and trading front, was reflected in a $503 billion annual trade deficit (5% of GDP), a $6.4 trillion accumulated state debt (60% of GDP), and hundreds of billions of dollars in annual government deficits for the foreseeable future. From 1997–2002, a fifth of all US manufacturing jobs were lost. The US dollar crashed by more than 30% against the euro between late 2001 and late 2003.

A small GDP increase of 5.05% between 2001 and the middle of 2003 was entirely due to personal consumption (5.84%) and state spending (2.29%), as military Keynesianism outweighed social programme cuts. GDP was dragged down by negative private sector investment (-2.01%) and net exports (-1.36%). For households, the big financial factor, even outweighing the $5 trillion of personal savings lost in the crash of the New York stock markets, was the housing bubble. US households' real estate 'wealth' rose from $11 trillion to $16 trillion, partly thanks to what Brenner terms 'the greatest macroeconomic stimulus in US history'. From 2000–03, interest rates declined from 6.5% to 1%, luring more consumers into massive debt. The state budget surplus of 1.4% of GDP became a deficit of 4.5%. Yet 'the economy barely budged'. In late 2003, quarterly GDP finally rose quicker (8.2% annualised). But, as Brenner shows, 'US economic advances in the third quarter broke in a decisive way from its dependence on bubbles, debt and consumption.' Even after the 2000–03 slowdown and dramatic shakeout of manufacturing, by late 2003 overaccumulation remained acute. Manufacturing capacity utilisation (73%) was still lower than at any time since World War II, except the 1975 and 1982–3 recessions. Foreign inflows of capital finally began to reflect this weakness, falling from $110 billion in May 2003 to $4.2 billion in September. Japan and China may decline to finance further US current account deficits. Brenner poses other thorny questions:

Can an economy move forward by way of the expansion of service and financial sectors catering to consumption, when key goods-producing sectors remain weighed down by overcapacity and reduced profitability, when overseas producers are grabbing ever-greater shares of the US goods market, when exports are falling ever further behind imports with no hope of closing the gap at current exchange rates, and when the US depends upon the largesse of East Asian governments to cover its international obligations?

A longer-term problem also loomed, becoming the most important incentive to the petro-military wing of US imperialism: the need to loot the world's fossil fuels, especially Middle Eastern, African and Central Asian oil reserves. Former Democratic Party presidential security advisor Zbigniew Brzezinski wrote in his 1997 book, *The Grand Chessboard*, about the 'chief geopolitical prize':

> How America 'manages' Eurasia is critical. Eurasia is the globe's largest continent and is geopolitically axial. A power that dominates Eurasia would control two of the world's three most advanced and economically productive regions... control over Eurasia would almost automatically entail Africa's subordination, rendering the Western Hemisphere and Oceania geopolitically peripheral to the world's central continent. About 75% of the world's people live in Eurasia, and most of the world's physical wealth is there in its enterprises and underneath its soil. Eurasia accounts for 60% of the world's GNP and about three-fourths of the world's known energy resources...
>
> The world's energy consumption is bound to vastly increase over the next two or three decades. Estimates by the US Department of Energy anticipate that world demand will rise by more than 50% between 1993 and 2015, with the most significant increase in consumption occurring in the Far East. The momentum of Asia's economic development is already generating massive pressures for the exploration and exploitation of new sources of energy and the Central Asian region and the Caspian Sea basin are known to contain reserves of natural gas and oil that dwarf those of Kuwait, the Gulf of Mexico, or the North Sea...
>
> America's primary interest is to help ensure that no single power comes to control this geopolitical space and that the global community has unhindered financial and economic access to it... The three grand imperatives of imperial geostrategy are to prevent collusion and maintain security dependence among the

vassals, to keep tributaries pliant and protected, and to keep the barbarians from coming together.[19]

Barbarians are multiplying on Washington's radar screen. There are problems for the US in maintaining control over an interstate system which may be experiencing involuntary deglobalisation outside the 'functioning core' of global capital. Panitch and Gindin cite a publication of the US Naval War College which, under the title 'The Pentagon's New Map', lists countries considered danger zones for imperialism: Argentina, Brazil, Colombia and Venezuela, and smaller Latin American states not coping with social protest; most of the Arab regimes; and Afghanistan, Pakistan, India, China, North Korea, Russia, Angola, Burundi, the DRC, Rwanda, Somalia, and South Africa.[20] These potential rebels against US Empire represent most of the world. They may not only 'incubate the next generation of global terrorists', according to the Naval War College, but also fall prey to poverty, disease and routine mass murder.

Optimistically, Panitch and Gindin conclude, 'an American imperialism that is so blatantly imperialistic risks losing the very appearance that historically made it plausible and attractive.'[21] According to Brzezinski, the message was clear:

> The attitude of the American public toward the external projection of American power has been ambivalent. The public supported America's engagement in World War II largely because of the shock effect of the Japanese attack on Pearl Harbor . . . America is too democratic at home to be autocratic abroad. This limits the use of America's power, especially its capacity for military intimidation. Never before has a populist democracy attained international supremacy. But the pursuit of power is not a goal that commands popular passion, except in conditions of a sudden threat or challenge . . . The economic self-denial (that is, defence spending) and the human sacrifice (casualties, even among professional soldiers) required are uncongenial to democratic instincts. Democracy is inimical to imperial mobilisation . . . Moreover, as America becomes an increasingly multi-cultural society, it may find it more difficult to fashion a consensus on foreign policy issues, except in the circumstance of a truly massive and widely perceived direct external threat.[22]

On September 11 2001, that threat emerged, but contradictions have not been resolved.

Starting from scratch

Damage by the Bush regime hardly needs repeating, but fatal flaws in the Washington Consensus are also increasingly recognised by disillusioned insiders. David Ellerman is among several well-meaning economists who tried to change the World Bank from the inside. From his vantagepoint in the chief economist's office during the late 1990s and early 2000s, Ellerman saw more than his share of gambits. Finally, he threw up his hands:

> Agencies such as the World Bank and the IMF are now almost entirely motivated by big power politics and their own internal organisational imperatives. All their energies are consumed in doing whatever is necessary to perpetuate their global status. Intellectual and political energies spent trying to 'reform' these agencies are largely a waste of time and a misdirection of energies. Dominant global institutions, like monopolies or oligopolies in the private sector, can be counted on to use the power to maintain their dominance – yet that dominance or monopolistic power is the root of the problem.[23]

IMF abuse of power and dogmatic ideology were Joseph Stiglitz' long-standing justification for his August 2002 call to abolition:

> I used to say that since we are going to need these institutions it is better to reform them than to start from scratch. I'm beginning to have second thoughts. I'm beginning to ask, has the credibility of the IMF been so eroded that maybe it's better to start from scratch? Is the institution so resistant to learning to change, to becoming a more democratic institution, that maybe it is time to think about creating some new institutions that really reflect today's reality, today's greater sense of democracy. It is really time to re-ask the question: should we reform or should we build from start?[24]

A Columbia University colleague, Jeffrey Sachs, argued that low-income countries should *not repay World Bank and IMF loans*, and should redirect debt servicing toward health and education. Decapitalisation of the Bretton Woods Institutions through a sovereign defaults would be a sensible and direct closure tactic. Sachs insisted, no one 'in the creditor world, including the White House, believes that those countries can service these debts without extreme human cost. The money should instead be rerouted as grants to be spent on more demanding social needs at home. Poor countries should take the first step by demanding that all outstanding debt service payments to official creditors be reprocessed as grants for the fight against HIV/ AIDS.'[25] The idea was not as outlandish as it appeared at first blush, according to the *Boston Globe*, for during the 1980s Bolivia and Poland both got away with this strategy: 'Because the two countries used that money for social causes both were later able to win debt forgiveness.'[26]

The other reason elite Post-Washington reformers like Stiglitz and Sachs propose radical reforms such as closure of the IMF and debt defaults is that there is an economic necessity to clear unpayable loans. If we return to the 1820s, the 1870s and the 1930s, it is obvious that the periodic build-up of foreign debt required mass defaults, typically involving a third of all borrowing countries. Figure 9, prepared by orthodox economist Barry Eichengren for the World Bank, illustrates an extraordinary difference between earlier default waves and the more recent period: 1980s–90s defaults were avoided through debt restructuring processes arranged by the Bank and IMF.

As Chapter Five showed, the structural adjustment pain associated with debt restructuring was far worse than the meagre gains from the deals. The actual debt relief derived from restructuring was negligible, because new financing added to the outstanding debt pile. The main reason that the 'restructuring' line replaces the 'default' line in Figure 9 is because the World Bank and IMF have centralised creditor power since the early 1980s. During earlier mass default episodes, no such centralising device existed, so individual sovereign-debt bondholders in London, Paris and New York took the hit. During the 1980s–90s, in

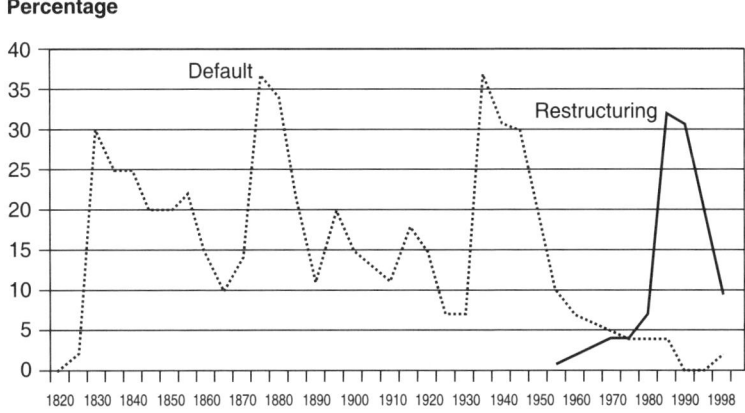

Figure 9: The long-term record of sovereign bankruptcy: Percentage of countries in default, 1820–1999.

Source: World Bank[27]

contrast, Washington ensured that creditors were repaid, and the hit was taken by the people of the Third World. Dictators or other rogue leaders who borrowed the money were generally left unscathed.

Default may be the logical option, since so few HIPC resources are allocated for debt relief. One important writer who straddles the Post-Washington and global justice movement standpoints is *The Guardian* columnist George Monbiot. His 2003 book, *The Age of Consent*, endorses a mass Third World default. Likewise, George Soros has complained about the inadequate debt cancellation on offer from the Bretton Woods Institutions. Their 'failure to bring the required relief indicates that there is something fundamentally wrong with the international financial system as currently constituted . . . In recent years, the so-called Washington Consensus has put its faith in the self-correcting nature of financial markets. That faith has been misplaced.'[28]

Pretoria's sleeping elite

Trevor Manuel retains the faith, despite evidence to the contrary. With Post-Washington voices of such credibility, why doesn't Pretoria realise the necessity of abolishing the institutions of global financial apartheid?[29] At his Rand Afrikaans University lecture in October 2000, Manuel showed he was not only out of step, but apparently incapable of answering his own simple question:

> It might be very fashionable among protesters in the richer countries to demand that they be closed down, but the reality of the world we live in is that, at most, four countries in – Africa have access to private capital markets, even though many African governments have reduced deficits and increased growth rates. If the world closes its doors on Africa, are the poor countries to get the capital necessary to launch sustainable development?[30]

The simple answer remains: first, lock down local capital instead of letting it run footloose and fancy free across the world. Application of capital controls as a strategy applies as much to the Mozambiques and Zimbabwes of the world as it does to Malaysia or South Africa. Although neoliberalism has decapacitated many states, it is not difficult to imagine the establishment of a rigorous exchange control regime in low-income African countries, if the will existed. Second, use the diverse powers of a central bank and finance ministry to ensure more rapid circulation of domestic funds. The means to do so are widely known and don't require repetition.[31]

Fashionable protesters supported Manuel when he fought racial apartheid. They have won the respect of *serious* reformers. 'Until the protesters came along there was little hope for change and no outlets for complaint,' Stiglitz wrote in his book *Globalisation and its Discontents.* 'It is the trade unionists, students, environmentalists, ordinary citizens, marching in the streets in Prague, Seattle, Washington and Genoa who put the need for reform on the agenda of the developed world.' Nor, Stiglitz continues, is the radical agenda as trivial as Manuel alleges: 'It used to be that subjects such as structural adjustment loans and banana quotas were of interest to only a few. Now sixteen-year-old kids from the suburbs have strong opinions on such esoteric treaties at GATT and NAFTA. These protests have provoked an enormous amount of soul-searching from those in power.'[32]

Whether due to protests or persistent failure, Manuel has had to soul search the economic record of government's Growth, Employment and Redistribution (GEAR) strategy. His period in office has been characterised by negative per capita GDP, a massive decline in jobs and a degeneration in the world's worst wealth distribution system. GEAR should have been renamed Decline, Unemployment and Polarisation Economics (DUPE).

In an April 2002 article entitled, 'Great leap into stagnation courtesy of World Bank,' Bloomberg News Service reported that Manuel advocated 'spending cuts, the dismantling of trade barriers and fighting inflation . . . under the guidance of World Bank economists. He is still waiting for the payoff. Now, Manuel and even some World Bank officials say Africa's largest economy has not gained as expected from the lender's advice.' Manuel conceded to Bloomberg, 'developing countries have undertaken many reforms, but the benefits are slim . . . We [undertook] substantial macroeconomic reform. But the rewards are few.'[33]

Was Manuel pushed into such substantial 'reforms', a bizarre expression for the imposition of job-killing austerity, or did he jump? He claims the former. In a May 2003 speech, Manuel admitted that 'economic integration must be managed because it carries the possibility to severely restrict the degree of policy choice that a country has. It is worth reminding ourselves that the extent of limitation of choice and country's demand for access to capital, are in direct proportionality. The key variables are firstly, the financing of the fiscal deficit and secondly, the dependence on external capital for financing economic expansion.' Manuel warned that 'countries which are entirely dependent on the Bretton Woods Institutions for finance would have policy limitations imposed through the Washington

Consensus or its derivatives. This is quite a formal limitation. Alternatively, the restrictions are imposed informally by virtue of interconnectedness.'[34]

This assertion of policy impotence in the face of global finance was sound at a superficial level, but Manuel did not make attempts to remedy the power imbalance. The 'informal' limitations were partly a function of currency fluctuations. Manuel continued, 'the key issue is the extent of capital mobility and a country's demand for a portion of the free float.' Yet, the crucial lever of counterpower is the application of stronger exchange controls. Consistent with his zig-zag approach to international financial management, Manuel loosened controls further in 2003. The contrast with the fashionable activist agenda could not be greater.

Notes

1. I set this case out in Bond, P. (2000), 'From Reconstruction and Development to Neo-Liberal Modernization in South Africa', in H. Othman (ed.), *Reflections on Leadership in Africa: 40 Years after Independence: Essays in Honour of Mwalimu Julius K. Nyerere on the Occasion of his 75th Birthday*, Dar es Salaam, University of Dar es Salaam Institute of Development Studies and Brussels, VUB University Press. Seminal works include Wolpe, H. (1972),

'Capitalism and Cheap Labour Power', *Economy and Society*, 1; Legassick, M. (1974), 'South Africa: Capital Accumulation and Violence', *Economy and Society*, 3; and O'Meara, D. (1996), *Forty Lost Years*, Indiana, Indiana University Press, for a wider analysis of gender issues drawn from a growing feminist literature.
2. A useful survey is found in Brewer, A. (1980), *Marxist Theories of Imperialism: A Critical Survey*, London, Routledge and Kegan Paul. Original texts include Bukharin, N. (1972) [1917], *Imperialism and the World Economy*, New York, Monthly Review; Grossmann, H. (1992) [1929], *The Law of Accumulation and Breakdown of the Capitalist System*, London, Pluto; Hilferding, R. (1981) [1910], *Finance Capital*, London, Routledge and Kegan Paul; and Lenin, V. (1986) [1917], *Imperialism*, Moscow, Progress Publishers.
3. Luxemburg, R. (1968) [1923], *The Accumulation of Capital*, New York, Monthly Review Press, p. 347.
4. Luxemburg, *The Accumulation of Capital*, pp. 396, 452–453.
5. Luxemburg, *The Accumulation of Capital*, p. 370. Updates of the theme that capitalism requires pre-capitalist 'articulations' are found in Seddon, D. (ed.), *Relations of Production: Marxist Approaches to Economic Anthropology*, London, Frank Cass; and Wolpe, H. (ed.) (1980), *The Articulations of Modes of Production*, London, Routledge and Kegan Paul.
6. For more theoretical and empirical information on primitive accumulation, see Moore, D. (2002), 'Zimbabwe's Triple Crisis: Primitive Accumulation, Nation-State Formation and Democratisation in the Age of Neoliberal Globalisation', Paper presented to the conference on Transition and Crisis in Zimbabwe, Centre of African Studies, University of Florida, Gainesville, 2 March; Perelman, M. (2000), *The Invention of Capitalism: Classical Political Economy and the Secret History of Primitive Accumulation*, Durham, Duke University Press; Von Werlhof, C. (2000), 'Globalisation and the Permanent Process of Primitive Accumulation: The Example of the MAI, the Multilateral Agreement on Investment', *Journal of World Systems Research*, 6, 3; Zarembka, P. (2000), 'Accumulation of Capital, Its Definition: A Century after Lenin and Luxemburg', in P. Zarembka (ed.), *Value, Capitalist Dynamics and Money: Research in Political Economy, Volume 18*, Stamford and Amsterdam, JAI/Elsevere; and Zarembka, P. (2002), 'Primitive Accumulation in Marxism, Historical or Trans-historical Separation from Means of Production?', *The Commoner*, http://www.thecommoner.org, March.
7. Harvey, D. (2003), 'The "New" Imperialism: On Spatio-temporal Fixes and Accumulation by Dispossession', in L. Panitch and C. Leys, *Socialist Register 2004*, London, Merlin Press and New York, Monthly Review Press. A longer version is elabourated in Harvey, D. (2003), *The New Imperialism*, Oxford and New York, Oxford University Press.
8. Harvey, 'The "New" Imperialism'. A longer version is elaborated in Harvey, *The New Imperialism*.
9. Harvey, 'The "New" Imperialism'.
10. Amin, S. (2003), 'Confronting the Empire', presented to the conference on The Work of Karl Marx and the Challenges of the 21st Century, Institute of Philosophy of the Ministry of Science, Technology and the Environment, the

National Association of Economists of Cuba, the Cuban Trade Union Federation and the Centre for the Study of Economy and Planning, Havana, 5–8 May.
11. Krugman, P. (2003), 'Looting the Future', *New York Times*, 5 December.
12. This same multifaceted point was made to South African audiences in an important intervention by leading ANC and Alliance intellectuals in late 1998: 'The present crisis is, in fact, a global capitalist crisis, rooted in a classical crisis of overaccumulation and declining profitability. Declining profitability has been a general feature of the most developed economies over the last 25 years. It is precisely declining profitability in the most advanced economies that has spurred the last quarter of a century of intensified globalisation. These trends have resulted in the greatly increased dominance (and exponential growth in the sheer quantity) of speculative finance capital, ranging uncontrolled over the globe in pursuit of higher returns' (ANC Alliance (1998), 'The Global Economic Crisis and its Implications for South Africa', *African Communist*, Fourth Quarter).
13. Panitch, L. and S. Gindin (2003), 'Global Capitalism and American Empire', in L. Panitch and C. Leys, *Socialist Register 2004*, London, Merlin Press and New York, Monthly Review Press.
14. Panitch and Gindin, 'Global Capitalism and American Empire'.
15. Amin, 'Confronting the Empire'.
16. Amin, 'Confronting the Empire'.
17. United Steel Workers of America (2003), 'Press Release', Washington, 4 December.
18. Wallach, L. (2003), 'U.S. to Comply with WTO Order; Bush Retracting Steel Tariffs Early Shows Americans that WTO is Boss', Washington, Public Citizen Global Trade Watch, 4 December.
19 Brzezinski, Z. (1997), *The Grand Chessboard*, New York, pp. 30–31, 125, 40.
20. United States Naval War College (2003), 'The Pentagon's New Map', http://www.nwc.navy.mil/newrules/ThePentagonsNewMap.htm.
21. Panitch and Gindin, 'Global Capitalism and American Empire'.
22. Brzezinski, *The Grand Chessboard*, pp. 24–25, 211.
23. Ellerman, D. (2004), *Helping People Help Themselves: From the World Bank to an Alternative Philosophy of Development*, Ann Arbor, University of Michigan Press. Persuasion by reformists within the chief economist's office did not affect the institution, agreed William Easterly, a former senior staffer: 'There's a big disconnect between World Bank operations and World Bank research. There's almost an organisational feud between the research wing and the rest of the Bank. The rest of the Bank thinks research people are just talking about irrelevant things and don't know the reality of what's going on' (*New York Times*, 7 June 2003).
24. *Financial Times*, 21 August 2002. Stiglitz was interviewed by Doug Henwood on WBAI in New York. Because the idea is such an important one and the social forces of the global justice movements are mobilising, it is not surprising that the mainstream press and the South African media have been so wary about allowing this idea to spread.
25. InterPress Service, 2 August 2002.
26. Not surprisingly (because his prior job was public relations director for the

World Bank), the UNDP's Mark Malloch Brown insisted, 'It would be an absurdity for countries that are so dependent on financial assistance to poke the donors in the eye.' Mozambican prime minister, Pascoal Mocumbi agreed: 'If I stopped paying debt service, all my poverty-reduction money would stop from the World Bank and IMF. Fifty percent of our budget is from donors. I can't not pay. The country would stop.' UN special AIDS envoy Stephen Lewis retorted, 'There are some donors who would be privately pleased, although they would never publicly take this stand' (*Boston Globe*, 4 August 2002).

27. World Bank (2000), *Global Finance Tables 2000*, Appendix G, Washington.
28. *Financial Times*, 13 August 2002.
29. ANC policy head Michael Sachs put this bluntly in a 2001 interview: 'We don't oppose the WTO. We'd never join a call to abolish it, or to abolish the World Bank or the IMF. We think you have to engage with these institutions' (Kingsnorth, *One No, Many Yeses*, p. 119).
30. Manuel, 'Address to the Seminar on South Africa's Relations and Creation of National Wealth and Social Welfare'.
31. See Bond, *Against Global Apartheid*, Chapter Twelve. The implications for a country like Zimbabwe, in many ways the most difficult case of all for the 'anti-globalisation' position (as *The Economist*, 20 November 2002, points out), are addressed in Bond and Manyanya, *Zimbabwe's Plunge*, pp. 162–193.
32. Stiglitz, *Globalisation and its Discontents*, pp. 3–4.
33. Bloomberg News Service, 25 April 2002.
34. Manuel, T. (2003), 'Input to the HSRC Conference', Kleinmond, 4 May 2003.

11
Movement strategy
Abolish global apartheid

Thabo Mbeki, Trevor Manuel and Alec Erwin are not unusual: they posture in populist ways but shirk confrontation with the US Empire, especially in red-carpeted conference habitats, in Green Rooms and other corridors of power.

As the ANC prepared to win the 2004 election, rumours circulated that Manuel might find a Washington job or relocate to the South African private sector; and that Erwin was being considered as World Trade Organisation diretor general in 2005. Their eventual replacements (e.g., Jabu Moleketi in finance) may not necessarily be as effective, but it's fair to predict they would follow a similar path. Only very rarely are politicians willing to take advantage of contradictions associated with the Resurgent Rightwing and Washington Consensus.

That leaves us, finally, to enquire whether a critical mass of Africa's people is ready to fight? If so, will their struggle have a coherent political strategy? What allies might be found, and at what scale should they fight? What institutions should they target? What strategies and tactics do they need to employ? Are the global justice movements capable of advancing such struggles?

African anti-capitalisms

We have asked of ANC leaders, will you polish or abolish global apartheid? There has been no satisfactory response.

'Amilcar Cabral's injunction,' Nigerian sociologist Jimi Adesina reminds us, was 'that for the African petit bourgeois class to become one with the people, it must *commit class suicide*. It must turn its back on its natural instinct to [become] a bourgeois class and share in the aspiration of the people – not only in nation building, widening of social access, but in the area of resource accumulation and control.'[1]

The potential for a revolutionary civil service cadreship in Africa was never realised for more than a brief, romantic moment, unlike, for example, in Cuba. It reflected, as Adesina laments, the ascendancy 'of a *petty bourgeoisie with bourgeois aspirations*. This shift has been at the level of the state and the civil society (or societies), voluntary and compelled.' He continues:

> The sociological effect was to (a) shift the balance of forces within the state itself in favour of neoliberal fellow-travellers, and (b) to establish neoliberal principles as the underlining framework of policy discussions. In many cases this involved personnel changes. In other cases, it was a matter of a dominant ideology becoming hegemonic. Government unites with economic mandates: Ministries of Finance, central banks, bureaux with oversight mandate for privatisation and commercialisation, often became the first line soldiers for the emergent neoliberal orthodoxy. 'Capacity building' projects by the Bretton Woods Institutions and similarly oriented western agencies focused on reinforcing this ideological commitment.[2]

Under existing conditions, most Africans who request democracy and basic socio-economic services from their regimes will be frustrated. Progress will be forged not from good ideas, technicist interventions and insider persuasion tactics, but in movement campaigns from the grassroots and shopfloors.[3] Across Africa, there is evidence to allow us to move from inspiring historical examples to diverse ecological, community, feminist and labour struggles.

Africa was and remains the world's leading example of accumulation by appropriation and dispossession. There have been waves of resistance that correspond to international struggles. The anti-slavery and anti-colonial uprisings of the 18th and 19th centuries were suppressed by the Europeans' military superiority. Twentieth century settler-capitalism could only take hold through coercive mechanisms that dragged Africans out of traditional modes of production into mines, fields and factories. Many rural women had the added burden of subsidising capitalism with their own migrant-labour survival system, since schools, medical schemes and pensions for urban families were largely non-existent. The nexus of racial patriarchy and capitalism was an ingenious way to reproduce cheap black labour. Aspects of superexploitative migrant labour systems remain important to this day in many of Africa's extractive and settler economies.

Africa's interrelated radical traditions grew and intermingled. They included vibrant nationalist liberation insurgencies, political parties that claimed one or another variant of socialism, mass movements (sometimes peasant-based, sometimes emerging from degraded urban ghettoes), and powerful unions. Religious protesters, womens groups, students and youth played catalytic roles that changed history. If Luxemburg's critique of imperialism was based upon pressures building up throughout the world, then these were some of the most important anti-capitalist campaigns ever. The 1885 meeting in Berlin that carved up Africa between the main colonial powers reflected pressures directly related to capitalist crises during the 1870s–90s emanating from the financial centres of London and Paris. Soon, stock markets would react as badly to news of, for example, Ndebele raids on Cecil John Rhodes' mine surveyors in Zimbabwe, as modern brokers did to the Zapatista uprising and the failure of WTO negotiations in Seattle a century later.[4]

What kinds of globalised resistance can be retraced? Anti-slavery was one of the most important international solidarity movements ever. A century later, African nationalist movements established pan-Africanist ties with northern critics of colonialism, apartheid and racism. Actions against colonialism in Africa, in particular, from the 1950s to the liberation of South Africa in 1994, inspired leftists and anti-racists, from militants like Malcolm X and Stokely Carmichael to church-basement activists. Although as Che Guevara found out during 1965, organising and occasionally fighting in what was then Mobutu's Congo, not all peasant societies proved ripe for the struggle.

In contemporary times, we must first note the continent's increasingly desperate and militant labour movement.[5] Labour, and much of African civil society was, by the turn of the 21st century, largely civilised, tamed and channelled into serving neoliberalism. The potentially anti-capitalist remnants of the 'old left' (as Nzimande puts it) were prevaricating about the new movements, when not actively trying to discredit, demobilise and repress their left challengers.

Resistance to malgovernance and to accumulation by dispossession was never stamped out or entirely co-opted. In recent years, Egypt, Ghana, Kenya, Mauritius, Nigeria, Senegal, South Africa, Zambia and Zimbabwe have been among the most intense sites of conflict between anti-capitalists and ruling parties (some of which played out over differential resistance to the Iraq war). Across the continent, the contradictions between global justice movements and Third World nationalism are endemic, and the continuation of IMF riots suggests that the leftist critique of neoliberalism remains intact.

The micro-developmental and ecological damage of neoliberal policies is also widely recognised. Some of the most impressive recent upsurges of protest have been in areas of 'environmental justice'. In mid-2002, as an example, women in the oil rich Nigerian

Delta conducted sit-ins at the offices of multinationals prior to the World Summit on Sustainable Development. Subsequently, oil workers protesting at several Delta platforms over wages and broader community demands took multinational corporate managers hostage for a time.

In Botswana, indigenous-rights campaigners, aided by Survival International, targeted the De Beers diamond corporation, the World Bank and the Botswana government for the displacement of Basarwa/ San Bushmen from the central Kalahari in 2002. Removals from the central Kalahari were allegedly coerced to facilitate $2 million worth of diamond explorations under the auspices of the World Bank. According to *The Guardian*, the San targeted for relocation away from diamond mining areas, 'had their water supplies cut off before being dumped in bleak settlements with derisory compensation'.[6] The impact was so great that by August 2002, the *Botswana Gazette* described the government as a 'disease-ridden international polecat'. A San activist explained, 'Basarwa in this country are ill-treated and looked down upon. We want the world to know that.' The response from government officials was that San organisers were 'highly seditious' for drawing in 'fringe, lunatic and racist' allies in Britain.[7] As capital globalised, these struggles found increasing international support. South Africans in the Environmental Justice Networking Forum and far-sighted NGOs like Durban-based groundWork began working with counterparts elsewhere around environmental racism, dumping of toxics, compensation for asbestos, anti-incinerator campaigns and air pollution. Movements against privatisation of Africa's basic services – mainly water and electricity, but also municipal waste, health and education – began in Accra and Johannesburg in 2000 and quickly attracted global solidarity. Their influence is spawning similar campaigns across southern and west Africa. The Soweto Electricity Crisis Committee's Operation Khanyisa ('Switch On') illegally reconnects people whose supplies were cut because of poverty and rising prices associated with services commercialisation. Similar community-based protests in Durban and Cape Town against disconnections, evictions and landlessness have won recognition across the world.[8]

Can such specific, 'particularist' protests and campaigns graduate to a more generalised programme and mature anti-capitalist ideology? If so, it is possible that the African Social Forum will be the site. In January 2002, dozens of African social movements met in Bamako, Mali, in preparation for the Porto Alegre World Social Forum. It was one of the first substantial conferences since the era of African liberation, to combine progressive NGOs and social movements from the whole continent. It was followed by African Social Forum sessions in Johannesburg (August 2002), Addis Ababa (January 2003) and

Maputo (December 2003). The Bamako Declaration included the following paragraphs:

> A strong consensus emerged at the Bamako Forum that the values, practices, structures and institutions of the currently dominant neoliberal order are incompatible with the realisation of Africa's dignity, values and aspirations.
>
> The Forum rejected neo-liberal globalisation and further integration of Africa into an unjust system as a basis for its growth and development . . . there was a strong consensus that initiatives such as NEPAD that are inspired by the IMF-WB strategies of Structural Adjustment Programmes, trade liberalisation that continues to subject Africa to an unequal exchange, and strictures on governance borrowed from the practices of Western countries and not rooted in the culture and history of the peoples of Africa.[9]

The difficulty of pulling together a continental initiative is profound. Just as great a challenge remains to weed out neoliberal philosophy in Africa. According to Adesina,

> At the level of civil society, concerted efforts were put in place to develop a new generation, committed to the neoliberal vision. The African Economic Research Consortium is such an initiative. The neoliberal counter-revolution took the Maoist principle on revolutionary insurgency; burrow deep within the population. The collapse in public sector wages and the secular decline in formal sector employment stimulated the growth of the NGO sector and the drift into the informal sector. The emergence of the governance argument initiated the campaign to extend and deepen 'civil society' of a neoliberal hue.[10]

Ideas will be important as the embryonic anti-capitalist movement expands. African intellectuals appear hungry for contributions to a more open, thoroughly deStalinised, brand of socialism. A re-emerging interest in the *praxis* of historical materialism, i.e., theoretically-grounded explanation and political-strategic guidance grounded in concrete struggles for justice, was evident at the April 2002 Accra meeting of the Council for Development and Social Research in Africa and Third World Network-Africa. Codesria/TWN-Africa called upon 'Africa's scholars and activist intellectuals within African and in the Diaspora, to join forces with social groups whose interests and needs are central to the development of Africa'.[11]

Deglobalisation and decommodification

Dakar-based political economist Samir Amin argues for a 'delinking' strategy that 'is not synonymous with autarky, but rather with the subordination of external relations to the logic of internal development . . . permeated with the multiplicity of divergent interests.'[12] In 2002, a restatement of Amin's delinking theme came from Bangkok-based Focus on the Global South director Walden Bello, in his book *Deglobalisation*: 'I am not talking about withdrawing from the international economy. I am speaking about reorienting our economies from production for export to production for the local market.'[13]

There was no question of overthrowing the capitalist mode of production, merely the *scale* at which it operated. The possibility of attracting potential allies among a (mainly mythical) 'national patriotic bourgeoisie' still exists in some formulations of delinking, which coincides with reformist tendencies among the African intelligentsia and some currents of anti-capitalism, especially trade unions. The challenge in any such conversation is to establish the difference between 'reformist reforms' and change that advances a 'non-reformist' agenda. The latter would include generous social policies stressing decommodification, capital controls and inward-oriented industrialisation strategies allowing democratic control of finance and production. These would strengthen democratic movements, empower producers (especially rural women), and open the door to contesting capitalism as a more general system of multiple oppressions.

A first step toward such objectives is an effective form of deglobalisation. The strategic formula which the South African independent left has broadly adopted – internationalism combined with rigorous demands upon the national state[14] – could begin by removing the boot of the World Bank from Third World necks. If uneven development is amplified by a shift from national to global determination of political economy, part of the anti-capitalist project must be to wrest control of the national state from current ruling elites. These struggles must occur simultaneously, otherwise Washington will continue to prop up comprador elements who in turn, like Mbeki, will empower Washington and reproduce neoliberalism locally.

Even if sensible deglobalisation policies were adopted to 'lock capital down',[15] a national capitalist strategy in a society like South Africa would still be insufficient to halt or reverse uneven global development.[16] South Africa's independent left fully understands the need to transcend national-scale capitalism. One way is via 'decommodification'.

The South African decommodification agenda entails struggles to

turn basic needs into human rights, including: free antiretroviral medicines to fight AIDS; 50 litres of free water per person per day; 1 kiloWatt hour of free electricity for each individual every day; extensive land reform; prohibitions on service disconnections and evictions; free education; and the 'Basic Income Grant', as advocated by churches, NGOs and trade unions. All such services should be universal and financed through higher prices that penalise luxury consumption. This potentially unifying agenda could serve as a basis for widescale social change.

Deglobalisation and delinking from the most destructive circuits of global capital will be necessary. Those circuits rely upon the three main multilateral agencies, all of which promote commodification with a vengeance. Hence a strategy is urgently required to close the World Bank, IMF and WTO.

The limits of World Bank reformism

If men like Trevor Manuel won't concede the need for strategies such as defaulting on illegitimate foreign debt (Jeffrey Sachs) or closure of the IMF (Joseph Stiglitz), then South Africa's grassroots activists will have to take leadership. Cape Town's Anglican Archbishop Njongonkulu Ndungane makes this point in no uncertain terms:

> [If] we must release ourselves from debt peonage – by demanding the repudiation and cancellation of debt – we will campaign to

that end. And if the World Bank and IMF continue to stand in the way of social progress, movements like Jubilee South Africa will have no regrets about calling for their abolition. To that end, the World Bank Bonds Boycott movement is gaining even great momentum. Even a money centre city like San Francisco decided to redirect funds away from Bank bonds into other investments, on the moral grounds that taking profits from World Bank operations contributes to poverty, misery and ecological degradation. More and more investors are realising that profiting from poverty through World Bank bonds is not only immoral, but will not make good financial sense as the market shrinks.[17]

Some global justice movement activists and strategists still hold out hope for the kinds of reforms that Manuel claims to support: transparency, mass participation, a Post-Washington Consensus approach, gender equity and stronger environmental consciousness.

Since 2001, however, there have been virtually no successes and considerable backsliding. The three major recent processes in which well-meaning civil society advocates went inside the Bank were the World Commission on Dams (chaired by then water minister Kader Asmal), the Structural Adjustment Participatory Review Initiative (Sapri) and the Extractive Industries Review. In the first case, a South Africa Bank water expert, John Briscoe, actively lobbied southern governments to reject the findings of a vast, multi-stakeholder research team in 2001.[18] According to Patrick McCully of International Rivers Network, 'The World Bank's singularly negative and non-committal response to the WCD Report means that the Bank will no longer be accepted as an honest broker in any further multi-stakeholder dialogues.'[19]

As for Sapri, hundreds of organisations and scholars became involved in nine countries: Bangladesh, Ecuador, El Salvador, Ghana, Hungary, Mexico, the Philippines, Uganda and Zimbabwe. They engaged in detailed analysis from 1997–2002, often alongside local Bank and IMF officials. Bank staff withdrew from the process in August 2001.[20] In April 2002, when the research, a 188-page report, *The Policy Roots of Economic Crisis and Poverty*, was tabled for action, civil society groups found that Washington ignored them:

> The Bank's continual calls to street protesters to talk were denounced as disingenuous, and increased public pressure . . . to make the institution more open, democratic and responsive to the people of the Global South . . . 'This Sapri investigation has shown that the same policies are being applied everywhere, with very similar

results,' said Lidy Nacpil of the Freedom from Debt Coalition, Sapri's lead organisation in the Philippines. 'The Bank may claim that it has changed, but these policies remain firmly entrenched. It is imperative that we maintain the pressure on the Bank and the IMF.'[21]

Richard Peet, author of a recent book on the Bank, observed:

> In 2000, the World Bank published a report entitled *Voices of the Poor: Can Anyone Hear Us?* with an introduction by Clare Short, UK Secretary of State for International Development and James Wolfensohn, President of the World Bank. The report reached safe, moralistic conclusions like 'poverty is multidimensional' and 'households are crumbling under the stresses of poverty.' The last sentence of the introduction reads: 'Our hope is that the voices in this book will call you to action as they have us.'
>
> But in the case of Sapri, where thousands of civil society movements called on the World Bank to listen, its action was simply to leave the discussion. Why might this be? What these social movements were telling the Bank was that the poverty they sought to 'alleviate' had been produced by the structural adjustments they themselves had imposed – that they were merely rectifying a small part of their own massive mistakes. This made everything they had done in the way of structural adjustment over the previous 20 years . . . not meaningless (if only we were dealing with mere existential angst!), but pernicious, even malevolent, given that thousands of people active in development had been telling them for years to stop 'structurally adjusting' desperate countries. So the President of the World Bank did not listen to Sapri, because he could not. For he would hear, and he even might learn, that his finest, most splendid ideas had produced the worst, most harmful effects.[22]

The Extractive Industries Review (EIR) also nearly went off the rails when an April 2003 incident in Bali, Indonesia delegitimised the exercise before a final report was drawn up. A meeting between the Bank, international mining industry and civil society ended in an uproar when 15 environmental and human rights groups left in protest. According to the *New York Times*, 'The reviewers set up by the Bank had already circulated its draft conclusions supporting the Bank's oil, gas and mining investments, even though conferences organised to gather information from concerned groups and individuals in Asia, the Middle East and Africa had not yet taken place.'[23] This was a clear abuse of power, Oilwatch Africa warned, because 'international financial institutions, northern governments and transnational oil and gas companies force African countries to weaken or abolish laws and regulations on the oil and gas industries and this leads to the violation of community rights.'[24]

From the outset, the EIR was a dubious venue to address such concerns, activists found, even at the level of talk-shop etiquette during an April 2001 Rio de Janeiro session:

> The facilitators tried to cut off a presentation by a Bank staff member that had run overtime. The staff member ignored the facilitator and gave the microphone to another Bank colleague who in turn (despite pleas from the facilitators) turned it over to another Bank staff member . . . Bank staff had an overwhelming presence at the meeting, crowding out other stakeholders and providing information that was neither objective nor appropriate for the Review.[25]

In the meantime, the Bank approved loans for two infamous pipelines, Chad-Cameroon and Caspian, despite objections from the environmental, human rights and social justice communities.

By late 2003, civil societies indignation saw EIR leader, former environment minister Emil Salim of Indonesia, encounter another legitimacy crisis for World Bank participation politics. As a result, he ensured the civil society group message made it into the December 2003 draft findings. The report made it clear that public funds should not be used to facilitate private fossil-fuel profits.

The recommendations would have meant an end to World Bank coal lending by 2008 (worth billions in countries like India and China); mandatory revenue sharing with local communities; extensive environmental and social impact assessments; 'no go' zones for mining or drilling in environmentally sensitive areas; no new mining projects that dump tailings in rivers; obligatory environmental restructuring and increased renewable energy investments. The recommendations suggested that a dent could be made in global warming and energy-related oppression.

No one was surprised when lead Bank energy staffer Rashad Kaldany disagreed with the recommendations.[26] Several major environmental NGOs blasted the institution: 'One of the Bank's most important environmental reforms of the 1990s was its more cautious approach to high-risk infrastructure and forestry projects. This policy is now being reversed. The World Bank recently announced that it would re-engage in contentious water projects such as large dams in what it refers to as a "high risk/high reward" strategy. In 2002, the Bank dismissed its "risk-averse" approach to the forest sector when it approved a new forest policy. The World Bank is also considering support for new oil, mining, and gas projects in unstable and poorly governed countries, against the recommendations of its own evaluation unit.'[27]

Meanwhile, Pretoria's minister of minerals and energy, Phumzile Mlambo-Ngcuka, made it clear to senior World Bank staff in February 2004 that they should oppose 'green lobbyists' on the EIR. Mlambo-Ngucka instead preferred the African Mining Partnership, under the auspices of the New Partnership for Africa's Development, which stated its intention to establish an alternative sustainable mining strategy. The minister's spokesperson claimed, 'We are already implementing sustainable development programmes,' notwithstanding evidence of massive corruption and eco-destruction in countries like Angola and Nigeria, and a failure to trickle benefits of mining down in even the best-case country, Botswana.[28]

Forcing the World Bank and related lenders out of environmentally destructive activities is not likely to succeed without a financial threat to the institution. Minor concessions won through multi-stakeholder forums can be ignored or reversed when the Bank takes unilateral decisions.

For example, the good-governance and anti-corruption hype that Bank president Wolfensohn introduced at a Durban Transparency International Congress in 1999, was shown to be merely rhetoric when Bank staff ignored the need to 'debar' (ban) companies that bribed the key Lesotho Highlands Water Project official, Masupe Sole, from 1994–98. The Bank initially found companies like Canada's huge consultancy, Acres International, innocent. When the Lesotho courts found Acres guilty of corruption, the World Bank failed for several years to debar the firm. Others on the prosecution list include big South African companies doing Bank contracts across Africa and the world's biggest construction company, ABB.

Breaking the chains of global financial apartheid

Removing the Bretton Woods component of global apartheid is a central strategy for the global justice movements, especially those based in the Third World. Many Africans, especially in the Jubilee movement, argue the merits of 'nixing' not 'fixing' the Washington financial agencies, because they are:
- global neoliberalism's 'brains' *and* policemen;
- active across the African continent;

- reliant upon unreformed neoliberal logic, from macroeconomics to micro development policy;
- responsible for project-level conditionality;
- capable of commodifying even the most vital public services; and
- experience periodic IMF riots and other activism, with a severe legitimacy crisis.

Campaigning has become quite surgical:
- several local, African and international lobbies aim to force the WB/IMF and WTO to stop commodifying water, health, education and other services, and to remove the institutions from destructive roles in mega-projects, such as large dams or energy financing. They have achieved partial success because of citizen advocacy, the US Congress now prohibits user-fee requirements on some Bank/IMF financing;
- global justice movement components such as Anti-Privatisation Forums and environmental justice groups exist in many southern African cities, and their local struggles, such as those against Suez in Johannesburg, directly confront World Bank neoliberalism;
- the Southern African People's Solidarity Network links progressive activists, churches, and others in an explicit ideological challenge to the Washington Consensus;
- Jubilee movements across Africa continue fighting for debt repudiation;
- the African Social Forum is developing tough positions on debt and development, with the Southern African Social Forum demanding in November 2003 that Bretton Woods personnel pack up and leave; and
- reparations protests and lawsuits are underway against financiers – including, potentially, the Bank and IMF – which supported apartheid and African dictatorships.

In mid-2003, South African activists began considering how to make Bretton Woods Institutions accountable. They would have joined the Bank and IMF to the New York court cases, but their staff enjoy diplomatic immunity. Whether or not suing the World Bank and IMF to compensate South African society for the agencies' generous 1950s–80s loans to the apartheid regime will ever recoup money, campaigning along such lines could provide a disincentive to stop financing brutal or illegitimate regimes, such as US-occupied Iraq (beneficiary of $8 billion in 2003 IMF/Bank loan pledges).

US groups like the Center for Economic Justice and Global Exchange continued to work with Jubilee South Africa and Brazil's Movement of the Landless, among others, to ask of their northern comrades: is it ethical for socially-conscious people to invest in the World Bank by buying its bonds (responsible for 80% of the Bank's resources), hence drawing out dividends which represent the fruits of enormous suffering? The boycott impressed a London *Evening Standard* financial markets commentator during the IMF/Bank spring 2002 meetings: 'The growing sophistication of radical activists increases the likelihood that once-accepted fixed-income investment practices can no longer be taken as off limits from the threat of moral suasion.'[29]

In the short term, the boycott campaign sends a clear signal to the Bank: end anti-social, environmentally-destructive activities, and cancel the debt. When enough investors endorse the campaign, the Bank will suffer a declining bond rating, making it fiduciarily irresponsible to invest. In turn, some organisers hope, this lays the basis for a 'run on the Bank', to defund the institution entirely. This will happen initially through a collapsed bond market and then through northern taxpayer revolt, as the campaign gathers momentum and publicity.

The World Bank Bonds Boycott is only one of a variety of campaigns that could become more explicitly anti-capitalist, or that could rest at a comfortable populist, moral level. South Africans like Dennis Brutus, Trevor Ngwane, George Dor, Virginia Setshedi and Richard 'Bricks' Mokolo have been touring North America and Europe since 2000 to promote the Boycott so that the politics of solidarity become as strong as during an earlier period of anti-apartheid boycotting. Brutus was a leader of campaigns that forced apartheid South Africa out of the Olympics in 1968, and his subsequent extrapolation of the social justice agenda to the world scale has been of enormous benefit to the global justice movements. In contrast, Thabo Mbeki worked very hard to promote anti-apartheid disinvestment campaigns, but his about-turn re-emphasises the need for consistent, clear politics. The fact that Mbeki, Mugabe, Arafat and Aristide have broken the hearts of former solidarity allies, shows the limits of Third World nationalism as a vehicle for change and indicates that the global justice movements will continue to set the agenda.

The anti-capitalist component of the global justice movements understands that the World Bank and IMF may have changed their rhetoric but not their structural adjustment programmes. The rhetoric of 'pro-poor' development does not conceal that virtually everywhere, the Bretton Woods Institutions maintain their commitment to accumulation by appropriation and dispossession. The institutions' legitimacy is the only target that the African social movements can aim at. They have done so in recent years with an increasingly militant perspective that worries *not* about the World Bank's 'failure to consult' or 'lack of transparency' or 'undemocratic governance' – all easy populist critiques. Most of the attention that leading African activists pay to the Washington Consensus ideology is to the core content: *commodification*, whether in relation to water, electricity, housing, land, antiretroviral medicines and health services, education, basic income grant support or other social services, ideally all at once and in cross-sectoral combinations.

The fiercest debates that I see in the progressive African movements tend to be over the extent to which co-option is a threat: e.g., in the African Social Forum's potential work within the African Union structures; in social movements being sucked into World Bank/IMF PRSP processes; or in Mbeki's attempts to draw South African civil society (especially Cosatu and the South African Council of Churches) into worthless NEPAD seminars. Dembe Dembele of Dakar's Forum for African Alternatives warns:

> Some African NGOs, which have been among the leading critics of Structural Adjustment Programmes and in the forefront of the struggle for debt cancellation, have been misled by the Bretton Woods Institutions' (BWIs') rhetoric on PRSPs. These NGOs have found some 'merit' to the PRSPs and think that with the emphasis on more spending for social sectors, like education, health and nutrition, the PRSPs could help 'alleviate poverty.' This is a big mistake. One cannot trust the BWIs to reduce poverty in Africa or elsewhere. So long as they avoid challenging the unequal power relations that define the unfair rules of the international financial and trading system, these institutions will never be in a position to 'help' Africa or other developing countries. In reality, what the IMF and World Bank try to achieve with the PRSPs is to create the illusion of 'poverty reduction' while pursuing the same failed and discredited policies, with even more conditionalities; promote a superficial 'national consensus' on short-term 'poverty reduction' programmes at the expense of a serious and deep reflection on long-term development policies; drive a wedge between 'reasonable' and 'radical' civil society organisations in Africa; and shift the blame to HIPC countries' governments and citizens for the inevitable failure of the PRSPs.[30]

The highest stakes are bound up in maintaining the momentum of these movements. Who are their most reliable allies? Is it premature to propose alliances between global justice movements and Post-Washington (maybe neo-Keynesian?) 'leaders' or Third World nationalists or even merely anti-US Europeans? And would those alliances find optimal scale politics locally, nationally or globally?

For or against global apartheid

Having reviewed the evidence of Pretoria's floundering international economic policy role, and witnessing a general deterioration in political conditions since September 2001, this book concludes that the fight against global apartheid will continue to come most forcefully from the social, labour, women's, community, environmental, youth, disabled, indigenous and similar movements aggrieved by neoliberalism and its parallel oppressions. Unfortunately, that means that the most likely near-future re-alignment of the global forces discussed in Table 1 appears deeply unsatisfying if radical social and ecological change is desired in the short to medium term.

It is likely that, as in the 1930s, the Rightwing Resurgence will grow and will fuse with the economic interests of the Washington Consensus (and its US/UK corporate and banking backers), notwithstanding the ideological contradictions. Supporters of the Post-Washington Consensus will probably seek closer alignment with more 'responsible' Third World nationalists (e.g. Lula), and will tackle the more principled, radical forces within the global justice movements.

Is there any chance that the three left flanks might unite against the Rightwing Resurgence and Washington neoliberals? Perhaps a US Democratic Party president would, in view of citizen backlash against corporate malfeasance and imperialism, take a more left-populist position (such as was hinted at in the early stages of campaigning to unseat Bush by Howard Dean, but especially by Dennis Kucinich and Al Sharpton). As David Harvey posits,

> The construction of a new 'New Deal' led by the US and Europe, both domestically and internationally, in the face of overwhelming class forces and special interests ranged against it, is surely enough to fight for in the present conjucture. The thought that it might, by adequate pursuit of some long-term spatio-temporal fix, actually assuage the problems of overaccumulation for at least a few years and diminish the need to accumulate by dispossession might encourage democratic, progressive and humane forces to align behind it and turn it into some kind of practical reality. This does seem to propose a far less violent and far more benevolent imperial trajectory than the raw militaristic imperialism currently offered up by the neo-conservative movement in the US.[31]

It is not inconceivable that a 'global-Keynesian' approach to allow for genuine wealth and income transfers to poor people, alongside more ecologically-sound industrialisation, may emerge as a philosophy acceptable to the liberal wing of the US polity.[32] I remain sceptical, however, that the 'global' part can be realised at a time of such exceptionally unequal power relations, or that the Democratic Party's main financial and commercial elites would allow such a leftward drift.

Moving then to more explicitly anti-imperialist tasks, Samir Amin argues the necessity of a broadly unifying political project. Beginning with the global justice movements and Third World nationalists, he observes, 'The reconstruction of a Southern Front capable of giving the peoples of Asia and Africa, together with their solidarity across three continents, the capacity to make their voices heard will come about by liberating ourselves from the illusions of a "non-asymmetric" globalised liberal system, that will allow the nations of the Third World to make up their "backwardness".'[33] Drawing inspiration from the February 2003 Kuala Lumpur meeting of the Non-Aligned Movement, at which Mbeki turned over the chair to Mahathir, Amin elaborates: 'The Southern countries are becoming aware of the fact that the neoliberal globalised management has nothing to offer them and that being the case, the neo-liberal system had to use military violence to be established, thereby playing the game enshrined in the American project. The [Non-Aligned] Movement is becoming – as suggested – that of "non-alignment with liberal globalisation and US hegemony."'

Moreover, contended Amin, the January 2003 'Franco-African Summit strengthened the eventual alliance taking shape between Europe and the South'.[34] Post-Washington Consensus advocates in a 'social Europe' would, in this scenario, join the Southern Front: 'There exist conditions capable of promoting closer relations between at least all the peoples of the ancient world. This union could be given concrete expression at the international diplomatic level by thickening the Paris-Berlin-Moscow-Peking axis . . . by developing friendly relations between this axis and the reconstituted Afro-Asian front.'[35] On the surface, it appears that Bush's mid-2003 diplomacy with Putin and the Evian meeting, which stitched together G8 unity and showed no signs of European solidarity to Africa, negate that option. Nevertheless, Amin's is an attractive scenario: a global popular front against the United States: '[With] an authentic cohesion between Europe, Russia, China, the whole of Asia and Africa will constitute the foundation on which will be constructed a multi-centrist, democratic and pacific world.'[36]

University of KwaZulu-Natal researcher Peter Dwyer reacts:

> Are we to seriously believe that we can enter into (or rely upon for more than a nano-second) some sort of alliance with 'some members of the military,' intelligence political and business elites. Even if some of the above were against the war, their reasons for doing so are rarely if ever progressive ones. Whilst we must always exploit contradictions, tensions and differences among the ruling classes, this should not mean entering into alliances with them, they should not be part of the global peace movement. France *et al* were never going to be reliable allies for the global peace movement.[37]

Amin conceded:

> The political regimes set up in many Southern countries are not democratic, to say the least, and are sometimes really odious. These authoritarian power structures favour comprador groups whose interests consist in expanding the global imperialist capitalism. The alternative – construction of a front comprising peoples of the South – can materialise through democratisation. This necessary democratisation will be a difficult and long process but it certainly cannot be realised by establishing puppet regimes to open their countries' resources to plunder by North American multinational companies, regimes that will consequently be even more fragile, less credible and less legitimate than those they succeeded under protection by the American invader.[38]

A stronger case for the global popular front comes from Jeremy Brecher, a US-based activist and writer:

> If the Bush program is regarded as little but the continuation of US imperialism, then I understand the logic of saying that popular movements require no new alliances with national elites and governments. But if it represents a greatly augmented threat to the peace and future well-being of the world – as the (very different) phenomenon of Nazism represented something far more threatening than traditional German capitalism and militarism – then one must consider all the forces that could possibly be brought to bear to defeat it.
>
> I entirely agree that various governments and elites I discuss as potential coalition partners 'should not be part of the global peace movement' and they are 'never going to be reliable allies.'

Indeed, there were other errors of the left in the 1930s and 1940s that grew in part from subservience to the state interests of one or another power (the capitalist powers for the Social Democrats; the USSR for the Communists). I emphasise the need for the new global peace movement to remain independent of the dominance of any of the various forces with whom alliances need to be constructed. The movement's independence from elites and governments should go hand in hand with its effort to move them toward collective resistance to US dictation and aggression.[39]

These formulations require very close attention to the dynamics of state power. Is that, though, the direction in which most global justice movements are actually heading?

Retrieving a lost word

World-systems theorist William Martin points out that, 'for at least several hundred years there have been successive, waves of movements which have attacked and destabilised the capitalist world-economy, its hegemonic powers, and yet, at the same time, come to provide the foundation for a new ordering of accumulation and political rule on a world scale. Seen from this perspective, present movements take on a distinctive meaning, and pose for us quite different possible futures.'[40] Martin and his Binghamton University colleagues have identified four 'waves of movements': 1760–1848, 1848–1917, 1917–68, and 1968–2001.[41]

The most recent left movements have 'a solid understanding that capturing national power could not be equated with capturing control over economic or cultural lives, embedded in the much deeper and wider domains of the capitalist world-economy', Martin insists. 'This strategic advance presented a dilemma, however, that remained unresolved: how does one organise and attack capital and inequality, if even the capture of state power leaves its global foundations unchecked? Inability to resolve this dilemma was considerably complicated by faltering attempts to bridge the differences of race and gender across the core-periphery divide.'[42]

The answer lies in the actual grassroots struggles of what Michael Hardt and Toni Negri term the 'multitudes', namely, as Martin puts it, in 'the demands for the decommodification of land, labour, and cultural life, demands so prominent in the local, but increasingly globally-integrated, struggles against the privatisation of basic human needs (land, water, education, health). Late-capitalist antisystemic movements may find much to learn from earlier movements against incorporation into the capitalist world, movements which have often been dismissed as attempts to retain "pre-capitalist" modes of life and production.' In addition to their new perspective on the state, for Martin, the 'very different' nature of the contemporary global justice movements is that they are based upon 'attempts to construct a new strategy suited precisely to the fundamental structures of governance within a single, expanding, capitalist world-economy'.

In opposition to uneven global capitalist development, this point is indisputable, and reflected not only in the big protests from Seattle onwards, but also in surgical campaigning against international targets, as exemplified by the World Bank Bonds Boycott. Nevertheless, we might begin to part company with Martin (and Hardt/Negri in their book *Empire*), if it means posing 'the problem as one of democratically embedding society in a *world*-economy, as opposed to the liberal's fictitious, mid-twentieth century national economies, [which] poses a much sharper challenge to the structures and central powers of the capitalist world-economy'. He concludes, 'there can be no return to the nationalist programs of the twentieth century.'[43]

Opposing national*ism* as a motivating force and political philosophy is not the same, however, as dismissing the most potentially substantial counterweight to global capital in the world today: the national state. Elsewhere, I've provided evidence to support a different interpretation of the probable trajectory of global justice movements, based upon nixing, or at least disempowering, the embryonic world economic state, and making intensifying demands upon states and capital for the decommodification of basic goods, services and labour power.[44] The way that Soweto revolutionary Trevor Ngwane puts it is instructive: 'Some people attack the idea of targeting state power. The argument that globalisation undermines the role of the nation state gets translated into an excuse for avoiding the fight with your own national bourgeoisie. But we in South Africa cannot (fail to) confront the ANC and Mbeki. American activists can't (fail to) confront Bush.'[45]

Yet we must frankly acknowledge, that political *scale* remains a point of great contention. While a formula of 'internationalism plus the state' is probably most appropriate for the short term, there are potentially important experiments that continue in local settings, such as the neighbourhood assemblies and factory occupations of crisis-ridden Argentina. Amory Starr and Jason Adams are North American academic-activists who promote a localist 'autonomism' that explicitly endorses Amin, so as to extend the logic of delinking and deglobalisation to the very local level:

> The most resolute of these are the now-famous indigenous movements, such as the U'wa and the Ogoni, who expel

'development' from their lands . . . They affirm the possibility and necessity of collaboration among autonomous communities when necessary. These movements don't just want 'another world' but 'a world in which many worlds fit' (a phrase of the Zapatistas) . . .

Drawing on Rousseau, Gandhian development, anarchism, indigenous culture, and village anthropology, a diverse range of scholars emphasise the benefits of 'decentralised political institutions' which would protect people from exploitation, alleviate unemployment through 'complementary small-scale industry,' prioritise 'solving the problems of poverty' rather than 'compatibility with the world market,' and 'protect the local globally.'[46]

It is sometimes suggested that one component of autonomist struggle is the Soweto activist campaign, Operation Khanyisa, or 'light up': the illegal reconnection of electricity in the wake of Eskom's massive price increases. However, Ngwane has carefully considered the ideology of autonomism in the case of the Western Cape Anti-Eviction Campaign (AEC), and found it wanting. He describes the AEC cadres'

> insistence that they do not want leaders and are opposed to 'representative democracy' in their organisation, including the establishment of sub-committees. In 2002, I had the privilege of spending some time with the AEC, and my impression is that this is

a 'received ideology' which the leaders acquired from a prolonged visit by an autonomist comrade from the US. This is not to say that the comrades were not already thinking or acting along the same lines, but in politics the formal doctrine or line adopted by a group or movement, especially its leadership, is crucial. In my own interventions with the AEC, I attempted to mitigate the most damaging and debilitating aspects of this ideology, and was able to win the comrades on certain issues. For example, it was soon demonstrated in a meeting that the agenda was not drawn up collectively with the masses, as is often claimed. Instead, everyone looked to the leaders to suggest the items for discussion. It was also easy to illustrate the utter impracticality of refusing to send delegates or representatives to carry out tasks, when it is necessary to organise support in other areas.

My concern is also that the ideology of no leadership means, by default, the principle of 'self-selection' and thus encourages a lack of accountability. There is also the danger of the AEC drowning in its own militancy, because of its refusal to develop long-term political projects in favour of immediate and short-term and militant actions.

The Marxist method of distinguishing between immediate, democratic and transitional demands can be used as an antidote to the disease of 'pure' militancy, and can win militants by its usefulness. Marx teaches us that our aim, in taking up immediate problems of the class, is to show the power of collective working-class action and the need to ultimately overthrow the capitalist system. Without such a perspective there is a danger of co-option, once the enemy accedes to our demands, as they did with the SECC stopping disconnections, or once demoralisation and tiredness set in when the enemy stands firm and people don't see a solution despite their efforts.

The most important lesson is, in the words of the Anti-Privatisation Forum, to 'draw a class line' between us and the class enemy. This class line should not just be drawn by word of mouth but by the nature of our demands, our methods of struggle and the solutions we propose to the problems faced by the working class.

As to the ideology of the Soweto Electricity Crisis Committee, 'these are ordinary people, like millions of other ordinary working people in SA. They have rescued a word which was disappearing into history, or being lost in books and discussions of a few people from the middle class: socialism.'[47]

The global scale of struggle

To be as formidable an opponent as is required, the global justice movements will have to not only build from below, in places like Soweto, but also deconstruct global apartheid from the top down. The Washington Consensus neoliberals and their Washington neighbours who adhere to the Rightwing Resurgence remain too powerful a bloc. Post-Washington reformers have had a desperately unsuccessful recent period, in virtually all spheres of activity: preventing the Iraq War; making the bureaucratised and increasingly neoliberal United Nations relevant and constructive; reforming governance and economic policy at the international financial institutions; solving environment problems with Kyoto-style market mechanisms; establishing genuine anti-poverty programmes; and even protecting traditional bourgeois-liberal civil rights. Neither can success be claimed by Third World nationalists, who are terribly uneven, with some, like Lula of Brazil and, to some degree, Mbeki, ascendant but only at the cost of their core constituencies. However, most such leaders, especially African elites like Mbeki and Obasanjo, cannot be taken terribly seriously. Not only is hypocrisy a debilitating problem; they are, even on their own limited terms, unable to move a decisive agenda.

Usually, the global justice movements stand resolutely against both exhausted Third World state elites and unimaginative global-scale Post-Washington Consensus reformers. Their main enemies, in the Washington Consensus and Resurgent Rightwing, have reason to be worried about the global justice activists. As Fidel Castro explained to a May 2003 Havana conference of Marxist economists,

> These are fighters, and that's what we must call them. They won at Seattle. At Quebec, they forced the elites into a fortified position. It was more than a demonstration, it was an insurgency. The leaders of the world must now meet inside a bunker. They had to meet on a ship in Italy, and on a mountain in Canada. They needed police barriers in Davos, in peaceful Switzerland. The most important thing is that the fighters have created a real fear. The IMF and World Bank cannot meet properly.[48]

It is easy to predict continuing militancy and independent honing of strategies and tactics for the left. Already, the popular and intellectual texts on the global justice movements are overwhelming, and it is difficult to pin down the ideological orientations and strategic trajectories.[49] Alex Callinicos breaks up the movements into 'localist', 'reformist', 'autonomist' and 'socialist' ideologies. Christophe Aguiton cites three currents: 'radical internationalist', 'nationalist', and 'neo-reformist'. Peter Waterman argues against these categories, by *surpassing* traditional left internationalism. "Emancipation" might seem a more appropriate term than "left" when discussing the transformation of society, nature, culture, work and psychology, and that increasingly important but nether-place, cyberspace.'[50]

What this means in terms of political mapping (with reference to Table 1) is apparently diminishing patience between at least three blocks: a) global justice movements, b) Third World nationalists and Post-Washington Consensus reformers, and c) the two most obdurate *status quo* tendencies: the Washington Consensus and Resurgent Rightwing. The latter two appear to be working in harmony, with only the Washington institutions' adoption of somewhat more 'sustainable' rhetoric distinguishing its main implementing institutions (World Bank, IMF and WTO) from prior years. The Resurgent Rightwing often continues to express rhetorical support for both 'sustainability' and free markets, yet adopted a post-September 11 programme of protectionism, racism, xenophobia, bailouts, and unilateralism on most eco-social grounds. The combination of the Washington Consensus and Resurgent Rightwing is intimidating.

For the sake of future political strategy, therefore, the major question is whether the global justice movements will provide not only delegitimisation of the Washington Consensus and Resurgent Rightwing, but also continue to express hostility to the Post-Washington Consensus and fight Third World nationalists on home turf. Presently, this configuration of forces applies to South Africa, Nigeria and Zimbabwe, as well as strategically important countries in Asia and Latin America. If proponents of a strengthened WSSD-type gathering aim to continue holding summits of this type, it is unlikely that they will have an easier time of it in places characterised by conflicts between the global justice movements and Third World nationalists.

Next steps for the global justice movements?

The rise of the global justice movements as the world's first-ever multi-issue political convergence was profoundly important, and South Africa has been the scene of crucial, productive developments in the movement's growth. The time may well come for a formalisation of the character of these movements in explicitly *political* terms, such as within the traditions of international socialism, for which the first four 'internationals' provide a host of lessons, largely negative, about world-scale co-ordination.[51]

The period from September 2001 to late 2003 witnessed impressive alliances, no matter how brief, between the various global justice movements fighting for both economic progress and peace. The merits of various related causes coming together, as they did at the WSSD, will be reflected to some extent in wide-ranging protests at future events. Lasting possibilities for linkages of eco-social issues are evident in other sectoral processes, as well as at the World Social Forum and its decentralised offshoots. The strength of the linkages depends, in future, in part upon more national-level civil societies having the chance to learn and experience the sorts of political dynamics that were on display, in many ways, at the WSSD.

Even within progressive civil society there remain a good many Post-Washington Consensus-type development NGOs, labour movements and environmentalists who have ambitions for making an impact upon global apartheid in the same spirit as Pretoria. By and large they have been disappointed by the weak outcomes of their endeavours. International global justice movements and individuals are increasingly delighted with the power and vision of South Africa's social movements, and how *undaunted* they are when confronting neoliberalism.

The best terms to describe the various components of international civil society are probably no longer based on 'north' and 'south' geographic standpoints, and not even 'Global North' and 'Global South' (to make allowance for uneven development within societies). Instead, the two main competing ideologies of civil society, global justice movements and Post-Washington Consensus, seem to have settled in as the more permanent and important divisions. There are some NGOs that work closely with Third World nationalists, and others that even advocate policies of a Washington Consensus character such as unsubsidised microfinance for vulnerable women, but it is likely that neither group will profoundly influence future relationships between civil societies of the north and south.

The differences between the global justice movements and the Post-Washington Consensus approaches are widening. Global justice movements often advocate more forceful 'nixing' of institutions, which the Post-Washington Consensus would rather 'fix'. Nevertheless, Amin and Brecher, among others, argue that opposition to US unilateralism in the military, diplomatic, economic and environmental spheres would be an important basis for pulling such a broad-based alliance together, similar to that during World War II against the Axis powers. Arundhati Roy's January 2004 speech to the Mumbai World Social Forum suggested that the movements choose two US corporations that are profiting from the Iraq occupation, and targeting them in numerous cities across the world.[52]

Yet, our final word must be one of caution. The importance of empowering local and national 'affiliates' of the global justice movements, such as the South African social movements and their regional allies, cannot be emphasised enough. My sense is that this process will occur unevenly in coming years via Social Forum initiatives now being established. In South Africa, the split between Cosatu and most independent-left social movements, means that it is not likely that a national 'social forum' branding exercise will be successful, until a wide-ranging challenge to the ruling party occurs. Precedents from trade unions emerged in Zambia and Zimbabwe over the past 12 years.

South African social movements will help lead a Southern African Social Forum headquartered at the Lusaka NGO Women for Change in 2004. Zimbabwe and Niger were the first countries in Africa to establish genuine national Social Forums, with the Central African Republic, Ethiopia and a Horn of Africa Social Forum not far behind. The rise of national and regional Social Forums in most parts of the world bode well for more co-ordinated civil society inputs into global governance. My sense is that state priorities will be seen as overriding, because the balance of forces at the international scale simply do not offer progressive social movements any real scope for durable reforms, as efforts on debt, trade, environment, militarism and other examples continually prove. Quite intense protests will continue at WTO, World Bank, IMF, G8, Davos and other elite meetings.

Optimistic outcomes depend upon an obvious prerequisite: the hard work of local, then national, then regional and finally global-scale organising. Skipping any steps through top-down interventions will never make more than a momentary dent, and may divert these new and enthusiastic forms of organising into a technicist cul-de-sac. The approach of the South African social movements, namely thinking globally and acting locally first, while the balance of forces change nationally and internationally, appears a wise route toward a final attack on global apartheid, and capitalism itself.

Simultaneously, anti-capitalists from the Global South must not merely reject the international character of neoliberalism, but must also confront its local champions. I tend to think that this negates prospects for alliances between global justice movements and Third World nationalists, unless more radically left-leaning governments, such as Cuba and Venezuela, invent a model that convinces anti-capitalists that the state won't necessarily repress or co-opt their initiatives.

The opportunities to take up these challenges, and link them across countries and sectors of struggle, is now greater than at any time in memory. If the bulk of work lies in activism, however, that does not mean the intellectual project can be set aside. Even if the theory of uneven development is explored from many angles,[53] it will still be necessary to expand our case studies of concrete forms of unevenness, and to demonstrate in both intellectual and political terms that the theory can easily jump scale from local to global and back. As for reversing uneven development, when Mbeki tells world leaders that 'out of Johannesburg and out of Africa, must emerge something new that takes the world forward away from the entrenchment of global apartheid', as he did at the outset of the WSSD, it is only possible to agree ... to disagree.[54]

And in so doing, we hear two eloquent testimonies that warn us about the real role played by Mbeki, Manuel, Erwin and the others. Arundhati Roy talks of the insidious function men like them play today:

> The vulgar, hands-on racism of Old Imperialism is outdated. The cornerstone of New Imperialism is New Racism. The tradition of 'turkey pardoning' in the US is a wonderful allegory for New Racism. Every year since 1947, the National Turkey Federation presents the US President with a turkey for Thanksgiving. Every year, in a show of ceremonial magnanimity, the President spares that particular bird (and eats another one). After receiving the presidential pardon, the Chosen One is sent to Frying Pan Park in Virginia to live out its natural life. The rest of the 50 million Turkeys raised for Thanksgiving are slaughtered and eaten on Thanksgiving Day. ConAgra Foods, the company that has won the Presidential Turkey contract, says it trains the lucky birds to be sociable, to interact with dignitaries, school children and the press. (Soon they'll even speak English!)
>
> That's how New Racism in the corporate era works. A few carefully bred turkeys – the local elites of various countries, a community of wealthy immigrants, investment bankers, the occasional Colin Powell, or Condoleezza Rice, some singers, some writers (like myself) – are given absolution and a pass to Frying Pan Park. The remaining millions lose their jobs, are evicted from their homes, have their water and electricity connections cut, and die of AIDS. Basically they're for the pot. But the Fortunate Fowls in Frying Pan Park are doing fine. Some of them even work for the IMF and the WTO – so who can accuse those organisations of being anti-turkey? Some serve as board members on the Turkey Choosing Committee – so who can say that turkeys are against Thanksgiving? They participate in it! Who

can say the poor are anti-corporate globalization? There's a stampede to get into Frying Pan Park. So what if most perish on the way?[55]

Finally, consider these last furious words about Pretoria's role as accomplice to global apartheid, in the poetry of Vonani wa ka Bila, an anti-capitalist activist from Elim Hospital in Limpopo:

> Mr. President, let the babies die
>
> The fat men in parliament sleep in broad daylight.
> They've lost the dream to free the starving bellies of the masses.
> Street fighter! Bull-fighter!
> Don't inconvenience Mr. President.
> He has an important meeting in Washington DC.
>
> Buy him houses in all cities of the world.
> Don't forget to buy him a private jet, a balloon.
> He'll jump, clad and stomp like a well-fed baboon.
> Don't worry about the price,
> Ties with the US and G-8 must be tightened.
> The poor labour under the burden of tax
> While Third World debt heralds irreversible death.
>
> Mr. President, bodies decompose in run down public hospitals,
> At Ga-Nchabeleng we need doctors, x-ray plates, water and electricity,
> Mothers give birth in open bushes,
> At Zava we need condoms and femidoms,
> The girl-mother-child's future is uncertain,
> You told us victory is certain,
> That the people shall govern . . .
> Mr. President, your hospital has become a white elephant,
> A slaughter house.
>
> Boom! Boom!
> We blew horns when exiles returned –
> We did not know you befriended Ronald Reagan and Margaret Thatcher.
> We strummed guitars when prisoners walked free –
> We did not know the mind got frozen in prison winter.
> We shouted power to the people!
> But business sucked the power of the state.

Preacher man! Miracle man!

Get the demons out of my body!
Ghetto babies die of AIDS and cholera –
Multinational pharmaceutical companies
Rake billions with their expensive drugs.

Preacher man! Miracle man!
Get the devil out of my country's skull!
Ghetto babies die of kwashiokor and marasmum –
The rich squeeze the last ounce of blood of Mother Africa.

Street fighter! Bull-fighter!
Don't inconvenience Mr. President.
He has an important meeting in Geneva,
He must brush shoulders with the high and mighty.
Dollars, will overflow my table,
Bread and butter!

This is the millennium plan,
Followed by declarations and slogans,
Poor men and women goaded by the western whip.
Dawn of a new century.
Money talks.
The rich get richer,
We can only sell our breasts and thighs for a living.
I'm scared of urban beasts.
Their tongues are too sweet.
Their knives are too sharp.
In the meantime –
Ghetto babies die in public toilets.[56]

Notes

1. Adesina, J. (2002), 'NEPAD and the Challenge of Africa's Development: Towards the Political Economy of a Discourse', Unpublished paper, Rhodes University Department of Sociology, Grahamstown.
2. Adesina, 'NEPAD and the Challenge of Africa's Development'.
3. This is a perpetual theme in Bond, *Unsustainable South Africa.*
4. Bond, *Against Global Apartheid,* Chapter Twelve.
5. Fisher, J. (2002), 'Africa', in E. Bircham and J. Charlton (eds) (2002), *Anti-Capitalism: A Guide to the Movement,* London, Bookmarks; Zeilig, L. (ed.) (2002), *Class Struggle and Resistance in Africa,* Cheltenham, New Clarion.
6. *Guardian,* 20 February 2003.

7. Taylor, I. and G. Mokhawa (2003), 'Not Forever: Botswana, Conflict Diamonds and the Bushmen', *African Affairs*, 102. The UN Committee on the Elimination of Racial Discrimination also condemned Botswana. On the other side, the permanent secretary in Botswana's Ministry of Mineral Resources and Water Affairs (and deputy Chairman of Debswana), called Survival a 'terrorist organisation' in 2003.
8. Community campaigns are well covered on the South African Indymedia website, which is one in Africa that periodically reports on anti-capitalist activism.
9. Cited in Bond, *Fanon's Warning*, p. 48.
10. Adesina, 'NEPAD and the Challenge of Africa's Development'.
11. Report of the Codesria/TWN Conference on Africa and the Challenge of the 21st Century, Accra, 23–26 April, excerpted from Bond, *Fanon's Warning*. Such a revival would, in my opinion, have to be grounded in classical theories of commodity-form and value, accumulation and overaccumulation, spatio-temporal crisis and crisis displacement, accumulation by dispossession, and the untenable rise of finance and commerce, augmented to better incorporate the reproductive aspects and gender dynamics of capitalism, systemic environmental degradation, aspects of social resistance, and many other ethnic and cultural factors that have been used by critics to illegitimately denounce Marxism as a holistic theory of social relations.
12. Amin, S. (1985), *Delinking: Towards a Polycentric World*, London, Zed Books.
13. Bello, W. (2002), *Deglobalisation: Ideas for a New World Economy*, London, Zed Books.
14. Bond, *Against Global Apartheid*, Part Four.
15. Bond, *Against Global Apartheid*, Chapter Twelve.
16. This was also the position taken in Bond, P. (1991), *Commanding Heights and Community Control*. No reform projects during subsequent years have been convincing.
17. Ndungane, N. (2003), *A World with a Human Face: A Voice from Africa*, Cape Town, David Philip, p. 31.
18. *Mail & Guardian*, 27 April 2001.
19. McCully, P. (2002), 'Avoiding Solutions, Worsening Problems', San Francisco, International Rivers Network, http://www.irn.org, p. 40. For more on the background and South African politics associated with the Commission, see Bond, *Unsustainable South Africa*, Chapters Three and Seven.
20. Sapri provided six conclusions from the studies:
    (1) Trade liberalisation, financial sector liberalisation, the weakening of state support and reduction of demand for local goods and services have devastated local industries especially small and medium sized enterprises providing most national employment.
    (2) Structural and sectoral policy reforms in agriculture and mining have undermined the viability of small farms, weakened food security and damaged the natural environment.
    (3) A combination of labour market reforms, lay-offs resulting from privatisation and the shrinking of labour-intensive productive sectors have undermined the position of workers causing employment to drop, real wages to fall, and workers' rights to weaken.

(4) Privatisation of public utilities and the application of user fees to health care and education have disproportionately reduced the poor's access to affordable services.
(5) Increased impoverishment caused by structural adjustment has affected women more than men.
(6) Anticipated gains in efficiency, competitiveness, savings and revenues from privatisation have failed to materialise. Trade liberalisation has increased rather than decreased current-account deficits and external debt, while transnational corporations have become more powerful in the structurally adjusted countries.

21. http://www.saprin.org/
22. Peet, R. (2003), *The World Bank, IMF and WTO*, London, Zed Books, Chapter Four.
23. *New York Times*, 7 June 2003.
24. http://www.brettonwoodsproject.org/topic/governance/g2801eir.html.
25. http://www.brettonwoodsproject.org/topic/governance/g2801eir.html.
26. World Bank Press Review, 10 December 2003.
27. Environmental Defence, Friends of the Earth, and International Rivers Network (2003), *Gambling With People's Lives*, Washington and Berkeley, 19 September.
28. http://www.irinnews.org/report.asp?ReportID=39413&SelectRegion=Southern_Africa&SelectCountry=south%20africa.
29. *London Evening Standard*, 17 April 2002.
30. Dembele, 'PRSPS: Poverty Reduction or Poverty Reinforcement?'
31. Harvey, *The New Imperialism*, pp. 210–211.
32. For more on the concept, see, for example, Mosley, P. (1997), 'The World Bank, "Global Keynesianism" and the Distribution of the Gains from Growth', *World Development*, 25, 11; Koehler, G. (1999), 'Global Keynesianism and Beyond', *Journal of World-Systems Research*, 5, http://csf.colorado.edu/wsystems/jwsr.html; Koehler, G. and A. Tausch (2002), *Global Keynesianism: Unequal Exchange and Global Exploitation*, Huntington, USA, Nova Science.
33. Amin, 'Confronting the Empire'.
34. Amin, S. (2003), 'Laying New Foundations for Solidarity Among Peoples of the South', presented to the conference on The Work of Karl Marx and the Challenges of the 21st Century, Institute of Philosophy of the Ministry of Science, Technology and the Environment, the National Association of Economists of Cuba, the Cuban Trade Union Federation and the Centre for the Study of Economy and Planning, Havana, 5–8 May.
35. Amin, 'Laying New Foundations for Solidarity Among Peoples of the South'.
36. Amin, 'Laying New Foundations for Solidarity Among Peoples of the South'.
37. Dwyer, P. (2003), 'The New Global Peace Movement vs. the Bush Juggernaut', http://www.lists.kabissa.org/mailman/listinfo/debate, 26 May.
38. Amin, 'Laying New Foundations for Solidarity Among Peoples of the South'.
39. Brecher, J. (2003), 'The New Global Peace Movement vs. the Bush Juggernaut', http://www.lists.kabissa.org/mailman/listinfo/debate, 6 June. See also Brecher's longer analysis: http://www.foreignpolicy-infocus.org/papers/juggernaut/index.html.
40. Martin, W. (2003), 'Three Hundred Years of World Movements: Towards the End of the Capitalist World-Economy?', presented at the Sociology Seminar,

Rand Afrikaans University, Johannesburg, 13 June. See also Frank, A.G. and M. Fuentes (1990), 'Civil Democracy: Social Movements in Recent World History', in S. Amin, G. Arrighi, A.G. Frank and I. Wallerstein, *Transforming the Revolution: Social Movements and the World-System*, New York, Monthly Review.

41. Going back to the Hapsburg and Ottoman Empires, Martin continues, 'It is possible to trace trans-national networks of not only ideological opposition to older imperial networks, but also increasingly inter-connected revolt against core agents of the rising capitalist world-economy ... Merchants, mariners and diasporic networks, integrally tied to global economic processes and political struggles, began to fuel nationalist and revivalist revolts' that reached as far as Indonesia. In the 18th century, 'a rising tide of revolts against the central, proletarian base of the eighteenth century existed, leading to the destruction of a world-wide system of enslavement and slave-based commodity production.' This entailed 'extensive networking and clustering of emancipatory struggles across colonial boundaries prior to, rather than derived from, the French (and American) Revolution', of which Haiti was a crucial example. The mid-nineteenth century was the period of state-oriented party-building, and from 1917 national independence revolutions were common, all based upon the 'expectation that state power would bring emancipation' (Martin, 'Three Hundred Years of World Movements').
42. Martin, 'Three Hundred Years of World Movements'.
43. Martin, 'Three Hundred Years of World Movements'. In an otherwise excellent US economic analysis by Doug Henwood, straw figures are set up to criticise localist and national-based strategies, *even though it is at these scales that the actual social movements in motion struggle around*, with no indication as yet that the leading Third World strategists envisage any sort of global-scale construction, at least prior to changing local and national power relations (Henwood, D. (2003), *After the New Economy*, New York, New Press).
44. Bond, *Against Global Apartheid*, Part Four; and Bond, *Unsustainable South Africa*.
45. Ngwane, 'Sparks in the Townships'.
46. Starr, A. and J. Adams (2003), 'Anti-globalisation: The Global Fight for Local Autonomy', *New Political Science*, 25, 1. In view of Amin's historic orientation to Third World revolutions that require national state control, and the need for economies of scale to assure provision of basic goods and necessary services, this is not a particularly convincing stretch of the word delinking.
47. Ngwane, T. (2004), 'The New Social Movements and Working Class Politics in Post-Apartheid South Africa', *Historical Materialism*.
48. Transcribed by the author and cited in Bond, 'Cuba Dares'.
49. Numerous books analyse the global justice movements. Aside from Naomi Klein's seminal *NoLogo*, the one broad overview that has sold the most copies in English is Bircham, E. and J. Charlton (eds) (2002), *Anti-Capitalism: A Guide to the Movement*, London, Bookmarks. Recent English-language movement analyses include Aguiton, C. (2003), *The World Belongs to Us!*, London, Verso; Alvarez, S., E. Dagnino and A. Escobar (eds) (1998),

Cultures of Politics, Politics of Cultures: Re-visioning Latin American Social Movements, Boulder, Westview; Amin, S. and F. Houtart (eds) (2003), *The Globalisation of Resistance: The State of the Struggles*, London, Zed Books; Anand, A., A. Escobar, J. Sen and P. Waterman (eds) (2003), *Are Other Worlds Possible? The Past, Present, and Futures of the World Social Forum*, New Delhi, Viveka; Callinicos, A. (2003), *An Anti-Capitalist Manifesto*, Cambridge, Polity; Fisher, W. and T. Ponniah (eds) (2003), *Another World is Possible: Popular Alternatives to Globalisation at the World Social Forum*, London, Zed Books; Kingsnorth, *One No, Many Yesses*; Mertes, T. (ed.) (2003), *A Movement of Movements: Is Another World Really Possible?*, London, Verso; Smith, J. and H. Johnston (eds) (2002), *Globalisation and Resistance: Transnational Dimensions of Social Movements*, Lanham, Rowman and Littlefield; Starr, A. (2000), *Naming the Enemy: Anti-Corporate Movements Confront Globalisation*, London, Zed Books; Waterman, P. (2001), *Globalisation, Social Movements and the New Internationalisms*, London, Continuum.

50. Waterman, P. (2003), 'The Global Justice and Solidarity Movement', http://groups.yahoo.com/group/GloSoDia/
51. The first international was the International Working Men's Association which Marx and Engels helped kickstart with the *Communist Manifesto* in 1848. The second was the social democratic flop which did not prevent workers from turning nationalistic at the time of World War I. The third was a Stalinist merger of Soviet defensiveness and nationalist liberation, which exhausted itself long before the Berlin Wall fell. The fourth represented one key strand of the Trotskyist tradition which survived Stalin's murder of Trotsky, but faded by the 1990s (though still alive in Mbeki's nightmares and the laudable journal *International Viewpoint*). A fifth international would have to innovate in terms of avoiding sectarianism, vanguardism, dogmatism, patriarchy, anthropocentrism, and other classic sins of the 'groupuscule' left.
52. Roy, A. (2004), 'Do Turkeys enjoy Thanksgiving?', *The Hindu*, 18 January, http://www.hindu.com/2004/01/18/stories/2004011800181400.htm.
53. See, for example, Aglietta, M. (1976), *A Theory of Capitalist Regulation*, London, New Left Books; Bond, P. (1999), 'Uneven Development', in P. O'Hara (ed.), *Encyclopaedia of Political Economy*, London, Routledge; Harvey, *The Limits to Capital*; Mandel, E. (1962), *Marxist Economic Theory*, Volume 1, London, Merlin Press. Smith, N. (1990), *Uneven Development*, Oxford, Basil Blackwell.
54. Mbeki, 'Address by President Mbeki at the Welcome Ceremony of the WSSD'.
55. Roy, 'Do Turkeys enjoy Thanksgiving?'
56. wa ka Bila, V. (2002), 'Mr. President, Let the Babies Die', in V. wa ka Bila and W. Nghalaluma (eds), *Timbila 2002: A Journal of Onion Skin Poetry*, Elim Hospital, Timbila Poetry Project.

References

Adams, S. (2001), *Comrade Minister*, New York, Nova Science Publishers.
Adedeji, A. (2002), 'From the Lagos Plan of Action to the New Partnership for Africa's Development, and from the Final Act of Lagos to the Constitutive Act: Whither Africa?', Keynote Address prepared for the African Forum for Envisioning Africa, Nairobi, 26–29 April.
Adesina, J. (2002), 'Development and the Challenge of Poverty: NEPAD, Post-Washington Consensus and Beyond', Paper presented to the Codesria/TWN Conference on Africa and the Challenge of the 21st Century, Accra, 23–26 April.
_____ (2002), 'NEPAD and the Challenge of Africa's Development: Towards the Political Economy of a Discourse', Unpublished paper, Rhodes University Department of Sociology, Grahamstown.
African National Congress (2002), 'People's Power in Action: Preface to the Strategy and Tactics of the ANC', 51st National Conference, Stellenbosch, December.
African National Congress Political Education Unit (2002), 'Contribution to the NEC/NWC Response to the "Cronin Interviews" on the Issue of Neoliberalism', Johannesburg, September.
African National Congress and ANC Alliance Partners (1998), 'The Global Economic Crisis and its Implications for South Africa', *African Communist*, Fourth Quarter.
African Womens Communication and Development Network, African Womens Empowerment Network, Congress of South African Trade Unions, Council for the Development of Social Science Research in Africa, Crisis in Zimbabwe Coalition and Mwelekeo wa NGO (2003), 'Joint Statement: G8 Summits 2002 to 2003: From a Trickle to a Drop', Geneva, 3 June.
Afrodad (2001), 'Civil Society Participation in the Poverty Reduction Strategy Paper Process: A Synthesis of Five Studies conducted in Burkina Faso, Mauritania, Mozambique, Tanzania and Uganda', Harare, April.
Aglietta, M. (1976), *A Theory of Capitalist Regulation*, London, New Left Books.
Aguiton, C. (2003), *The World Belongs to Us!*, London, Verso.
Alexander, N. (1993), *Some are More Equal than Others*, Cape Town, Buchu.
_____ (2002), *An Ordinary Country*, Pietermaritzburg, University of Natal Press.
Ali, T. (2002), *The Clash of Fundamentalisms*, London, Verso.
_____ (2003), 'Business as Usual', *The Guardian*, 24 May 2003.
Alvarez, S., E. Dagnino and A. Escobar (eds) (1998), *Cultures of Politics, Politics of Cultures: Re-visioning Latin American Social Movements*, Boulder, Westview.
Amin, S. (1985), *Delinking: Towards a Polycentric World*, London, Zed Books.
_____ (2003), 'Confronting the Empire', presented to the conference on The Work of Karl Marx and the Challenges of the 21st Century, Institute of Philosophy of the Ministry of Science, Technology and the Environment, the National Association of Economists of Cuba, the Cuban Trade Union Federation and the Centre for the Study of Economy and Planning, Havana, 5–8 May.

_____ (2003), 'Laying New Foundations for Solidarity Among Peoples of the South', presented to the conference on The Work of Karl Marx and the Challenges of the 21st Century, Institute of Philosophy of the Ministry of Science, Technology and the Environment, the National Association of Economists of Cuba, the Cuban Trade Union Federation and the Centre for the Study of Economy and Planning, Havana, 5–8 May.
_____ and F. Houtart (eds) (2003), *The Globalisation of Resistance: The State of the Struggles*, London, Zed Books.
Anand, A., A. Escobar, J. Sen and P. Waterman (eds) (2003), *Are Other Worlds Possible? The Past, Present, and Futures of the World Social Forum*, New Delhi, Viveka.
Anonymous (2001), 'Angolan Civil Society Debates Way Forward', *World Bank Watch SA? SA Watch WB!*, December.
Anyang'Nyong'o, P. et al (eds) (2002), *NEPAD: A New Path?*, Nairobi, Heinrich Böll Foundation.
Appollis, J. (2002), 'The Political Significance of August 31', *Khanya Journal*, 2.
Armijo, L. (2001), 'The Political Geography of Financial Reform: Who Wants What and Why?', *Global Governance*, 7, 4.
Arrighi, G. (2002), 'The African Crisis: World Systemic and Regional Aspects', *New Left Review* 2, 15.
Asmal, K. (2003), 'Report of the World Panel on Financing Infrastructure: Letter to Dr Margaret Catley-Carson', Pretoria, 10 April.
Barchiesi, F. and T. Bramble (eds) (2003), *Rethinking the Labour Movement in the 'New South Africa'*, Aldershot, Ashgate.
Barlow, M. and T. Clarke (2002), *Blue Gold: The Battle Against Corporate Theft of the World's Water*, Toronto, Stoddard.
Bell, T. and D. Ntsebeza (2001), *Unfinished Business*, Cape Town, RedWorks.
Bello, W. (2002), *Deglobalisation: Ideas for a New World Economy*, London, Zed Books.
Bendaña, A. (2002), 'Byebye Poverty Reduction Strategy Papers, and Hello Good Governance', Unpublished paper, Managua.
Bernstein, H. (ed.) (1996), *The Agrarian Question in South Africa*, London, Frank Cass.
Bircham, E. and J. Charlton (eds) (2002), *Anti-Capitalism: A Guide to the Movement*, London, Bookmarks.
Bodibe, O., P. Craven and V. Mde (2002), 'Black Shadows and Red Herrings: A Rejoinder to the Moleketi-Jele Pamphlet', Johannesburg, personal discussion paper, October.
Bond, P. (1991), *Commanding Heights and Community Control*, Johannesburg, Ravan Press.
_____ (1993), 'If and When the New South Africa Looks North', *Financial Gazette*, 22 November.
_____ (1998), *Uneven Zimbabwe: A Study of Finance, Development and Underdevelopment*, Trenton, Africa World Press.
_____ (1999), 'Uneven Development', in P. O'Hara (ed.), *Encyclopaedia of Political Economy*, London, Routledge.
_____ (2000), *Cities of Gold, Townships of Coal*, Trenton, Africa World Press.
_____ (2002), *Unsustainable South Africa: Development and Social Protest*, London, The Merlin Press and Pietermaritzburg, University of Natal Press.

_____ (ed.) (2002), *Fanon's Warning: A Civil Society Reader on the New Partnership for Africa's Development*, Trenton, Africa World Press and AIDC.

_____ (2002), 'The Social Costs of Corporate HIV/AIDS Policies', *Sowetan/Sunday World*, 14 July.

_____ (2002), 'Globalisation hits the Poor', *City Press*, 8 September.

_____ (2003) [2001], *Against Global Apartheid: South Africa Meets the World Bank, IMF and International Finance*, Cape Town, University of Cape Town Press and London, Zed Books.

_____ (2003), 'Labour, Social Movements and South African Foreign Economic Policy', in P. Nel and J. van der Westhuizen (eds), *Democratising South African Foreign Policy*, New York, Lexington Books and Cape Town, University of Cape Town Press.

_____ (2003), 'Can the New Partnership for Africa's Development Work?', in K. Wohlmuth (ed.), *African Development Perspective Yearbook: African Entrepreneurship and Private Sector Development*, Bremen, Institute for World Economics and International Management.

_____ (2003), 'The Neoliberal Roots of South Africa's Cholera Epidemic', in M. Fort (ed.), *Globalisation and Health*, Boston, South End Press.

_____ (2003), 'Battle of the Trevors', *Sowetan*, 7 February.

_____ (2003), 'Cuba dares to Resist Washington and Resurrect the Ideas of Marx', *ZNet Commentary*, http://www.zmag.org, 31 May.

_____ (2003), 'Can AIDS Medicines Victory Catalyse Deeper Changes?', *ZNet Commentary*, http://www.zmag.org, 1 December.

_____ (2004) [2000], *Elite Transition: From Apartheid to Neoliberalism in South Africa*, London, Pluto Press and Pietermaritzburg, University of Natal Press.

_____ and G. Dor (2003), 'Uneven Health Outcomes and Political Resistance under Residual Neoliberalism in Africa', *International Journal of Health Services*, 33, 3.

_____ and G. Dor (2003), 'The Residual Dominance of Neoliberalism in Africa', in A. Osmanovic (ed.), *Transforming South Africa*, Hamburg, Institute of African Affairs.

_____ and T. Guliwe (2003), 'Contesting "Sustainable Development": South African Civil Society Critiques and Advocacy', in O. Edigheji and G. Mhone (eds), *Governance in the New South Africa: The Challenges of Globalisation*, Cape Town, University of Cape Town Press.

_____ and M. Khosa (eds) (1999), *An RDP Policy Audit*, Pretoria, HSRC Publications.

_____ and M. Manyanya (2003), *Zimbabwe's Plunge: Exhausted Nationalism, Neoliberalism and the Search for Social Justice*, London, The Merlin Press, Pietermaritzburg, University of Natal Press and Harare, Weaver Press.

_____ and T. Ngwane (2003), 'African Anti-Capitalism', in R. Neumann and A. Hsiao (eds), *Anti-Capitalism: A Field Guide to the Global Justice Movement*, New York, New Press.

Booker, S. and W. Minter (2001), 'AIDS is a Consequence of Global Apartheid', *The Nation*, July 2.

Boyce, J. and L. Ndikumana (2000), 'Is Africa a Net Creditor? New Estimates of Capital Flight from Severely Indebted Sub-Saharan African Countries, 1970–1996', Occasional Paper, University of Massachusetts/Amherst Political Economy Research Institute.

Brecher, J. (2003), 'The New Global Peace Movement vs. the Bush Juggernaut', http://www.lists.kabissa.org/mailman/listinfo/debate, 6 June. See also Brecher's longer analysis: http://www.foreignpolicy-infocus.org/ papers/juggernaut/ index.html.
Brewer, A. (1980), *Marxist Theories of Imperialism: A Critical Survey*, London, Routledge and Kegan Paul.
Brutus, D. (2002), 'Global Agendas are Set by the Usual Suspects', *Business Day*, 27 June.
Brzezinski, Z. (1997), *The Grand Chessboard*, New York.
Bukharin, N. (1972) [1917], *Imperialism and the World Economy*, New York, Monthly Review Press.
Bush, G. (2003), 'Remarks by the President to the Corporate Council on Africa's US-Africa Business Summit', Washington, 26 June.
Cafod, Oxfam, Christian Aid and Eurodad (2002), 'A Joint Submission to the World Bank and IMF Review of HIPC and Debt Sustainability', London, Oxford and Brussels, August.
Callinicos, A. (1992), *South Africa Between Apartheid and Capitalism*, London, Bookmarks.
_____ (2003), *An Anti-Capitalist Manifesto*, Cambridge, Polity.
Campbell, H. (2003), *Reclaiming Zimbabwe: The Exhaustion of the Patriarchal Model of Liberation*, Cape Town, David Philip.
Carroll, R. (2002), 'More Blacks believe Apartheid Country ran Better', *Mail & Guardian*, 13 December.
Cashdan, B. (2002), *Globalisation and Africa: Whose Side are We On?*, video, Johannesburg, Seipone Productions.
_____ (2002), *Down to Earth: Water*, SABC ChannelAfrica documentary, 6 September.
Center of Concern, International Gender and Trade Network and Institute for Agriculture and Trade Policy (2003), 'IMF-World Bank-WTO Close Ranks Around Flawed Economic Policies', Washington, Geneva and Minneapolis, http://www.coc.org/resources/articles/display.html?ID=484.
Cheru, F. (2001), *The Highly Indebted Poor Countries Initiative: A Human Rights Assessment of the Poverty Reduction Strategy Papers*, Report sub-mitted to the United Nations Economic and Social Council, New York, January.
Clarke, J. (2002), *Coming Back to Earth: South Africa's Changing Environment*, Johannesburg, Jacana.
Clarno, A. (2003), 'Denel and the South African Government: Profiting from the War on Iraq', *Khanya Journal*, 3, March.
Cock, J. (2003), 'A Better or Worse World? Report on the Third World Social Forum, Porto Alegre 2003', University of the Witwatersrand Department of Sociology, paper prepared for the University of Natal Centre for Civil Society (http://www.nu.ac.za/ccs), Durban, February.
Cockburn, A. and K. Silverstein (1996), *Washington Babylon*, London, Verso.
Corporate Europe Observatory (2003), 'Anti-privatisation Wave Sinks Corporate Lobby Group', Amsterdam.
Cosatu (2003), 'Statement on the Anti-Terrorism Bill', Johannesburg, 25 June.
_____ (2003), 'End of Year Statement', Johannesburg, 22 December.
Costello, A., F. Watson and D. Woodward (1994), *Human Face or Human Facade? Adjustment and the Health of Mothers and Children*, London, Centre for International Child Health.

Darrow, M. (2003), *Between Light and Shadow: The World Bank, International Monetary Fund and International Human Rights Law*, Portland, Hart Publishing.
Dembele, D. (2003), 'PRSPS: Poverty Reduction or Poverty Reinforcement?', *Pambezuka News* 136, 11 December.
Desai, A. (1999), *South Africa Still Revolting*, Durban, Natal Newspapers.
_____ (2002), *We are the Poors*, New York, Monthly Review Press.
_____ (2003), 'Neoliberalism and Resistance in South Africa', *Monthly Review*, January.
Dovers, S., R. Edgecombe and B. Guest (eds) (2002), *South Africa's Environmental History: Cases and Comparisons*, Cape Town, David Philip and Athens, Ohio University Press.
Draper, P. (2003), 'To Liberalise or Not to Liberalise? A Review of the South African Government's Trade Policy', South African Institute of International Affairs Working Paper, Johannesburg.
Duncan, J. (2002), *Broadcasting and the National Question*, Johannesburg, Freedom of Expression Institute.
_____ (2003), 'A Flash in the Pan? The Relevance of the WSSD for Freedom of Expression', in S. Kimani (ed.), *The Right to Dissent: Freedom of Expression, Assembly and Demonstration in the New South Africa*, Johannesburg, Freedom of Expression Institute.
Dwyer, P. (2003), 'The New Global Peace Movement vs. the Bush Juggernaut', http://www.lists.kabissa.org/mailman/listinfo/debate, 26 May.
Economist, The, 'Survey of Water', 19 July 2003.
Edigheji, O. and K. Gostner (2000), 'Social Dialogue: The South African Experience', *Labour Education*, 3, 120.
Ellerman, D. (2004), *Helping People Help Themselves: From the World Bank to an Alternative Philosophy of Development*, Ann Arbor, University of Michigan Press.
Ellis-Jones, M. (2003), 'States of Unrest III: Resistance to IMF and World Bank Policies in Poor Countries', London, World Development Movement, April.
Elson, D. (1991), 'The Impact of Structural Adjustment on Women: Concepts and Issues', in B. Onimode (ed.), *The IMF, the World Bank and the African Debt*, London, Zed Books.
Environmental Defence, Friends of the Earth, and International Rivers Network (2003), *Gambling With People's Lives*, Washington and Berkeley, 19 September.
Erwin, A. (1999), 'Statement to the World Trade Organisation Plenary', Seattle, 1 December.
Fanon, F. (1961), *The Wretched of the Earth*, New York, Grove Press.
Feldman, G. (2002), 'US-African Trade Profile', US Department of Commerce, Washington, March.
Fiil-Flynn, M. (2003), 'Report from Kyoto', e-debate listserve, 27 March.
Financial Stability Forum (2001), *International Standards and Codes to Strengthen Financial Systems*, Basle, www.fsforum.org/Standards/Reiscfs.html.
Fine, B. and Z. Rustomjee (1996), *The Political Economy of South Africa*, London, Christopher Hurst and Johannesburg, Wits University Press.
Fine, R. and D. Davies (1991), *Beyond Apartheid*, London, Pluto Press.
Fisher, J. (2002), 'Africa', in E. Bircham and J. Charlton (eds) (2002), *Anti-Capitalism: A Guide to the Movement*, London, Bookmarks.

Fisher, W. and T. Ponniah (eds) (2003), *Another World is Possible: Popular Alternatives to Globalisation at the World Social Forum*, London, Zed Books.

Frank, A.G. and M. Fuentes (1990), 'Civil Democracy: Social Movements in Recent World History', in S. Amin, G. Arrighi, A.G. Frank and I. Wallerstein, *Transforming the Revolution: Social Movements and the World-System*, New York, Monthly Review Press.

Friends of the Earth and Halifax Initiative (2002), *Marketing the Earth: The World Bank and Sustainable Development*, Washington, DC and Ottawa, August.

Focus on the Global South (2002), 'The Road to Monterrey Passes through Washington', *Focus on Trade*, 75, March.

Foster, J. (2003), 'A Planetary Defeat: The Failure of Global Environmental Reform', *Monthly Review*, January.

Freedom of Expression Institute (2003), 'FXI urges Parliament to Withdraw Anti-Terrorism Bill', Johannesburg, 25 June.

Gabriel, N. (2002), 'Monterrey: Spinning the Washington Consensus All the Way to Johannesburg', Pretoria, Southern African Catholic Bishops' Conference.

Gender and Trade Network in Africa (2003), 'Mohau Pheko in Mexican Gov't Leaked "Enemies List" of Activists toward Cancun', Johannesburg, email alert, 22 August.

Gomes, R.P., S. Lakhani and J. Woodman (2002), 'Economic Policy Empower-ment Programme', Brussels, Eurodad.

Gopinath, D. (2003), 'Doubt of Africa', *Institutional Investor Magazine*, May.

Gowan, P. (1999), *The Global Gamble: Washington's Faustian Bid for Global Dominance*, London, Verso.

Griffith-Jones, S. (2002), 'Suggestions on Reforming the Governance of the World Bank', Sussex, University of Sussex Institute of Development Studies, http://www.gapresearch.org.

Grossmann, H. (1992) [1929], *The Law of Accumulation and Breakdown of the Capitalist System*, London, Pluto Press.

Hall, D. (2003), 'Water Multinationals in Retreat', London, Public Services International Research Unit, University of Greenwich. http://www.psiru.org.

Hart, G. (2002), *Disabling Globalisation*, Pietermaritzburg, University of Natal Press and Berkeley, University of California Press.

Harvey, D. (1999) [1982], *The Limits to Capital*, London, Verso.

_____ (2003), *The New Imperialism*, Oxford, Oxford University Press.

_____ (2003), 'The 'New' Imperialism: On Spatio-temporal Fixes and Accumu-lation by Dispossession', in L. Panitch and C. Leys, *Socialist Register 2004*, London, The Merlin Press and New York, Monthly Review Press.

Harvey, E. (2003), 'A Critical Analysis of the Decision to Corporatise the Water and Wastewater Services in the City of Johannesburg', University of the Witwatersrand Graduate School of Public and Development Manage-ment Masters Dissertation, Johannesburg.

Hemson, D. (2003), 'Rural Poor Play a Role in Water Projects', *Business Day*, 1 July.

Henwood, D. (2003), *After the New Economy*, New York, New Press.

Hilferding, R. (1981) [1910], *Finance Capital*, London, Routledge and Kegan Paul.

Hormeku, T. (2001), 'Text a Slap in the Face for African Countries', *Business Day*, 8 November.

Institute of Development Studies (2002), 'A Foresight and Policy Study of Multilateral Development Banks', Prepared for the Swedish Ministry of Foreign Affairs, Stockholm, November.

International Monetary Fund (1998), *Report of the Working Group on Transparency and Accountability*, *Report of the Working Group on Strengthening Financial Systems*, and *Report of the Working Group on International Financial Crises*, Washington, www.imf.org/external/np/g22/index.htm.

____ and International Development Association (2001), 'The Impact of Debt Reduction under the HIPC Initiative on External Debt Service and Social Expenditures', Washington, 16 November.

International Rivers Network (2003), 'Who's Behind the World Water Forums? A Brief Guide to the World Water Mafia', Berkeley, March.

____ (2003), 'Some Preliminary Comments on the Camdessus Report', Berkeley, 10 March.

Jacobs, N. (2002), *Environment, Power and Injustice: A South African History*, Cambridge, Cambridge University Press.

Jacobs, S. and R. Calland (eds) (2002), *Thabo Mbeki's World*, London, Zed Books and Pietermaritzburg, University of Natal Press.

Johannesburg (2001), 'Budget 2001–2002: City Development Plan 2001/2002', Johannesburg.

____ (2001), 'Johannesburg Metropolitan Council Attitude Survey', Johan-nesburg.

____ (2002), *Joburg 2030*, Johannesburg.

Johannesburg Water (2001), *Business Plan*, Johannesburg.

Jubilee Plus (2003), 'Real Progress Report on HIPC', London, September.

Jubilee South (2001), 'Pan-African Declaration on PRSPs', Kampala, 12 May.

Kasrils, R. (2000), 'A Desiccated Vision of Water Delivery', *Business Day*, 22 August.

____ (2003), 'South Africans' Water', *New York Times*, 5 June.

____ (2003), 'Report on Water Cut-offs a Case of Sour Grapes among US Populists', *Sunday Independent*, 8 June.

____ (2003), 'From Myth to Reality in the Great Water Debate', *Sunday Independent*, 29 June 2003.

Keet, D. (2002), *South Africa's Official Role and Position in Promoting the World Trade Organisation*, Cape Town, Alternative Information and Development Centre.

____ (2003), 'Contrasts and Counter-Positions in Cancun', Report on behalf of the African Peoples Caucus, Cancun, 16 September.

Khor, M. (2002), 'A Disappointing Summit', *Third World Resurgence*, December 2002.

Kimani, S. (ed.) (2003), *The Right to Dissent: Freedom of Expression, Assembly and Demonstration in the New South Africa*, Johannesburg, Freedom of Expression Institute.

____ (2003), 'South Africa at the Crossroads: Dissent and the New Political Agenda', in S. Kimani (ed.), *The Right to Dissent: Freedom of Expression, Assembly and Demonstration in the New South Africa*, Johannesburg, Freedom of Expression Institute.

Kingsnorth, P. (2003), *One No, Many Yeses: A Journey to the Heart of the Global Resistance Movement*, London, The Free Press.

Koehler, G. (1999), 'Global Keynesianism and Beyond', *Journal of World-Systems Research*, 5, http://csf.colorado.edu/wsystems/jwsr.html.

____ and A. Tausch (2002), *Global Keynesianism: Unequal Exchange and Global Exploitation*, Huntington, USA, Nova Science.

Krugman, P. (2003), 'Looting the Future', *New York Times*, 5 December.

Kwa, A. (2002), *Power Politics in the WTO*, Bangkok, Focus on the Global South.
Lallah, R. (2003), 'AGOA – Consolidating US Imperialism in Africa', *Khanya Journal*, 3, March.
Lee, S. (2002), 'Global Monitor: The International Monetary Fund', *New Political Economy*, 7, 2.
Legassick, M. (forthcoming), *Towards Socialist Democracy*, Pietermaritzburg, University of KwaZulu-Natal Press.
Lenin, V. (1986) [1917], *Imperialism*, Moscow, Progress Publishers.
Leon, T. (2003), 'South Africa's Policy Conundrum', *South African Journal of International Affairs*.
Levin, R. and D. Weiner (eds) (1997), *'No More Tears'*, Trenton, Africa World Press.
Logan, M. (2003), 'Multinationals Ride Wave of Water Privatisation', OneWorld US, 4 February.
Longwe, S. (1991), 'The Evaporation of Policies for Women's Advancement', in N. Heyzer et al (eds), *A Commitment to the World's Women*, New York, UNIFEM.
Luxemburg, R. (1968) [1923], *The Accumulation of Capital*, New York, Monthly Review Press.
Lynas, M. (2003), 'Playing Dirty at the WTO', *Third World Network Features*, Penang, Malaysia, June.
Mahmoud, F. (1996), 'Building a Pan-African Women's Movement', in T. Abdul-Raheem (ed.), *Pan-Africanism: Politics, Economy and Social Change in the 21st Century*, Trenton, Africa World Press.
Makhaye, D. (2002), 'Left Factionalism and the NDR: The ANC must Respond to Professionals of the "Left" ', ANC Today, http://www.anc.org.za, 29 November.
Malawi Economic Justice Network (2001), 'Civil Society PRSP Briefing', Issue 8, 21 December, Lilongwe.
Mandel, E. (1962), *Marxist Economic Theory*, Volume 1. London, The Merlin Press.
Mann, E. (2002), *Dispatches from Durban*, Los Angeles, Frontline Books.
Manuel, T. (2000), 'Address to the Seminar on South Africa's Relations and Creation of National Wealth and Social Welfare', Rand Afrikaans University Centre for European Study in Africa, Johannesburg, 20 October.
_____ (2002), 'Remarks to the International Business Forum at the International Conference on Financing for Development', Monterrey, 18 March.
_____ (2002), 'Remarks at the Finance Minister's Retreat', International Conference on Financing for Development, Monterrey, Mexico, 19 March.
_____ (2002), 'Mobilizing International Investment Flows: The New Global Outlook', Speech to the Commonwealth Business Council, 24 September.
_____ (2003), 'Input to the HSRC Conference', Kleinmond, 4 May.
Manyanya, M. (ed.) (2003), *NEPAD's Zimbabwe Test: Why the New Partnership for Africa's Development is Already Failing*, Harare, Zimbabwe Coalition on Debt and Development.
Marais, H. (2000), *South Africa Limits to Change*, London, Zed Books and Cape Town, University of Cape Town Press.
Martin, W. (2003), 'Three Hundred Years of World Movements: Towards the End of the Capitalist World-Economy?', presented at the Sociology Seminar, Rand Afrikaans University, Johannesburg, 13 June.
Mathiason, N. (2003), 'Left High and Dry by the Water Companies', *The Observer*, 16 March.

Mayekiso, M. (1996), *Township Politics*, New York, Monthly Review Press.
Mbeki, T. (2002), 'Address by President Mbeki at the Welcome Ceremony of the WSSD', Johannesburg, 25 August.
____ (2002), 'Response to Questions in the National Assembly of Parliament', Cape Town, 19 September.
____ (2002), 'Statement of the President of the African National Congress, Thabo Mbeki, at the ANC Policy Conference', Kempton Park, 27 September.
____ (2003), 'Address by the President of South Africa at the SA National Editors Forum Conference on the Media, the AU, NEPAD and Democracy', Johannesburg, 12 April.
____ (2003), 'Letter from the President', *ANC Today*, http://www.anc.org.za, 31 October.
____ (2003), 'We Will Resist the Upside-Down View of Africa', *ANC Today* 49, http://www.anc.org.za, 12 December.
McCandless, E. and E. Pajibo (2003), 'Can Participation Advance Poverty Reduction? PRSP Process and Content in Four Countries', Afrodad PRSP Series, Harare, January.
McDonald, D. (ed.) (2002), *Environmental Justice in South Africa*, Cape Town, University of Cape Town Press.
____ (2003), 'Attack the Problem Not the Data', *Sunday Independent*, 15 June.
____ and J. Pape (eds) (2002), *Cost Recovery and the Crisis of Service Delivery in South Africa*, London, Zed Books and Pretoria, HSRC Publications.
McGee, R. (2002), 'Assessing Participation in Poverty Reduction Strategy Papers: A Desk-Based Synthesis of Experience in Sub-Saharan Africa', Sussex, University of Sussex Institute for Development Studies.
McKinley, D. (1997), *The ANC and the Liberation Struggle*, London, Pluto Press.
____ (2003), 'Trying to "Kill" the Messenger, and Failing: Experiences of the Anti-Privatisation Forum during the WSSD', in S. Kimani (ed.), *The Right to Dissent: Freedom of Expression, Assembly and Demonstration in the New South Africa*, Johannesburg, Freedom of Expression Institute.
McCully, P. (2002), 'Avoiding Solutions, Worsening Problems', San Francisco, International Rivers Network, http://www.irn.org.
Medecins Sans Frontieres, Health GAP, Health Action International, ACT UP Paris, Peoples Health Movement, Oxfam (2003), 'Joint NGO response to US proposal on Intellectual Property Rights, Innovation and Public Health at the 56th World Health Assembly', Geneva, 21 May.
Mertes, T. (ed.) (2003), *A Movement of Movements: Is Another World Really Possible?*, London, Verso.
Milanovic, B. (2002), 'Can we Discern the Effect of Globalisation on Income Distribution?, Evidence from Household Budget Surveys', World Bank Policy Research Working Paper 2876, April.
Mokonyane, D. (1994), *The Big Sell Out*, London, Nakong ya Rena.
Moleketi, J. and J. Jele (2002), 'Two Strategies of the National Liberation Movement in the Struggle for the Victory of the National Democratic Revolution', Discussion document distributed by the African National Congress, Johannesburg, October.
Moore, D. (2002), 'Zimbabwe's Triple Crisis: Primitive Accumulation, Nation-State Formation and Democratisation in the Age of Neoliberal Globalisation', Paper presented to the conference on Transition and Crisis in Zimbabwe, Centre of African Studies, University of Florida, Gainesville, 2 March.

Mosley, P. (1997), 'The World Bank, "Global Keynesianism" and the Distribution of the Gains from Growth', *World Development*, 25, 11.
Muller, M. (2003), 'Water 2003 – What Should be Done: Lessons from Johannesburg and Pointers for the Future', Speech given at various international fora, Pretoria, Department of Water Affairs and Forestry.
Munnik, V. and J. Wilson (2003), *The World Comes to One Country*, Berlin and Johannesburg, Heinrich Boell Stiftung.
Murerwa, H. (2002), 'The 2003 National Budget Statement', Presented to Parliament, Harare, 14 November.
Murray, M. (1994), *Revolution Deferred*, London, Verso.
_____ (forthcoming), *City of Extremes: The Spatial Politics of Johannesburg After Apartheid*, London, Verso.
Myburgh Commission (2002), *Commission of Inquiry into the Rapid Deprecia-tion of the Exchange Rate of the Rand and Related Matters*, Pretoria, 30 June.
Nabudere, D. (2002), 'NEPAD: Historical Background and its Prospects', in P. Anyang'Nyong'o, et al (eds), *NEPAD: A New Path?* Nairobi, Heinrich Böll Foundation.
Ndungane, N. (2003), *A World with a Human Face: A Voice from Africa*, Cape Town, David Philip.
Ngcobo, C. (2003), 'Local Authorities and the Regulation of Assemblies and Demonstrations', in S. Kimani (ed.), *The Right to Dissent: Freedom of Expression, Assembly and Demonstration in the New South Africa*, Johannesburg, Freedom of Expression Institute.
Ngwane, T. (2003), 'Sparks in the Township', *New Left Review*, July–August 2003.
_____ (2003), 'A Tale of Two WSSD Demos', in R. Neumann and A. Hsiao (eds), *Anti-Capitalism: A Field Guide to the Global Justice Movement*, New York, New Press.
_____ (2004), 'The New Social Movements and Working Class Politics in Post-Apartheid South Africa', *Historical Materialism*.
Nyamugasira, W. and R. Rowden (2002), 'New Strategies, Old Loan Conditions: Do the IMF and World Bank Loans Support Countries' Poverty Reduction Strategies? The Case of Uganda', Uganda National NGO Forum and RESULTS Educational Fund, Kampala, April.
Nzimande, B. (2003), 'New Possibilities for a Progressive Global Politics', *Umsebenzi*, www.sacp.org.za, March.
O'Meara, D. (1996), *Forty Lost Years*, London, James Currey.
Ong'wen, 'O (2001), 'The PRSP in Kenya', *World Bank Watch SA? SA Watch WB!*, December.
Olukoshi, A. (2002), 'Governing the African Political Space for Sustainable Development: A Reflection on NEPAD', Paper prepared for the African Forum for Envisioning Africa, Nairobi, 26–29 April.
Panitch, L. and S. Gindin (2003), 'Global Capitalism and American Empire', in L. Panitch and C. Leys, *Socialist Register 2004*, London, The Merlin Press and New York, Monthly Review Press.
Panos (2002), 'Reducing Poverty: Is the World Bank's Strategy Working?', London, September.
Pauw, J. (2003), 'Metered to Death: How a Water Experiment Caused Riots and a Cholera Epidemic', International Consortium of Investigative Journalists, Washington, 5 February.

Peet, R. (2003), *The World Bank, IMF and WTO*, London, Zed Books.
Perelman, M. (2000), *The Invention of Capitalism: Classical Political Economy and the Secret History of Primitive Accumulation*, Durham, Duke University Press.
Petrella, R. (2001), *The Water Manifesto: Arguments for a World Water Contract*, London, Zed Books.
Pincus, J. and J. Winters (eds) (2002), *Re-inventing the World Bank*, Ithaca, Cornell University Press.
Prasad, E., K. Rogoff, S.J. Wei and M. Ayhan Kose (2003), 'Effects of Financial Globalisation on Developing Countries: Some Empirical Evidence', Washington, International Monetary Fund, 17 March.
Public Services International (2003), 'The Report of the World Panel on Financing Water Infrastructure', Geneva, 12 March.
Roome, J. (1995), 'Water Pricing and Management: World Bank Presentation to the SA Water Conservation Conference', unpublished paper, South Africa, 2 October.
Round, R. (2002), 'CBC Commentary', Toronto, 20 March.
Sachs, M. (2003), 'A Line in the Sand', *Khanya Journal*, 3, March.
Saul, J. (1993), *Recolonization and Resistance in Southern Africa*, Trenton, Africa World Press.
_____ (forthcoming), *The Next Liberation Struggle*, London, The Merlin Press, New York, Monthly Review Press and Pietermaritzburg, University of KwaZulu-Natal Press.
_____ and C. Leys (1999), 'Sub-Saharan Africa in Global Capitalism', *Monthly Review*, July.
Seddon, D. (ed.), *Relations of Production: Marxist Approaches to Economic Anthropology*, London, Frank Cass.
Shiva, V. (2002), *Water Wars: Privatization, Pollution and Profit*, Boston, South End Press.
_____ (2002), 'Savings Lives or Destroying Lives? World Bank Sells Synthetic Soap and Cleanliness to Kerala the Land of Health and Hygiene', Water Liberation Movement Press Statement, New Delhi, 17 September.
Smith, N. (1990), *Uneven Development*, Oxford, Basil Blackwell.
Soederberg, S. (2001), 'The Emperor's New Suit: The New International Financial Architecture as a Reinvention of the Washington Consensus', *Global Governance*, 7, 4.
_____ (2002), 'The New International Financial Architecture: Imposed Leadership and Emerging Markets', in L. Panitch and C. Leys (eds), *Socialist Register 2002*, London, The Merlin Press.
_____ (2004), *The Politics of the New International Financial Architecture: Reimposing Neoliberal Dominance in the South*, London, Zed Books.
_____ (2004), 'Recasting Neoliberal Dominance in the South? A Critique of the Monterrey Consensus', forthcoming in *Alternatives*.
Smith, J. and H. Johnston (eds) (2002), *Globalisation and Resistance: Transnational Dimensions of Social Movements*, Lanham, Rowman and Littlefield.
Sooka, Y. (2003), 'Defining the Constitutional Right to Freedom of Expression, Assembly and Demonstration', in S. Kimani (ed.), *The Right to Dissent: Freedom of Expression, Assembly and Demonstration in the New South Africa*, Johannesburg, Freedom of Expression Institute.
Social Movements Indaba (2002), 'Anti-Privatisation Activists Expose Corporate Takeover of W$$D at Waterdome', Johannesburg, 3 September.

South African Broadcasting Corporation News (2002), 'SA govt faces "global protest" over WSSD', Johannesburg, 27 August.
South African Civil Society Water Caucus (2002), 'Press Release', Pretoria, 5 August.
South African Institute of International Affairs (2003), 'NEPAD and WEF', *eAfrica*, July.
Spicer, D. (2003), 'More Resources Expected for African Water Projects, *Engineering News*, 28 March.
Starr, A. (2000), *Naming the Enemy: Anti-Corporate Movements Confront Globalisation*, London, Zed Books.
_____ and J. Adams (2003), 'Anti-globalisation: The Global Fight for Local Autonomy', *New Political Science*, 25, 1.
Statistics South Africa (2001), *South Africa in Transition*, Pretoria.
_____ (2002), *Earning and Spending in South Africa*, Pretoria.
_____ (2002), 'Database on Expenditure and Income, 2000', Pretoria.
_____ (2003), *Labour Force Survey, September 2002*, Pretoria.
Stiglitz, J. (2002), *Globalisation and its Discontents*, London, Penguin.
Tandon, Y. (1999), 'A Blip or a Turnaround?', *Journal of Social Change and Development*, 49, December.
Tanzanian Feminist Activism Coalition (2001), 'Position Paper', Dar es Salaam, 6 September.
Tayob, R. (2003), 'South Africa at Cancun', Unpublished paper, Seatini, Harare, 14 September.
Taylor, I. (2002), 'Obstacles to Change in Africa: NEPAD, Zimbabwe, and Elites', Foreign Policy in Focus Commentary, http://www.fpif.org/outside/commentary/2002/0204NEPAD.html.
_____ and G. Mokhawa (2003), 'Not Forever: Botswana, Conflict Diamonds and the Bushmen', *African Affairs*, 102.
Thale, T. (2003), 'Census gives Joburg a Clearer Picture', http://www.johannesburg.org.za, 11 July.
Thomson, G. (2003), 'Water Tap Often Shut to South Africa Poor', *New York Times*, 29 May.
Tibbett, S. (2003), 'The Spoils of the War on Poverty: The West's Rhetoric about Foreign Aid Conceals a Greedy Self-Interest', *The Guardian*, 2 July.
Trade Union Research Project and Center for Research on Multinational Corporations (2001), 'Taking the Devil's Rope: Findings from Swaziland', Durban and Amsterdam.
_____ (2003), *Made in Southern Africa*, Amsterdam and Durban.
Treatment Action Campaign (2003), 'The People's Docket: Indictment Against South African Government Ministers', Cape Town, 21 March.
Tskikata, D. and J. Kerr (eds) (2002), *Demanding Dignity: Women Confronting Economic Reforms in Africa*, Ottawa, The North-South Institute and Accra, Third World Network-Africa.
Tsunga, A. (2003), 'The Legal Profession and the Judiciary as Human Rights Defenders in Zimbabwe', Mutare, 24 December.
Tsvangirai, M. (2002), 'President of the MDC's Speech to MDC Parliamentarians', Harare, 18 December.
United Nations (2002), 'Report of the International Conference on Financing for Development', A/CONF.198/11, Monterrey, Mexico, 22 March.
United Nations Development Programme (2002), *Deepening Democracy in a Fragmented World*, New York, July.

United Nations University World Institute for Development Economics Research (2002), *Governing Globalisation: Issues and Institutions*, Helsinki, October.
United States Naval War College (2003), 'The Pentagon's New Map', http://www.nwc.navy.mil/newrules/ThePentagonsNewMap.htm.
United Steel Workers of America (2003), 'Press Release', Washington, 4 December.
Vally, S. (2003), 'The Political Economy of State Repression in South Africa', in S. Kimani (ed.), *The Right to Dissent: Freedom of Expression, Assembly and Demonstration in the New South Africa*, Johannesburg, Freedom of Expression Institute.
Varma, S. (2002), 'Improving Global Economic Governance', Geneva, South Centre, August.
Verheul, E. and G. Cooper, (2001), 'Poverty Reduction Strategy Papers (PRSP): What is at Stake for Health?', Amsterdam, Wemos, September.
Von Werlhof, C. (2000), 'Globalisation and the Permanent Process of Primitive Accumulation: The Example of the MAI, the Multilateral Agreement on Investment', *Journal of World Systems Research*, 6, 3.
wa ka Bila, V. (2002), 'Mr. President, Let the Babies Die', in V. wa ka Bila and W. Nghalaluma (eds), *Timbila 2002: A Journal of Onion Skin Poetry*, Elim Hospital, Timbila Poetry Project.
Wade, R. (2001), 'Capital and Revenge: The IMF and Ethiopia', *Challenge*, September/October.
_____ (2003), 'The Invisible Hand of the American Empire', *Open Democracy*, 13, 3.
Wallach, L. (2003), 'U.S. to Comply with WTO Order: Bush Retracting Steel Tariffs Early Shows Americans that WTO is Boss', Washington, Public Citizen Global Trade Watch, 4 December.
Waterman, P. (2001), *Globalisation, Social Movements and the New Inter-nationalisms*, London, Continuum.
_____ (2003), 'The Global Justice and Solidarity Movement', http://groups.yahoo.com/group/GloSoDia/
Weisbrot, M. (2002), 'Progress Postponed: The Economic Failure of the Last Two Decades of the Twentieth Century', Washington, http://www.cepr.org.
Werner, D. and D. Sanders (1997), *Questioning the Solution: The Politics of Primary Health Care and Child Survival*, California, Healthwrights.
Wilks, A. and F. Lefrançois (2002), 'Blinding with Science or Encouraging Debate? How World Bank Analysis Determines PRSP Policies', London, Bretton Woods Project.
Wolpe, H. (ed.) (1980), *The Articulations of Modes of Production*, London, Routledge and Kegan Paul.
World Bank (1999), *Country Assistance Strategy: South Africa*, Washington.
_____ (2000), *Global Finance Tables 2000*, Washington.
_____ (2002), *Global Finance Tables 2002*, Washington.
_____ (2002), 'South Africa: Monitoring Service Delivery in Johannesburg', Washington
_____ (2003), 'Issues Note: Enhancing the Voice of Developing and Transition Countries at the World Bank', Washington, 9 June.
_____ (2003), 'Proceedings of Press Conference', Dubai, http://www.worldbank.org, 22 September.
World Health Organisation (2001), 'Health in PRSPs: WHO Submission to World Bank/IMF Review of PRSPs', Department of Health and Development, Geneva, December.

Zarembka, P. (2000), 'Accumulation of Capital, Its Definition: A Century after Lenin and Luxemburg', in P. Zarembka (ed.), *Value, Capitalist Dynamics and Money: Research in Political Economy, Volume 18*, Stamford and Amsterdam, JAI/Elsevere.

_____ (2002), 'Primitive Accumulation in Marxism, Historical or Trans-historical Separation from Means of Production?', *The Commoner*, http://www.thecommoner.org, March.

Zeilig, L. (ed.) (2002), *Class Struggle and Resistance in Africa*, Cheltenham, New Clarion.

Index

ABB 221
Abuja 9, 10, 53, 113, 116, 117
Accra 215
Acres International 221
Adams, J. 229
Addis Ababa 10, 87, 120, 214
Adedeji, A. 116
Adesina, J. 211, 212, 215
Afghanistan 201
Africa Group 51, 55
Africa Growth and Opportunity Act 60
Africa Institute 105
Africa Trade Network 119
African-Caribbean-Pacific countries 64, 65
African Development Bank 115
African Economic Research Consortium 215
African National Congress (ANC) 9, 22, 28, 30, 32, 38, 40, 46, 47, 109, 110, 114, 117, 128, 132, 133, 138, 151, 160, 163, 164, 170, 179, 180, 181, 183–185, 187–189, 200, 211, 229
African Regional Technical Assistance Centre 103
African Social Forum 214, 222, 224
African Union 4, 10, 64, 103, 105, 108, 120, 224
Afrodad 82
Agbar 150
Agence France Press 158
Aguiton, C. 233
Akerlof, G. 195
Alexandra 128–132, 145, 161, 166, 167, 170
Algeria 30, 120
Ali, T. 8
Alien Tort Claims Act 41, 45, 46
All Nigeria People's Party 110
Amin, S. 195, 216, 226, 229, 234

anarchism 183, 185, 230
Anglo American Corporation 41
Angola 30, 60, 81, 201
Annan, K. 37, 75
Anti-Eviction Campaign 144
Anti-Privatisation Forum 129, 133, 134, 146, 167, 181, 183, 222, 231
antiretroviral medicines 11, 12, 66–68, 217, 224
Anti-War Coalition 22, 28, 30
Appollis, J. 181
Arafat, Y. 132, 223
Argentina 75, 79, 80, 153, 154, 201, 229
Aristide, J. 223
Asmal, K. 145, 157, 158, 169, 218
Atlanta 153, 154, 156

Baghdad 29
Bali 219
Bamako 215
Bangladesh 218
Bank for International Settlements 90
Bank Information Center 88
Barcelona 13
Barlow, M. 128
Barnard, N. 46
Basarwa/San Bushmen 214
Basic Income Grant 217
Basle 90
Battersby, J. 114
Bauer, O. 192
BBC 144
Bechtel 154
Beijing 31, 226
Belgium 39
Bello, W. 216
Bengu, M. 77
Benin 81
Berlin 31, 226
Bila, V. 237

257

Bill and Melinda Gates Foundation 67
Binghamton University 169, 228
biotechnology 60, 61, 125, 194
Biwater 151, 154, 155
Bizos, G. 48
Bloomberg News Service 205
Bodibe, O. 186
Bolivia 154, 203
Booker, S. 4
Boston Globe 143, 203
Botha, P.W. 47
Botswana 30, 94, 113, 214
Boyce, J. 107
Brandt, W. 182
Brazil 3, 11, 21, 58, 63, 64, 68, 75, 79, 109, 121, 127, 201, 223, 232
Brecher, J. 227, 234
Brenner, R. 196, 199
Bretton Woods Project 88
Briscoe, J. 218
Broederbond 116
Brooking, C. 86
Brown, G. 94
Brutus, D. 44, 121, 128–130, 223
Brzezinski, Z. 200, 201
Buenos Aires 143, 157
Bukharin, N. 192
Burkina Faso 60, 82, 83
Burma 45
Burundi 108, 109, 201
Bush, G.W. 8, 22, 28–31, 41, 56, 58, 60, 61, 66, 67, 86, 103, 120, 128, 137, 195, 198, 199, 202, 214, 225–227, 229, 237
Business Day 31, 40, 55, 66, 94, 105, 115, 172

Cabral, A. 211
Cairns Group 58
Cairo 53
Calland, R. 116
Callinicos, A. 232
Camdessus, M. 75, 91, 117, 155–158
Cameroon 113, 116, 220
Canada 10, 51, 55, 77, 95, 117, 144, 221, 232
Canadian Broadcasting Corporation 144
Canberra 113

Cancun 10, 48, 51–53, 56–58, 62–65
Cape Investment Bank 117
Cape Town 22, 41, 43, 146, 214, 217
capital flight 107, 151, 194
Carmichael, S. 213
Caspian Sea 200, 220
Castro, F. 132, 232
Center for Economic Justice 222
Center for Economic Policy Research 126
Central African Republic 235
Chad-Cameroon pipeline 220
Chamber of Mines 191
Chikane, F. 42
Chile 180
China 60, 93, 125, 139, 198, 199, 201, 220, 226
Chinamasa, P. 115
Chirac, J. 58
cholera 131, 152, 153, 160, 170, 238
Chretien, J. 115
Churchill, W. 47
Citibank 95, 157
City University of New York 193
Civil Liberties Organisation 110
Civil Society Water Caucus 144
Clarke, T. 128
Clinton, W. 46, 52, 91, 118
Coates, B. 158
Coega 56
Colgate Palmolive 147
Colombia 201
Columbia University 202
Commonwealth 4, 10, 90, 91, 111–114
Commonwealth Business Council 90, 91
Commuter Corporation 117
Congress of South African Trade Unions (Cosatu) 9, 14, 37, 38, 48, 57, 77, 78, 106, 132, 135, 183, 186, 224, 235
Constitutional Court 11
Convention on Biological Diversity 135, 136
Cornish, J-J. 108
Corporate Council on Africa 30
Corporate Europe Observatory 156
Council for Development and Social Research in Africa 215

Craven, P. 186
Cronin, J. 180
Cuba 53, 150–152, 212, 235
Curtin, M. 154

Da Silva, L. 21, 121, 225, 232
Dar es Salaam 57, 103
Davos 10, 104, 118, 121, 232, 235
De Villepin, D. 29
Dean, H. 225
De Beers 214
decommodification 8, 216, 228, 229
deglobalisation 8, 201, 216, 217, 229
Democratic Republic of the Congo 30, 105, 108, 201
Denel 28
Desai, A. 44, 104
Development Bank of Southern Africa 154
Djibouti 30
Dlamini-Zuma, N. 40, 108, 110, 112
Doha 9, 48, 52–58, 63–65, 121
Dolphin Coast 151, 154, 160
Dominican Republic 53
Dor, G. 223
Draper, P. 55
Dubai 10, 87
Duncan, J. 129
Durban 9, 10, 17, 22, 28, 37–40, 43, 44, 48, 68, 103–105, 110, 146, 152, 214, 221
Durban Concerned Community Forum 44
Durban Social Forum 38, 44
Dwyer, P. 227

Earthlife Africa 144
East Asia 16, 90, 107, 126, 200
East London 56
Eastern Cape 155
Economic Commission for Africa 87, 115
Economic Commission on Africa 10
Economist, The 159, 195
Ecuador 218
Egypt 53, 156, 157, 213
Eizenstat, S. 46
El Salvador 218

Ellerman, D. 202
Elliott, L. 94
Environmental Defence 156
Environmental Justice Networking Forum 134, 214
Environmental Monitoring Group 144
Equatorial Guinea 30
Ermelo 133
Erwin, A. 11, 22, 41, 42, 48, 51–59, 61, 63–66, 68, 69, 85, 103, 106, 211, 236
Ethiopia 90, 91, 235
Eurasia 200
European Bank for Reconstruction and Development 156
European Union 39, 40, 51, 54, 55, 58–60, 63–65, 75, 86, 87, 91, 104, 109, 121, 152, 156, 169, 171, 197, 198, 212, 223, 225, 226
Evening Standard 223
Evian 10, 58, 59, 80, 116–121, 158, 226
exchange controls 90, 91, 151, 204, 206
Extractive Industries Review 218, 220

Fanon, F. 22, 188
Fiil-Flynn, M. 155
Finance, Department of 165
Financial Stability Forum 90
Financing for Development Conference 9, 75, 77, 82, 95
First People 134
Fischer, S. 95
Fletcher, B. 30
Focus on the Global South 54, 216
Ford Motor Corporation 45
Ford, H. 45
Foreign Affairs, Department of 109
Foster, J. 125, 136
France 29, 31, 58, 117–120, 132, 143, 157, 158, 161, 227
Freedom of Expression Institute 48, 129, 167
Friends of the Earth 134, 135, 156

G8 77
G20 77, 90
G21 63–65
Gabriel, N. 45, 87, 88
Gaia Foundation 136

The Gambia 113
Gandhi, M. 147, 230
Gates, B. 67, 68
Gauteng Province 15, 133, 146, 181, 185
Gcin'amanzi 167, 168
Geffen, L. 15
General Agreement on Trade in Services 152
genetically-modified food 60, 61, 125, 194
Geneva 57, 63, 119, 158, 238
Genoa 104, 133, 134, 205
Ghana 30, 83, 113, 213, 218
Gilder, B. 129
Gindin, S. 196, 197, 201
Gini coefficient 5
global apartheid 3–5, 9, 15, 17, 33, 37, 87, 126, 135, 169, 170, 180, 181, 188, 191–193, 211, 221, 222, 225, 232, 234–237
Global Civil Society Forum 132
Global Exchange 222
Global Fund 66, 119
global justice movements 21, 22, 59, 76, 77, 128, 139, 172, 180, 181, 183, 204, 211, 213, 218, 221–226, 228, 229, 232–236
Global Water Partnership 155
Gokova, J. 112
Gold Fields 41
groundWork 214
Group for Environmental Monitoring 145
Group of 77 139
Group of 8 Summit 10, 17, 52, 58, 59, 63, 77, 80, 103–105, 116–121, 127, 144, 158, 226, 235
Growth, Employment and Redistribution (GEAR) 121, 205
Guardian, The 94, 204, 214
Guevara, C. 213

Hae, L. 62
The Hague 143, 148
Haiti 53
Halifax Initiative 95
Hall, D. 154
Harare 82, 111, 113, 115

Hardt, M. 228, 229
Harvey, D. 193, 194, 196, 225
Havana 150
Heavily Indebted Poor Countries initiative 78–80, 193, 204, 224
Hemson, D. 172
Hendrickse, L. 62
Hilary, J. 54
Hilferding, R. 192
Hillbrow hospital 83
Hitler, A. 45
HIV/AIDS 11–13, 22, 31, 66–69, 107, 117, 162, 203, 217, 238
Honduras 83
Horn of Africa 235
Houston Chronicle 143
Human Rights Foundation 133
Human Sciences Research Council 161, 171, 172
Hungary 218
Hussein, S. 22, 29

Igoli 2002 131
IMF Riot 81, 213, 222
India 51, 63, 127, 201, 220
Indonesia 60, 62, 75, 219, 220
Indymedia 134, 159
Institute for a Democratic Alternative in South Africa 13, 14
Institute for International Finance 76
Institutional Investor 103, 117, 118
intellectual property 16, 58, 66, 67, 194
International Business Machines 45
International Consortium of Investigative Journalists 144, 154, 156
International Criminal Court 30
International Development Association 87
International Finance Corporation 157
International Labour Organisation 84
International Monetary Fund 4, 9, 10, 75–77, 81–83, 85–95, 103, 104, 106, 115–117, 130, 152, 156, 185, 197, 202, 203, 213, 215, 217–219, 222–224, 232, 233, 235
International Private Water Association 156

International Rivers Network 156–158, 214, 218
InterPress Service 61
Iraq 8, 21, 22, 28–32, 119, 137, 195, 213, 222, 232, 235
Israel 28, 29, 31, 37, 39, 67, 129, 195
Ivory Coast 157
Ivory Park 167

Jakarta 154, 157
Jamaica 53
Japan 51, 55, 60, 65, 116, 197–199, 201
Jele, J. 185–188
Jewish Board of Deputies 129
Johannesburg 10, 11, 15, 22, 28, 31, 48, 52, 65, 76, 127, 128, 130, 131, 133, 135–137, 143, 148, 151, 153–155, 159–169, 183, 214, 222, 236
Johannesburg Metro Police Department 133
Johannesburg Water 161, 162, 166–168
Johannesburg Waterdome 143, 146, 148, 172
Jubilee Africa 119, 221, 222
Jubilee Plus 79
Jubilee South 39, 79, 81
Jubilee South Africa 40, 87, 134, 218, 222
Jukskei River 131, 168
Justice, Development and Peace Commission 110

Kadirgamar, L. 113
Kalahari 214
Kampala 81
Kananaskis 10, 105, 117, 118
Kansteiner, W. 29, 103
Kasrils, R. 131, 144–148, 150, 153, 155, 158–160, 163, 170–172
Katse Dam 55
Katzenellenbogen, J. 105, 115, 116
Keet, D. 52, 54, 56, 57, 62, 63
Kenya 53, 60, 62, 81, 83, 89, 105, 113, 116, 213
Kenyatta National Hospital 83
Kerala 147
Keys, D. 117
Khanya Journal 181
Khor, M. 139

Khulumani apartheid-victims group 40
Khumalo, B. 105
Kimani, S. 129
Kingsnorth, P. 180
Kiplegat, B. 116
Kissinger, H. 114
Klein, N. 128
Knollys, R. 46
Kose, M. 92
Krueger, A. 94
Krugman, P. 195
Kuala Lumpur 51, 226
Kucinich, D. 225
Kuwait 200
Kwa, A. 54
KwaZulu-Natal 153, 172
Kyoto 33, 136, 143, 148, 153, 155–157, 159, 232
Kyoto Protocol 136

L'Ecuyer, F. 159
L'Humanite 143
Lamy, P. 63, 65
Lancet, The 84
Landless People's Movement 14, 130, 133, 134
Latin America 63, 75, 89, 126, 131, 169, 198, 201, 233
Lausanne 119
Lawyers for Human Rights, Zimbabwe 114
Lazard Freres 157
Le Monde Diplomatique 143
League of Nations 32
Leigland, J. 154
Lekota, M. 56
Lengolo, E. 159, 160
Lenin, V. 179, 182, 185–188, 192, 194
Leon, T. 32
Lesotho 55, 131, 145, 146, 214, 221
Liberia 30
London 43, 79, 87, 88, 113, 143, 147, 151, 154, 172, 203, 213, 223
London Observer 143
London School of Economics 87
London School of Hygiene and Tropical Medicine 147
Louw, M. 46

Lusaka 235
Luxemburg, R. 192–194, 213

Machel, G. 116
Maduna, P. 42, 43, 47
Maharaj, M. 47
Mahathir M. 226
Mail & Guardian 10, 54, 65, 108, 116, 128, 129, 165
Makhan, V. 64
Makhaye, D. 180, 184
Malawi 83, 113
Malaysia 51, 62, 64, 75, 204, 216
Malcolm X 213
Malcomson, D. 112
Mali 30
Mandela, N. 28, 29, 31, 43, 48, 108, 109, 116, 117
Manila 143, 154, 156, 157
Mann, E. 37, 38, 44
Manuel, T. 22, 52, 65, 69, 75–81, 85–87, 90, 91, 93–95, 107, 118, 204, 205, 206, 211, 217, 218, 236
Maputo 103, 214
Marseilles 155
Martin, W. 228, 229
Mas, J-P. 162
Maseru 55
Mashatile, P. 15
Masterbond 117
Matanzima, K. 47
Mathiason, N. 153
Mauritania 82
Mauritius 65, 94, 113, 213
Mbeki, T. 3, 4, 9–11, 13, 15, 17, 21, 22, 28, 29, 31–33, 37–43, 46, 47, 51, 56, 75, 80, 103, 105, 106, 108–110, 112–119, 121, 127, 128–130, 132–134, 138, 179, 180, 184, 188, 211, 216, 223, 224, 226, 229, 232, 236
Mboweni, T. 93, 117
McCully, P. 218
McDonald, D. 161, 170
McKinley, D. 129
McKinnon, D. 113
Mde, V. 186
Medicins sans Frontiers 120
Meer, F. 44

Mestrallet, G. 154
Mexico 10, 51, 75, 76, 157, 200, 218
Michel, L. 39
Milanovic, B. 107
Minter, B. 4
Mittal, A. 128
Mobutu, S. 213
Mokolo, R. 160–163, 223
Moleketi, J. 185–188
Monterrey 10, 75–80, 82, 84–91, 94, 95
Montesquieu 53
Moore, M. 53
Moosa, M. 52, 138
Moriarity, M. 131
Morocco 30, 81
Moscow 31, 226
Mosley, O. 47
Mother Jones 143
Motlanthe, K. 22, 32
Movement for Democratic Change 111
Movement of the Landless 222–223
Mozambique 30, 82, 83, 116, 153, 155, 204, 214
Mpumalanga 133
Mudenge, S. 110
Mugabe, R. 103, 110, 113–115, 135, 179, 223
Muller, M. 148, 150, 152, 153, 155, 158–160, 172
Mumbai 127, 172, 234
Municipal Infrastructure Investment Unit 154
Murerwa, H. 110
Murray, M. 169
Muslim 8, 39, 129
Mvoko, V. 105
Mvula Trust 144
Mwanawasa, L. 61
Myburgh Commission of Inquiry into the Rapid Depreciation of the Exchange Rate 91

Namibia 214
National Economic Development and Labour Council 57, 106, 132
National Intelligence Agency 46, 47, 128, 129
National Land Committee 145
National Party 116

Naval War College 201
Ncube, W. 115
Ndikumana, L. 107
Ndungane, N. 41, 217, 222
Negri, M. 195, 228, 229
Nelspruit 151, 154, 155
Network for Advocacy on Water in Southern Africa 144
New Left Review 43
New Partnership for Africa's Development (NEPAD) 9, 21, 29, 32, 77, 78, 80, 90, 103–112, 115–119, 130, 134, 145, 182, 193, 215, 224
New York Stock Exchange 198
New York Times 13, 67, 143, 160, 170, 219
Ngcobo, C. 133
Ngcuka, B. 47
NGO Energy and Climate Caucus 135
Ngonyama, S. 180
Ngwane, T. 43, 128, 129, 134, 135, 223, 229, 230
Nicaragua 80, 180
Niger 81, 235
Nigeria 9, 30, 40, 53, 54, 60, 62, 79, 81, 106, 109, 110, 113, 115, 116, 211, 213, 233
Njehu, N. 128
Njeuma, D. 116
Nkonkobe 151, 155
Non-Aligned Movement 4, 226
North Korea 216
North Sea 200
Norway 65
Nqakula, C. 128
Nyerere, J. 109
Nzimande, B. 30, 181, 182, 213

Obasanjo, O. 40, 54, 106, 109–113, 232
Ogoni 229
Oilwatch Africa 220
Olver, C. 165
Ondeo 157
Operation Khanyisa 214, 230
Oppenheimer, N. 43
Orange Farm 159, 160, 166–168
Organisation of African Unity 4
Ottawa 77, 113

overaccumulation crisis 5, 199, 225
Overseas Private Investment Corporation 156
Oxfam 120, 136, 215

Pahad, A. 28, 116
Pahad, E. 129, 130
Pakistan 8, 53, 157, 201
Palast, G. 67
Palestine 38–40, 44, 129, 134
Palestinian Solidarity Committee 129, 134
Palme, O. 182
Panitch, L. 196, 197, 201
Paris 31, 46, 79, 160, 167, 172, 203, 213, 226
Paris Club 79
Patel, R. 56
Pauw, J. 154
Peet, R. 219
Pentagon 30, 77, 193, 201
People's Democratic Party 109
Peres, S. 129
Peru 53
Philippines 62, 80, 153, 218, 219
Poland 203
Porto Alegre 11, 127, 214
Post-Washington Consensus 21, 22, 32, 218, 225, 226, 233, 234
Poverty Reduction Strategy Papers 80–84, 89, 103, 193, 215, 224
Powell, C. 43
Prague 76
Prasad, E. 92
Princeton University 195
Private Eye 46
privatisation 37, 38, 60, 77, 85, 87, 129, 131–133, 135, 143–148, 150, 151, 153–156, 158–160, 167–170, 172, 180–183, 185, 186, 194, 195, 212, 214, 222, 228, 231
Procter and Gamble 147
protectionism 52, 58, 65, 199, 233
Provincial and Local Government, Department of 171
Public Citizen 61
Public Services International Research Unit 154

public-private partnerships 77, 78, 136, 145, 147, 156
Putin, V. 226

Qatar 9, 52–54, 57
Quebec 232

Radebe, J. 78
Rand Afrikaans University 76, 204
Rand Water Board 166
Reagan, R. 114
Reconstruction and Development Programme 165, 172
Red Ants 131
Regulation of Gatherings Act 129
reparations 37, 39–46, 80, 214, 222, 223
Resurgent Rightwing 21, 196, 198, 211, 232, 233
Rhodes, C.J. 43, 213
Rio de Janeiro 125, 136, 139, 220
Rio Earth Summit 136
Robinson, M. 39
Rogoff, K. 92
Roome, J. 169
Round, R. 95
Rousseau 230
Roy, A. 234, 236
Rural Development Services Network 134, 144, 145
Russia 75, 201, 226
Rwanda 201

Sachs, J. 202, 203, 217
Sachs, M. 22, 28, 180
Salim, E. 220
San Francisco 218
Sanders, D. 84
Sandton 128–132, 161, 168, 170
Sasol 41
Sasolburg 17
Saudi Arabia 60–61
Saul, J. 128, 180
Saur 151, 153, 154, 160
Savane, M-A. 116
Save the Children 54
Schroeder, G. 31, 114
Schuitema, B. 43
Seattle 51–54, 56, 57, 64, 133, 134, 137, 205, 213, 229, 232
Senegal 30, 116, 213
September, D. 46
Setshedi, V. 130, 223
Shakashead 160
Shandling, K. 156
Sharpton, A. 225
Shelter Rights Initiative 106
Shiva, V. 147
Short, C. 219
Sierra Leone 113
Singapore 51, 63, 64
Sisulu, L. 46, 47
Slovo, J. 15
Social Clause 57, 106
Social Movements Indaba 10, 13, 127, 128, 130, 132, 134, 135, 146, 181
Socialist International 3, 10
Socialist Register 196
Soldiers' Forum 133
Sole, M. 221
Solomon, H. 113–114
Somalia 201
Sooka, Y. 133
Soros, G. 204
South African Communist Party (SACP) 9, 30, 38, 78, 128, 135, 180–183, 186
South African Council of Churches 22, 105, 132, 224
South African Institute of International Affairs 55, 64
South African Municipal Workers Union 144, 145
South African National Defence Force 109
South African NGO Coalition 132
South African Reserve Bank 93, 116, 117
South Korea 51, 75, 198
Southern African Catholic Bishops Conference 61
Southern African Development Community 4, 53, 54, 114
Southern African People's Solidarity Network 222
Southern African Social Forum 222, 235
Southern and Eastern African Trade and Investment Negotiations Initiative 64

INDEX 265

Sowetan 129, 130
Soweto 43, 128, 131
Soweto Electricity Crisis Committee 134, 214, 231
Special Assignment 144
Stals, C. 116, 117
Starr, A. 229
Statistics South Africa 14
Steel Valley 17
Stiglitz, J. 42, 85, 91, 92, 95, 202, 203, 205, 217
Stockholm 148
Structural Adjustment Participatory Review Initiative 218, 219
Suez 132, 151, 153–157, 161, 163, 166, 167, 222
Summers, L. 90
Sun City 108
Sunday Independent 131
Sunday Times 57, 103, 118, 185
Sunday World 130
Survey Research Associates 88
Survivors of the Lesotho Dams 146
Suttner, R. 180
Swaziland 60
Swaziland Federation of Trade Unions 60
Sweden 89
Switzerland 65, 232

Taiwan 60
Tanzania 53, 62, 82, 83, 105
Taylor, C. 30
Taylor, J. 58
Tayob, R. 64
Thailand 75
Thames Water 155, 157
Third World nationalism 21, 22, 32, 172, 181, 213, 223–226, 232–235
Third World Network 139
Third World Network-Africa 215
Thompson, G. 160
Time 117
Tokyo 104
Trade-Related Intellectual Property Rights 58, 67, 68, 194
Transition Monitoring Group 111
Transparency International 157, 221

Treatment Action Campaign (TAC) 11–13, 68
Trotsky, L. 192
Truth and Reconciliation Commission (TRC) 41, 46
Tshabalala-Msimang, M. 11, 13, 22, 68
Tsunga, A. 114
Tsvangirai, M. 111, 114
Tunisia 30
Turkey 75, 89
Turok, B. 138
Tutu, D. 41, 42

U'wa 229
Ubani, C. 110
Uganda 13, 30, 53, 62, 82, 83, 114, 218
ultraleft 170, 179, 182, 185–188
UN Conference on Trade and Development 4, 59, 85
uneven development 5, 165, 216, 234, 236
Unilever 147
United Nations 4, 10, 22, 28, 31, 32, 37, 39, 59, 75, 77, 85, 87, 89, 95, 108, 109, 112, 115, 116, 119, 125, 138, 139, 145, 232
United Nations Development Programme 155
United Nations Millennium Development Goals 75, 76, 78
United Nations Research Institute for Social Development 85
United Nations Security Council 22, 29, 32, 108
United Social Movements 130
United States of America 8, 16, 28, 29, 44, 52, 65, 66, 90, 121, 125, 136, 137, 144, 152, 154, 198, 226
United States Agency for International Development 147
United States National Institutes for Health 13
United States-Africa Business Summit 61
University of KwaZulu-Natal 227
University of Pretoria 113
University of the Witwatersrand 128, 129, 138, 167

Usury Act 117

Vally, S. 129
Vavi, Z. 129
Venezuela 53, 139, 201, 235
Ventilated Improved Pitlatrines 168
Vivendi 153, 155
Voges, C. 55
Vorster, J. 128

Wade, R. 87, 90, 91
Wall Street Journal 66
Wallach, L. 61, 198, 199
Washington Consensus 21, 32, 88, 91, 103, 112, 155, 158, 164, 182, 183, 196, 199, 202, 204, 205–206, 211, 222, 224, 225, 232, 233, 234
Washington Post 143
WaterAid 157
Water Affairs, Department of 143–145, 148, 153, 158, 171
Watson, T. 45
Wei, S. 92
Weisbrot, M. 126
Werner, D. 84
Williamson, J. 76
Wolfensohn, J. 80, 219, 221
Women for Change 235
World Bank 4, 9, 10, 15, 75–77, 79–82, 84–89, 94, 95, 104, 106, 107, 115, 130, 131, 147, 148, 152, 154–157, 164, 165, 167, 169, 171, 185, 197, 202, 203, 205, 214, 216–224, 229, 232, 233, 235
World Bank Bonds Boycott 218, 222, 223, 229
World Bank Inspection Panel 131–132
World Coalition against Water Privatisation and Commodification 146
World Commission on Dams 218
World Conference Against Racism 9, 10, 37–40, 43, 44, 47, 48

World Development Movement 81, 158
World Economic Forum 10, 103–105, 118
World Health Organisation 84, 147
World Marxist Review 129
World Panel on Financing Infrastructure 156
World Social Forum 11, 127, 172, 214, 234
World Summit on Sustainable Development 10, 13, 15, 44, 48, 125, 127–133, 135, 136, 138–140, 143–148, 153, 158, 159, 160, 161, 172, 180–183, 214, 233, 234, 236
World Trade Centre 77
World Trade Organisation 9, 10, 48, 51–58, 62, 63, 77, 84, 85, 130, 136, 139, 152, 158, 198, 199, 213, 217, 222, 233, 235
World Water Council 155
World Water Forum 33, 143, 148, 155, 156, 172
World Wildlife Federation 138
Wozani Security 131

Zambia 61, 62, 81, 83, 213, 235
Zanzibar 53
Zapatistas 213, 230
Zedillo, E. 76
Zenawi, M. 91
Zimbabwe African National Union (Patriotic Front) 113, 114, 135, 179, 180
Zimbabwe 31, 53, 56, 62, 103, 109–114, 135, 155, 204, 218, 233, 235
Zimbabwe Coalition on Debt and Development 112, 135
Zoellick, R. 57, 59, 63, 64
Zulu, D. 15
Zuma, J. 47, 108